International Focus Group Research

A practical and authoritative guide to conducting focus group discussions in health and social science research, with particular emphasis on using focus groups in developing country settings. Monique M. Hennink describes the procedures and challenges of each stage of international focus group research. This book demonstrates how to balance scientific rigor with the challenges of the research context, and guides readers to making informed research decisions. It includes unique field perspectives and case study examples of research in practice.

Topics covered include:

- Planning international field research
- Developing a fieldwork timetable and budget
- Seeking research permissions
- Translating research instruments
- Training a field team
- Developing a culturally appropriate discussion guide
- Participant recruitment strategies
- Conducting focus groups in another language
- Managing discussions in outdoor locations
- Group size and composition issues
- Transcription and translation of the group discussions
- Data analysis and reporting focus group research

MONIQUE M. HENNINK is an Associate Professor in the Rollins School of Public Health at Emory University. She has extensive experience in conducting qualitative research in developing country settings and has trained researchers, professionals and students on qualitative techniques in China, India, Pakistan, Uganda, Malawi, South Africa, the Netherlands, the United Kingdom and the United States of America.

International Focus Group Research

A Handbook for the Health and Social Sciences

Monique M. Hennink

CAMBRIDGE
UNIVERSITY PRESS

CAMBRIDGE UNIVERSITY PRESS

Cambridge, New York, Melbourne, Madrid, Cape Town, Singapore, São Paulo

Cambridge University Press
The Edinburgh Building, Cambridge CB2 8RU, UK

Published in the United States of America by Cambridge University Press, New York

www.cambridge.org
Information on this title: www.cambridge.org/9780521607803

First published 2007

Printed in the United Kingdom at the University Press, Cambridge

A catalogue record for this publication is available from the British Library

ISBN 978-0-521-84561-8 hardback
ISBN 978-0-521-60780-3 paperback

Contents

Figures

Preface

There exist a large number of books on conducting focus group discussions, however, most texts have an implicit assumption that the focus group research will be conducted in western settings. These texts provide little guidance for those embarking on focus group research in developing countries. While many of the principles of focus group research remain the same despite the context, the practical application will often differ. Existing texts provide no guidance on conducting focus groups in another language, developing a culturally appropriate discussion guide, translation issues, training a field team, seeking research permissions, using tape-recorders in culturally conservative settings and a range of other practical issues. As a result novice users of the method remain uncertain of how to apply the principles of focus group research to developing country settings. Unfortunately, this uncertainty often leads to the absence of rigorous science with inevitably poor quality outcomes.

There exists a great deal of experiential knowledge amongst those who have conducted international focus group research, there are accepted procedures and common strategies that we use for applying the method and for managing difficult situations, but little of this knowledge is published to assist those embarking on focus group research in developing countries for the first time. Therefore, this book is written in response to frequent requests from researchers and research students for advice on how to conduct focus group discussions, particularly in developing country contexts, and to respond to the common concern 'Am I doing it right?' The intention of this book is to document the procedures, practices and challenges in applying the method to various research contexts. Following on from this, a second aim of the book is to encourage greater transparency in the conduct of focus group research. Often the application of focus group research is only superficially reported in research documents, so there is little indication of how the method was applied in practice. It is hoped that this book will assist researchers to report the use of the method and the decisions made during fieldwork with more confidence if there is a documented guide to good practice in international fieldwork.

The third aim of this book is to demonstrate how to balance methodological rigor with the challenges of the research context. Good quality focus group research, regardless of the context in which it is conducted, should reflect certain theoretical principles and be based on informed methodological decisions. Too often methodological rigor is overtaken by the management of fieldwork challenges. This book intends to assist researchers to understand the value of embracing theoretical issues in producing quality research outcomes and in guiding the numerous decisions throughout the research design and the data collection. It also highlights some of the methodological debates to enable researchers to anticipate certain decisions and make informed choices during the research process.

This book is for those who conduct, review and use focus group research. It is primarily intended for researchers (both academic and non-government), doctoral students and their supervisors, in both developed and developing countries. It is also useful for those who review focus group research or research proposals to identify whether appropriate methodological considerations have been included; and for those who use the results of focus group research to enable them to assess the quality of a study. This book is equally applicable for researchers new to the focus group method as well as those who have used the method but only in a developed country context. The structure of the book follows a basic task-chronology, with each chapter addressing a different stage or aspect of the method. The book begins by describing the range of tasks in planning international focus group research, the subsequent chapters detail various aspects in conducting the group discussions, data preparation and analysis, and the book finishes with issues relating to reporting the findings of focus group research. At the end of each chapter is a summary of the critical issues and a list of key terms that may not be familiar to all readers.

This book is based primarily on my own experience in conducting qualitative research in numerous developing countries over the last decade. However, in developing this book I also conducted interviews with other researchers and research students on their experiences in conducting focus group discussions. These were researchers from both developed and developing countries who conducted focus group research in developing country contexts. Learning from the experiences of others is extremely valuable and extracts from these interviews are included throughout the book to provide a unique field perspective of both positive and negative experiences. It is hoped that the inclusion of these experiences will help readers to better relate the issues described to the context in which their own focus group research is conducted.

Acknowledgements

I would like to express my sincere appreciation to all the people who spent time discussing their field experiences with me during the preparation of this book. I particularly appreciate the open discussions about the challenging aspects of focus group fieldwork and the reflections on issues to emphasise in the book. These contributions provide a unique field perspective in the book. I hope that you will appreciate why I cannot thank each of you by name.

I would like to thank the University of Southampton (Division of Social Statistics) in the United Kingdom, for providing support during the early development of this book, through the Department for International Development research programme 'Opportunities and Choices'. I would like to acknowledge the University of Adelaide (Department of Geographical and Environmental Studies) in Australia for providing me with office accommodation while writing several chapters. I would also like to thank the Department of Global Health at Emory University in the US, for allowing me the time needed to focus on completing this book.

Finally, I would like to express sincere thanks to my family and friends for their continuing support for my academic endeavours, particularly to Sarah and Andy.

1   Introduction to focus group research

Introduction

Focus group discussions have been in the toolkit of social scientists for some time now. In more recent decades the use of focus group discussions has increased amongst the health and social sciences as a tool to inform policy and practice. For example, focus group discussions have been used in health and behavioural research, strategic planning, health promotion, policy development and programme evaluation. The increased use of focus group discussions is partly due to a broader acceptability of qualitative methods in these disciplines, but also due to a greater emphasis on the inclusion of qualitative methods in mixed-method research designs, to respond to research issues not accessible by quantitative approaches. This more recent emphasis on integrating qualitative and quantitative approaches has been encouraged by research funding bodies and has led to a renewed focus on training in mixed-method research design for post-graduates in academic institutions.

The increased use of focus group discussions has led to a greater number and variety of researchers using the method. Focus group discussions are also being applied in a greater variety of settings than in the past. In particular, focus group discussions are often used in international research, particularly in developing country contexts. For example, health research on issues such as family planning, HIV/AIDS and the development of social and community initiatives now often include focus group discussions in the research methodology. Despite the broader application of focus group discussions in a wide variety of contexts, much of the existing methodological literature is written with an implicit assumption that the method is being applied only in western, developed country contexts. This is reflected in the guidance given for issues such as participant recruitment (i.e. written or telephone recruitment), the location of group discussions (i.e. indoors or formal settings), or the availability of professional moderators. However, when conducting focus group discussions in developing country contexts, often a different approach is taken or researchers are faced with different issues during the fieldwork process. For example, participant recruitment is often conducted verbally and through a community leader; and groups may be conducted outdoors, where the problem of onlookers and lack of privacy need to be addressed. The existing literature provides no guidance on conducting focus groups in another language, developing a culturally appropriate discussion guide, translation of the group discussion, training a field team, the use of tape recorders in culturally conservative settings and a range of other practical issues. As a result, novice users of the method remain uncertain of how to apply the principles of focus group research to developing country settings. Unfortunately, this often leads to the absence of rigorous science with inevitably poor quality outcomes. While many of the principles of focus group research remain the same despite the context, the practical application of the method will often differ. The aim of this book is, therefore, to provide guidance for researchers conducting focus group discussions in a variety of research contexts, with particular emphasis on application of the method in developing country settings.

This introductory chapter will outline the purpose of the book and its intended audiences. It will highlight the development of focus group discussions, define their characteristics, show the strengths and limitations of the method and describe appropriate applications of focus group research.

Purpose of this book

The purpose of this book is to guide readers through the procedures, practices and challenges in conducting focus group research in varying research contexts, with a particular emphasis on applying the method in developing country settings. An underlying objective of the book is to describe the conduct of focus group research which takes into consideration the context of the research but without compromising the rigor and scientific application of the method. A second aim of the book is to encourage greater transparency in the conduct of focus group research. Often focus group methodology is only superficially reported in research documents, so there is little indication of how the method was applied in practice. It is hoped that this book will provide a guide to good practice for using focus group discussions in international settings and give novice researchers more confidence in applying and documenting their own focus group research. The third aim of this book is to demonstrate how to balance methodological rigor with the challenges of the research context. Good quality focus group research, regardless of the context in which it is conducted, should reflect certain theoretical principles and be based on informed methodological decisions. Too often methodological rigor is overtaken by the management of fieldwork challenges. This book intends to assist researchers to understand the value of embracing theoretical issues in producing quality research outcomes and in guiding decisions throughout the research process. It also highlights some of the methodological debates to enable researchers to anticipate certain decisions and make informed choices during the research process.

This book is for those who conduct, review and use focus group research. It is primarily intended for researchers (both academic and non-government), doctoral students and their supervisors, in both developed and developing countries. It is also useful for those who review focus group research or research proposals to identify whether appropriate methodological considerations have been included; and for those who use the results of focus group research to enable them to assess the quality of a study. This book is equally applicable for researchers new to the focus group method as well as those who have used the method but only in a developed country context. This book is intended to provide a text on focus group research which embraces the application of the method in a variety of research contexts.

Structure and development of the book

The structure of this book follows the process of conducting focus group research, with each chapter addressing a different stage of the method. The first chapters detail the planning tasks prior to fieldwork (i.e. formalities, ethics, preparation of the discussion guide and training of the field team); subsequent chapters describe the field-based activities (i.e. participant recruitment, group composition and size, location, and conduct of the discussion), the issues of data management (i.e. recording the discussion, data preparation, translation and transcription) and data analysis and reporting. The book has only limited reference to qualitative study design, as these issues are covered sufficiently in other texts on qualitative research.

This book is primarily based on the experience of the author, who has conducted qualitative research in numerous developing countries over the past decade. In addition, the book includes extracts from interviews that the author conducted with other researchers and research students on their experiences of conducting focus group discussions in developing countries. The extracts include experiences of both expatriate researchers as well as those conducting focus group research in their own country. The extracts highlight specific issues, challenges and strategies in conducting focus group discussions in developing country contexts. Learning from the experience of others is extremely valuable; the extracts highlight not only positive field experiences, but also reflections on fieldwork problems, which provide the reader with a unique field perspective on the application of the research method in practice. The quotations from these interviews are referenced by the researcher's status and country in which the research was conducted, for example (Researcher, Mozambique), (Research Student, Cambodia).

What is a focus group discussion?

A focus group discussion is a unique method of qualitative research that involves discussing a specific set of issues with a pre-determined group of people. Focus group research differs from other qualitative methods in its purpose, composition and the process of data collection. The essential purpose of focus group research is to identify a range of different views around the research topic, and to gain an understanding of the issues from the perspective of the participants themselves. The group context is intended to collect more wide-ranging information in a single session than would result from one-to-one interviews.

Focus group methodology was formally developed in the social sciences during the 1940s (David and Sutton 2004), and for several decades its primary application was in the field of market research to determine consumer views, preferences and behaviour. The focus group method emerged due to the limitations of traditional forms of interviewing, such as the artificial nature of standard interview procedures, the influence of an interviewer on a respondent's comments and the limitations of pre-determined closed questioning on enabling spontaneous responses or identifying new issues (Hennink and Diamond 1999; Flick 2002). These drawbacks of traditional interviewing led to the development of a new approach of *non-directive interviewing*, whereby the interviewer plays a minimal role and the dynamics of a group discussion are used to gather information (Krueger 1988; Flick 2002). The context of a group discussion is thought to create greater spontaneity in the contributions of participants as it replicates everyday social interactions more than a traditional one-to-one interview. The function of non-directive interviewing is to shift the attention away from the dominance of an interviewer to focus on *generating a discussion* between participants on certain issues. The discussion element of the method gives participants greater control of the issues raised in the dialogue, as they are essentially discussing the issues between themselves rather than directly with an interviewer. It is important to recognise that it is the creation of a group dynamic that enables spontaneous issues to arise from the discussion and participants to highlight issues that are of importance to themselves. This element is less likely to occur in an interview that is more interviewer-directed. Ritchie and Lewis (2003: 171) state that, 'In a sense, the group participants take over some of the "interviewing" role, and the researcher is at times more in the position of listening in.' However, they stress that this situation does not lessen the researcher's burden, as focus groups need to be carefully managed for this to happen.

From the early 1980s, there has been a resurgence in the use of focus group discussions in the social sciences. Focus group research has provided valuable information for a wide range of research issues in the social sciences, including health and behavioural research, evaluation of social programs, shaping of public policy, developing health promotion strategies and conducting needs assessments. Focus group methodology is now embraced in the social sciences as one of the central tools of qualitative enquiry. During the 1990s, the use of focus groups in the public sphere became more prominent. Some high profile examples include the use of focus groups in 1997 by the newly elected Labour Party in the United Kingdom to gauge public perceptions of new government policies, in particular the introduction of fees for education. In the same year, focus group discussions were used to gauge public opinion on the role and image of the British royal family.

Focus group research may be defined as follows:

A focus group study is a carefully planned series of discussions designed to obtain perceptions on a defined area of interest in a permissive, non-threatening environment. Each group is conducted with six to eight people by a skilled interviewer ... Group members influence each other by responding to ideas and comments of others. (Krueger and Casey 2000: 5)

Focus group discussions have a number of characteristics which distinguish the method. Focus group discussions are comprised of pre-selected individuals who have similar characteristics or who share some experience of the research topic. Groups typically consist of six to eight participants, but may include anywhere from five to ten participants depending on the purpose of the study. The group discussion is focussed on a specific topic and usually explores only a limited number of issues to allow sufficient time for participants to discuss the issues in detail. The aim of a focus group is not to reach consensus on the issues discussed, but to encourage a range of responses which provide a greater understanding of the attitudes, behaviour, opinions or perceptions of participants on the research issues. The discussion between participants is a key element of focus group discussions, as this situation provides the opportunity for issues to emerge that are unanticipated by the researchers. The group discussion is guided by a trained moderator who introduces each issue and facilitates the discussion in such a way that detailed information is gained on each issue. The questions used by the moderator to stimulate the discussion are carefully designed to appear spontaneous and conversational, but are actually developed through considerable reflection and piloting. A key ingredient to successful focus group discussions is the development of a permissive, non-threatening environment within the group, whereby participants feel comfortable to share their views and experiences without the fear of judgement or ridicule from others.

Strengths and limitations of focus group discussions

The strengths and limitations of focus group discussions are summarised in Figure 1.1. There are many advantages in using focus group discussions, which may be summarised under three main headings; the socially oriented nature of the research procedure, the variety of applications of the method and the group environment of data collection. First, focus group discussions replicate people's natural social interaction rather than an artificial or

Strengths	Limitations
Social setting:	**Skills required:**
Replicates social interaction	Requires skilled moderator
Naturalistic setting	Less controlled environment
Comfortable and enjoyable	Need 'permissive environment'
	Risk of bias in participant selection
Application:	
Variable structure	**Group dynamics:**
Wide range of applications	Some participants may dominate
(exploratory, explanatory, evaluative)	Participants may agree
Suitable for stimulus material	Little discussion
Useful in multi-method research	Influence of social pressure
	Hierarchies may develop
Group environment:	Less confidential
Large volume of information	Few issues discussed
Range of views	
Limited researcher influence	**Data and analysis:**
Participants identify issues	Responses are not independent
Identify new issues	Not suitable for individual data
Spontaneous responses	Not for personal or sensitive topics
Considered responses	Large volume of textual data
Issues debated and justified	Data analysis complex and time consuming
Seek clarifications	Costly
Study group interaction	

Figure 1.1   Strengths and limitations of focus group discussions

experimental setting as in a quantitative survey or, to some extent, an in-depth interview. Therefore, participants may find the focus group environment comfortable and enjoyable, which is likely to impact on their contribution to the discussion.

Second, the level of structure in a focus group discussion can be varied to suit its application. For example, focus group research may be relatively structured and focussed to generate data that are easily comparable between different groups; it may also be largely unstructured and broadly focussed where the research is more exploratory and the issues unknown (David and Sutton 2004). Therefore, the method has a wide range of applications from unstructured exploratory research, to explanatory research that identifies motivations for certain behaviours or attitudes, and evaluative research to assess aspects of a service or social programme. The flexible application of the focus group method lends it well to incorporation into multi-method research designs, such as explaining quantitative survey findings or conducting exploratory research prior to in-depth interviews. The group format is also suitable for the introduction of stimulus material, such as posters, products, or video extracts, to discuss participants' opinions and reactions.

Third, perhaps the greatest advantage of this method comes from the group nature of the data collection. At a practical level, a one-hour focus group discussion can generate a large volume of data and identify a greater variety of views, opinions and experiences than the same time spent in individual interviews. Fern (1982) found that a focus group discussion generated about seventy percent of the original ideas that were identified in a set of individual interviews with the same number of people. Although a focus group discussion may identify a wide range of issues, this example also shows that the information gained in a focus group discussion is not equivalent to conducting the same number of in-depth interviews. The discussion element of the method enables participants to talk about the issues with little moderator involvement, participants are therefore able to build on the responses of other group members and debate various contributions. The comments of one participant may trigger a series of responses from others and reveal insights about an issue beyond that of a single interviewee. It is the group discussion which enables participants to reveal their own views and opinions of the topic discussed, which may uncover views, ideas or issues unanticipated by the researchers; the discussion also generates diversity of opinions amongst participants. All of these elements are important advantages of this method. Morgan (1998: 12 cited in Flick 2002: 120) states that 'The hallmark of focus groups is the explicit use of the group interaction to produce data and insights that would be less accessible without the interaction found in a group.' The interactive nature of a group discussion also influences the quality of data collected. As participants are able to react to the comments of others in the group this may lead to reflection, refinement or justification of the issues raised, which can provide a deeper insight into the issues and context in which these are discussed. The group environment also provides an opportunity for an explicit discussion of differences in opinion as they emerge in the group (Ritchie and Lewis 2003). Patton (1990: 335–6) states on this issue that focus group discussions can be a 'highly efficient qualitative data-collection technique [which provides] some quality checks on data collection in that participants tend to provide checks and balances on each other that weed out false or extreme views'. This type of social moderation of the discussion is not evident in individual interviews. A final advantage is that focus groups can be used to study group dynamics *per se*; to observe how ideas are shaped, generated or moderated in a discussion setting, or to identify influences on group consensus or conflict and the effect of dominant or passive individuals on the group dynamic (Ritchie and Lewis 2003; David and Sutton 2004). However, the most common use of focus groups is as a data collection tool rather than to study participant interactions.

As with all research methods there are also limitations in using focus group discussions (see Figure 1.1), which need to be considered before applying the method. Many of the limitations are the inverse aspects of the issues discussed as strengths of the method. The limitations in using focus group discussions relate to the skills required to conduct the groups, potential problems with the group dynamics and limitations related to the data and analysis. First, the flexible nature of focus group discussions, which enables participants to contribute freely to the discussion, also requires a skilled and experienced moderator. The moderator needs to facilitate a discussion that generates useful, detailed and varied responses on the research issues. In addition, the moderator needs to foster a comfortable and permissive environment in the group that will elicit open responses. The flexible and less controlled nature of focus group discussions can easily lead to the collection of redundant information if the moderator lacks the skills to effectively manage the discussion. Identifying skilled moderators or training them to conduct effective group discussion may be a limitation of using this method. There also exists a risk of bias in the selection of participants and in the delivery of questions by the moderator. If not carefully managed, these issues can affect the reliability and quality of the data collected.

Further limitations in the method may arise due to difficulties with group dynamics. Although group members may stimulate each other in the discussion, there is also a risk that some members may dominate the discussion, either due to an authoritarian tone or in the time spent talking. This may inhibit other members who remain quiet or simply agree with the views of a dominant participant. Clearly this situation will impact on the data quality. In other situations, participants may all simply agree with one another, perhaps due to social pressure to conform or discomfort in the group, resulting in little discussion of the issues. Poor recruitment of participants may contribute to a lack of group homogeneity and the formation of hierarchies within a focus group, which can have a negative impact on participant's contribution to the discussion. All these issues need to be carefully managed in the research design and by a moderator during the discussion to ensure quality data collection. The group setting may also afford less confidentiality than an individual interview. David and Sutton (2004) suggest that reduced confidentiality may lead participants to withhold certain information in the group, thus reducing the depth of information on some issues. Researchers need to be careful in the selection of discussion topics to counter this effect. Finally, the group discussion can only include a limited number of issues to enable sufficient time to discuss each issue in detail.

Finally, there are also limitations related to focus group data and data analysis. It must be remembered that focus group data are a product of interactive discussion with other participants, so that responses are not independent. Therefore, the method is not suitable for data on individuals or for gathering information on personal or sensitive topics. Focus group discussions also generate a large volume of textual data which can be complex and time-consuming to analyse, as data need to be analysed in the context of a group discussion whereby participants may change their views or provide contradictory opinions during the course of the discussion. Despite popular belief, focus group research is not a cheap and quick exercise; it requires a great deal of preparation, organisation, and time to collect, manage and analyse the data.

When to use focus group discussions

To clarify the appropriate application of focus group discussions, it may be useful to begin by contrasting when to use focus group discussion and in-depth interviews (Figure 1.2). The group context of a focus group makes it an ideal method when seeking a range of views on a topic, when debate and discussion on an issue is desired and for uncovering new insights or unanticipated issues. Focus group discussions are most suitable when seeking community-level information (as opposed to personal information), such as seeking information about social behaviour, cultural values or community opinions. Focus groups are suitable for provoking a discussion and are therefore useful when seeking justifications and explanations of issues or for studying group dynamics. The group context lacks confidentiality and so is less suitable for personal information or sensitive topics. Appropriate topics for a focus group discussion may be 'community perceptions about a proposed new health clinic', 'men's experiences in seeking paternity leave', or 'young people's use of

When to use focus group discussions	When to use in-depth interviews
To identify a range of views and experiences	To identify individual perspectives
To provoke discussion and explanation of issues	For personal experiences and opinions
To identify new issues and generate hypotheses	For detailed, in-depth information
To seek broad information about a community	For sensitive and complex topics
For less sensitive topics	For descriptive process information
To understand group interaction and decision-making	(e.g. life course issues, migration process)

Figure 1.2   When to use focus groups and in-depth interviews

family planning clinics'. These topics focus on seeking community-level views or experiences from a specific target population (e.g. young people, men). In contrast, in-depth interviews are more suitable for identifying individual perspectives, personal experiences or opinions, and for gaining detailed information on a research topic. In-depth interviews are more confidential and therefore suitable for discussing sensitive and personal topics. They can also be effective in exploring complex issues due to the greater time available to probe an individual for clarification or explanations. In-depth interviews are also a more suitable format for gaining process and event information about individuals, such as their experience of migration, marriage or a woman's childbirth history, as the respondent can take time to describe the process, the context and their experiences.

Focus group discussions have a wide variety of applications. They are an effective tool for exploratory, explanatory or evaluative research, and can provide useful information for policy and practice. Information from focus group discussions may be applied to health and behavioural research, strategic planning, health promotion, policy development, and programme evaluation. However, due to the qualitative method of enquiry focus groups are not suitable for research that requires identifying the prevalence of an issue within the community or for generalising the findings to a broader population.

Focus group discussions are suitable for exploratory research to identify new issues, to consolidate research hypotheses, or to provide background information about a topic or a study population about which little is known. The method may be used to provide baseline information prior to the development of a new social programme, to conduct community needs assessments, or to gauge opinions about proposed social policies. Focus groups may also be used to identify social norms or cultural practices amongst a specific population. The information from exploratory focus group discussions may provide useful information for decision-makers to develop policies, programmes or educational materials. For example, the Health Education Authority in the United Kingdom conducted focus group discussions amongst young people when developing posters for sexual health promotion. The focus groups were conducted to identify images, words and slogans to include (and exclude) on health education materials to capture the attention of young people (Pearson *et al.* 1996).

Second, focus group discussions may be used in evaluation research as a diagnostic tool to examine the effectiveness of a service or community programme. They may be used for program planning or re-development, to identify people's perceptions and experiences of a particular service, the barriers to using a service and strategies to recruit non-users. Focus groups can also be used to identify the positive or negative aspects of a service or policy. For example, the Civil Aviation Authority of the United Kingdom used focus group discussions to examine the effect of aircraft noise on sleep disturbance of residents near a major international airport. They needed this information to evaluate the potential impact of changing the current no-fly policy between midnight and 6 am (Diamond *et al.* 2000). Similarly, the Government of Malawi was considering replacing free family planning services with a fee-charging system. The Ministry of Health commissioned focus group research to assess the impact of this proposed change on poor communities (Hennink and Madise 2005).

Third, focus group discussions may be used to understand behaviour and provide explanations for certain beliefs, attitudes or behaviour amongst a target population. They may also be used to further explain, clarify or validate the findings of survey results. For example, Varga (2003) used focus group discussions amongst South African adolescents to explore the concepts of male and female gender norms and how these influence the reproductive health of adolescents. Borrayo *et al.* (2005) conducted focus group discussions amongst older Latino women to assess their perceptions about screening to detect breast cancer. This study revealed cultural and psychosocial explanations for a lack of preventative health behaviour, which were used in the design of health education programmes for this population group. Lennon *et al.* (2005) used focus group discussions to explore the social identities that influence young women's smoking behaviour, to develop smoking prevention initiatives aimed at young women.

Multi-method research designs

Focus group discussions may be used in multi-method research designs, which combine focus group research with quantitative methods or with other qualitative methods. The use of multi-method research is seen as increasingly valuable. Using a combination of research approaches can illuminate different aspects of a research problem, which can provide powerful evidence to inform policy and practice. Often mixed-method research focusses on combining quantitative and qualitative approaches. However, the same principles and advantages apply to using multiple qualitative methods in a study design, as each method brings a particular insight onto the research problem. For example, focus group discussions may be used to identify and refine issues that are later explored more fully in in-depth interviews. Alternatively, focus group discussions may be conducted subsequent to in-depth interviews to discuss the issues, debate strategies, or confirm experiences more broadly. Focus group research may also be combined with observation approaches. This is particularly useful in evaluation research, such as observing people's behaviour in a clinic waiting room and subsequently discussing the issues observed in a focus group discussion.

Many research issues in the health and social sciences require both the measurement of an issue and a greater understanding of the nature, context or influences on an issue. Combining qualitative and quantitative approaches enable this combination of results in a single research study. When combining both approaches it is important to recognise that each approach is rooted in different theoretical traditions and the data collection and analysis should reflect this, however the findings can be integrated to contribute to a fuller understanding of the research problem. Brannen (1992: 33 cited in Ritchie and Lewis 2003: 38) states that when combining quantitative and qualitative methods '... the researcher has to confront the tensions between different theoretical perspectives while at the same time considering the relationship between the data sets produced by the different methods'. The three most common approaches to combining qualitative and quantitative methods include conducting qualitative work prior to quantitative, in parallel to quantitative, or as a successor to quantitative work. These three approaches are described briefly below in relation to the use of focus group discussions. A more detailed discussion of combining qualitative and quantitative methods can be found in Tashakkori and Teddlie (1998), Ritchie and Lewis (2003), Green and Thorogood (2004), amongst other works.

First, focus group discussions may be used for exploratory research preceding quantitative work, such as a survey. This is particularly appropriate when the research topic is new or undefined, and the purpose of the group discussion is to identify salient issues, question strategies or to define concepts and terminology for the survey instrument. For example, in a study to evaluate the Marie Stopes family planning clinics in Pakistan (Hennink and Stephenson 2000), focus group discussions revealed that community members did not refer to the clinics as 'Marie Stopes' but used a range of local terms which translated as 'small family clinic', 'blue door clinic' and 'foreigners clinic'. These terms were incorporated into the survey instrument to improve clarity of the survey questions for respondents. Focus group discussions may also be conducted prior to a survey when the research topic is complex and requires some understanding of the underlying concepts before constructing relevant questions. The focus group discussions may also identify various sub-groups within the study population and their defining characteristics, which can be incorporated into the survey instrument to measure the size of these population elements (Ritchie and Lewis 2003).

A second approach is to use focus group discussions as a successor to quantitative work to provide greater insight or context to the quantitative findings. This explanatory capacity of focus group research is perhaps the most underutilised. There are many instances where survey findings may identify strong relationships between variables but the survey data are unable to identify the mechanisms for why the relationships exist (Green and Thorogood 2004). Focus group discussions may be conducted to uncover important influences, linkages or contextual information needed to fully understand the quantitative findings. Focus groups can also be used subsequent to a survey to investigate a specific sub-group of the study population, who exist in insufficient numbers in the survey data for statistical analysis but who may have an important perspective on the research issues (Ritchie and Lewis 2003). Ritchie and Lewis (2003) suggest further sequences, whereby qualitative approaches are used as a follow-up to a survey, but then the qualitative findings are used to directly inform analysis of the survey data. This may happen when the findings from focus group discussions identify a link between issues that may have been overlooked by the researchers. If there are variables in the survey data for the issues that are related, researchers can then re-analyse the survey data to model the relationships uncovered in the focus group discussions. This provides greater depth to the quantitative data analysis and integrates the qualitative findings into quantitative data analysis.

Third, focus group discussions and quantitative approaches may be used in parallel to investigate different research questions within the study or different perspectives of the same research issue. They may use the same or different participants, depending on the purpose of the investigation. The rationale for this combination of approaches is to achieve an extended understanding of the research issue that no one method alone can provide. Where both approaches are used to explore the same issue, quantitative methods often provide an indication of the prevalence or size of an issue, while qualitative approaches explore the nature of the same phenomenon. Qualitative approaches may be able to explore aspects of the research topic that are too complex or too sensitive to be investigated fully with a survey instrument. The findings of the focus group discussions may then dovetail closely into the quantitative findings to provide qualitative examples of the quantitative findings, clarify confusing or contradictory survey findings, or provide explanations of the associations found in the survey results.

Alternatively, focus group discussions may be used to contribute to a separate component of the research problem.

Types of focus group research

The evolution of focus group research over several decades has meant that there are now distinct approaches to using focus group discussions. Krueger and Casey (2000) highlight four distinct styles of focus group research; the market research approach, the academic application, use by non-profit organisations and participatory approaches. These will be briefly summarised below. Although this book is focussed primarily on the academic and non-profit approaches to focus group research, it is worthwhile to note that there exist various styles of focus group research which have variations in their purpose, procedure and outcomes.

The *market research approach* uses focus groups for practical problems, most often relating to improving consumer products and seeking consumer views. The approach is not concerned with the application of a methodology, but is based on seeking practical information, fast results and economic benefits. Typical market research focus groups are held in specially designed facilities with one-way mirrors to enable clients to observe the discussion, they use professional recruiting and screening strategies and professional moderators, the groups are large in size (i.e. ten to twelve participants) and cash incentives are offered to participants. The results of market research focus groups are often generated within days of the group discussions, from a moderator's notes, observations and memory.

The *academic research approach* to focus group discussions is much more focussed on the careful application of a research method, the generation of quality data and detailed, rigorous analysis of the information; therefore this approach takes considerable time. The academic approach involves conducting focus groups in the location of the target population and in community settings (e.g. meeting halls or homes) with a wide variety of study populations. The issues studied may vary from public health, education, environmental concerns or policy research. The academic approach provides transparency by detailing each stage of the process, to ensure rigor and validity in the application of the method. The information collected in the group discussions is treated as data and recorded in various forms, by notes, tape recording and transcription of the discussion. The written transcripts form the basis of data analysis, which follows an accepted scientific protocol, and may involve the use of specially designed software programs to code, categorise and interpret the findings. The research results are published in academic, technical or policy reports and the data are used to justify the findings. Monetary incentives for participants are less common with this approach.

The *public/non-profit approach* is generally used for applied research, often to inform decisions, determine the effectiveness of services and be responsive to public users of services and amenities. This approach is often applied to social marketing and public health issues to design, improve or evaluate policies, programmes or public services. The concept of this approach is similar to market research, only the focus is changed from consumer products to public services. The size of focus groups tends to be smaller (i.e. six to ten participants) than market research approaches to enable sufficient time to hear respondents' concerns, and groups are held in community locations. These types of groups are often moderated by a member of the public/non-profit organisation with skills in facilitation, interviewing or evaluation. The style of data analysis may vary from quick market research approaches to more detailed academic analysis, depending on the purpose of the research. Often the outcomes may be a summary of the key concerns or a ranking of the most important issues, with sufficient detail from the group discussions to convey the context of the issues.

The central tenet of the *participatory approach*, which emerged in the early 1990s, is to involve those who will use the results of focus group research in the actual process of conducting the groups. It involves training, co-operation and willingness on behalf of policy and programme personnel to be involved in the process of seeking information and applying the findings to practice. This approach does have some difficulties, in the less consistent application of the method to each group discussion (Krueger and Casey 2000).

Key terms

A *focus group discussion* is a unique method of qualitative research that involves discussing a specific set of issues with a pre-determined group of people.

Non-directive interviewing involves the interviewer playing a minimal role in the focus group, so that the dynamics of a group discussion are used to gather information.

Multi-method research involves combining several research methods in a single study design. This may involve combining quantitative and qualitative methods (e.g. survey and focus groups) or using multiple qualitative methods (e.g. focus groups and in-depth interviews).

Exploratory research is conducted when little is known about a research issue. It may be used to identify new issues, define research hypotheses, or to provide background information about a topic or study population.

Explanatory research is used when seeking to understand and provide explanations for certain beliefs, attitudes or behaviour amongst a target population. It may be used to explain or clarify the findings of survey results.

Evaluative research is conducted when assessing the effectiveness of a service, programme or initiative. It may be used in program planning or re-development.

Summary of key issues

- Focus group research can provide valuable information for a wide range of research issues, including: health and behavioural research, evaluation of social programmes, shaping of public policy, developing health promotion strategies, conducting needs assessments and programme evaluation.
- Focus group discussions are a unique method of qualitative research that involves discussing a specific set of issues with a pre-determined group of people.
- The essential purpose of focus group research is to identify a range of different views around the research topic, and to gain an understanding of the issues from the perspective of the participants themselves.
- Focus group discussions differ from other qualitative methods in their purpose, composition and the process of data collection.
- The group discussion element of the method is critical. It is the creation of a group dynamic that enables spontaneous issues to arise from the discussion and participants to highlight issues that are of importance to themselves.
- The advantages of focus group discussions are in the socially oriented nature of the research procedure, the variety of applications of the method and the group environment of data collection.
- The limitations in using focus group discussions relate to the skills required to conduct the groups, potential problems with the group dynamics and limitations related to the data and analysis.
- Focus group discussions may be used in multi-method research designs, which combine focus group research with quantitative methods or with other qualitative methods.
- There are several distinct styles of focus group research; the market research approach, the academic application, the approach of non-profit organisations and participatory approaches.

2 Planning international focus group research

Introduction

I think that seventy percent of the effort for focus group discussions is in the planning, because once you have planned everything you are able to better control when things go wrong. (Researcher, Zambia)

This chapter outlines the range of issues to be considered in planning international focus group research, highlighting the issues to be considered prior to beginning the fieldwork and once at the field location. Careful planning is fundamental to the successful implementation of focus group research, particularly when it is conducted in another country. The initial tasks involve clarifying the basic research issues, such as the research objectives, target population and utilisation of the research findings. Planning focus group research also involves seeking appropriate permissions, establishing local contacts, developing a suitable field team, providing training and organising logistics. All of these activities need to be conducted with sensitivity to local protocols, respect for cultural differences and a continued application of ethical principles. In addition, planning the research involves developing a realistic timetable and seeking an adequate budget. Conducting international focus group research also requires flexibility to meet the challenges that arise during the fieldwork process. However, with effective planning researchers can anticipate some of the difficulties that may occur and be in a better position to manage unexpected situations that may influence the quality of the research outcomes.

Defining the objectives, target population and outcomes of research

As with all scientific research, the first tasks in planning focus group research involve clarifying the purpose of the study, defining the target population and considering the utilisation of the research findings. The issues to be considered for each of these areas are highlighted in Figure 2.1. Clarity on these issues is important in guiding each of the activities concluded in the fieldwork.

Clarify the study purpose:
- Why is the study being conducted?
- What are the broad aims of the study?
- What are the specific objectives?
- How will focus group methodology achieve these objectives?
- Is the study exploratory, explanatory, evaluative, policy oriented?
- Is the study part of a mixed-method design? How will the focus group component contribute to the overall study objectives?
- Does the study have a conceptual framework?

Define the target population:
- Who will be the study participants?
- How are the study population defined (e.g. age, gender, experience, location, etc.)?
- Are there sub-groups of the study population?
- Will the study population be segmented for the group discussions? How?

Consider utilisation and target audience of findings:
- How will the study findings be used?
- Who will utilise the study findings?
- Are there different target audiences for the research findings?
- Will stakeholders be involved in the research process? How?

Figure 2.1   Considerations in planning focus group research

The first task involves defining the broad purpose of the research and the more specific research objectives. The purpose of the research needs to be clear, even for exploratory research. The research purpose will guide the development of the discussion questions and assist the moderator to keep the discussion focussed on the central areas of interest to the study. The purpose of the research may be broad, (e.g. attitudes towards immunisation); however, the specific objectives need to be more defined (e.g. type of immunisation, cost, side effects) as these will form the topics of discussion and provide the focus of the discussion.

Second, the target population of the research needs to be clearly defined. To some extent the target population may be identified by the research topic; for example, a study on 'young people's attitudes towards health insurance' will clearly focus on young people. However, the research team needs to define the exact characteristics of the target population, in terms of age, gender, employment, educational status, location of residence and so on. The target population for the study on health insurance may then be defined as young professionals, both male and female, aged eighteen to twenty-four, employed in urban areas. A clearly defined target population is necessary for designing appropriate discussion questions, for participant recruitment and for determining the composition of the discussion groups (e.g. male/female, age groups, etc.).

Finally, researchers need to consider how the information from the study will be used and by whom. This will help to focus the discussion questions, guide the data analysis and identify the various target audiences for the dissemination of research findings. For example, focus group discussions held prior to the conduct of a survey may be implemented to identify important issues and appropriate terminology for the survey instrument. Therefore, detailed data analysis is unlikely and the users of the data will be members of the research team itself. Alternatively, focus group research may be conducted to investigate substantive issues on a research topic, which may be relevant for the development of health policy or programme development. This type of utilisation of the research findings will require a substantially greater focus on data analysis and dissemination strategies that target policy audiences.

The process of focus group research

The typical process of conducting international focus group research involves a number of pre-fieldwork activities that require some forward planning, the

Pre-fieldwork activities:
- Develop research proposal and secure funding
- Design and pre-test research instruments
- Develop training materials for focus group team
- Identify research collaborators or host institution in study country
- Discuss joint research interests in study topic
- Gain appropriate research permissions
  (e.g. research clearance in study country, research visa)
- Gain ethical approval for study from institutional review board(s)
- Determine most suitable time period to conduct fieldwork
  (i.e. climate, seasonal availability of participants, research deadlines)
- Purchase necessary equipment
- Consider cultural setting (i.e. language assistance, culturally appropriate clothing, local protocols)

Fieldwork activities:
- Conduct in-country meetings
  (i.e. with collaborators, host organisation, sponsor organisations, etc.)
- Recruit a field team
- Provide training to field team
- Translate discussion guide into local language(s)
- Field-test discussion guide
- Arrange travel logistics to study sites (i.e. transport, accommodation)
- Follow local protocols in introductions and permissions
- Recruit focus group participants
- Conduct focus group discussions
- Follow local protocols before leaving study sites
  (i.e. debriefing, payments, follow-up)
- Translate and transcribe group discussions
- Debrief with in-country sponsor or host institution (if appropriate)
- Develop fieldwork report for in-country sponsor (if appropriate)

Post-fieldwork activities:
- Conduct data cleaning and analysis
- Write research report considering content, format, audiences and key messages
- Present research findings to key stakeholders
- Conduct dissemination activities
  (e.g. academic conferences, policy briefs, stakeholder meetings, press briefs, etc.)
- Provide in-country dissemination of research findings

Figure 2.2   The process of international focus group research

fieldwork stage of data collection, and a range of post-fieldwork activities that are generally conducted away from the study site or country. The activities in each of these stages are summarised in Figure 2.2 and described below. It is useful for novice researchers to become familiar with the range of activities to be conducted at each stage of international focus group research, to ensure that sufficient time is allocated to planning the activities.

The *pre-fieldwork stage* of the research involves developing the research proposal, securing funding, drafting the research instruments and developing training material for the field team. Researchers also need to gain the appropriate research permissions and ethical approval for the study. It is also valuable to identify a research collaborator or host institution in the study country early in the research process, as developing collaborative relationships can take time. Some of the pre-fieldwork activities will be dependent on formal procedures (e.g. visa application, research clearance, ethical approval), which can take time and are dependent on the speed of various review committees. Therefore, these activities need to be initiated well in advance of the planned fieldwork. The research team also needs to consider the most appropriate time period in which to conduct the fieldwork, which may be influenced by the climate of the study country, the seasonal availability of the target population or the research timetable; for example, the results may need to be available to coincide with the policy cycle of a particular government ministry. Finally, the research team needs to identify whether language assistance may be needed to conduct the fieldwork and researchers need to become familiar with any local protocols and procedures for conducting research in the study area, for example letters of introduction or study protocol documents may be expected by local officials.

The *fieldwork stage* of the research centres on the data collection activities. The initial tasks involve recruiting and training a field team, translating the research instruments and arranging fieldwork logistics, such as transportation, accommodation, local assistance and so on. Researchers need to become familiar with the appropriate local protocol for conducting research in the study area, such as informing regional authorities of the research and seeking endorsements from community gatekeepers in the intended study sites (see Seeking research permissions below). Once these preparatory activities have been completed, the focus group discussions can be conducted. Local protocol should also be followed in leaving the field sites, to debrief appropriate individuals and acknowledge any assistance received. The translation and transcription of the focus group discussions may also be conducted in-country to utilise local language skills and is a particularly time-consuming activity.

The *post-fieldwork* activities focus on data preparation, analysis and interpretation of the information, and the development of a research report or publication. Some of these activities may be conducted in collaboration with in-country research partners. The post-fieldwork stage may also involve returning to the study country to disseminate the research findings to appropriate government organisations or institutions and to the study communities themselves.

Estimating a fieldwork timetable

It is never easy to determine an accurate timetable for research, but for qualitative research this is particularly challenging due to the nature of the research. In focus group research the planned number of groups may change during the fieldwork process, groups may be held with additional target populations, the discussion issues may shift as the data collection progresses or other changes may occur as the fieldwork progresses. However, it is necessary to develop a fieldwork timetable for inclusion in a research proposal and to determine the cost of the research when seeking funding. In fact, the research budget or the time available to conduct the research may have been pre-determined and therefore influence the development of the fieldwork timetable. The fieldwork timetable will be different for each research project and is dependent on a range of factors, such as; the number of focus groups to be conducted, the geographic location of study sites, travel and logistics, the availability of the study population, ease of recruiting group participants, the size of the research team and so on. It is therefore impossible to suggest a generic fieldwork timetable for focus group research. However, Figure 2.2 shows the range of activities that are typically conducted in international focus group research, highlighting activities conducted prior to fieldwork, the fieldwork activities, and post-fieldwork tasks. The actual time needed for each of the listed activities will be dependent on the nature of the particular study and the context of the fieldwork, for example; the duration of gaining research permissions and ethical approval will differ for each study country, the duration of data collection will depend on the number of focus groups planned, the geographic proximity of each study site will determine the time required for travel and logistics, the size of the field team and their experience will determine the time required for training and the condition of the local infrastructure in the study sites will determine the time needed for travel and logistics. Figure 2.3 highlights a range of such issues to be considered in developing a realistic fieldwork timetable. The activities listed in Figure 2.2 and the issues in Figure 2.3 can be used to develop a project-specific timeframe for focus group research.

When scheduling the group discussions at the study sites it is critical to identify the most convenient times for participants to attend the group discussions rather than expect participants to fit into a research timetable. It is often easy to become too focussed on the research schedule and overlook the priorities and availability of the participants. Some participants may only be available in the evening or early morning before going to their daily tasks, these time restrictions on the availability of participants may affect the timetable of data collection. Researchers also need to consider that conducting focus group discussions is a tiring and intense exercise and scheduling too many group discussions per day may lead to moderator fatigue and have a

- How often does the institutional review board meet?
- How long does it take to receive research permissions for the study country?
- Is there an optimum time of year to conduct the fieldwork?
- Are in-country collaborators available to advise on fieldwork design and logistics?
- What is the geographic proximity of each field site?
- Is accommodation available near the field site or is travel required?
- How many focus groups will be conducted at each site?
- What is the most suitable time of day to conduct the group discussions?
- How many group discussions can be conducted per day?
- What is the size and experience of the field team?
- How much time will be needed to train the field team?
- Have the discussion guides been pre-tested?
- Will the transcription and translation of the discussion be conducted in-country?
- Are there any constraints on the researcher's time in the study country?
  (i.e. permissions, visas, availability of participants etc.)
- Are the research results required within a certain timeframe?
  (e.g. to inform a policy cycle or meet the dissertation deadline)

Figure 2.3   Considerations in developing a fieldwork timetable

negative impact on the quality of the information collected. It would be realistic to schedule one or two focus groups per day, and only plan more than this if a larger field team is available. If transcribing the focus group discussions while in the field, then no more than one group discussion plus transcription can be expected in a day. If possible, the timetable of data collection should include some time for reflecting on the information collected, so that the issues discussed in subsequent groups can be more refined. This is an important component of iterative qualitative research, and may be achieved by allocating time for transcription of the group discussions early in the data collection process, listening to the discussion tapes while in the field, or conducting debriefing meetings with the moderator, note-taker and observer after several group discussions have been conducted.

Developing a fieldwork budget

For focus group research, most of the items on the fieldwork budget will be for actual expenditure on items (e.g. cost of equipment, vehicle rental, etc.) or for payment of time, for field staff and other assistants. In developing an accurate fieldwork budget the research team will need estimates of in-country expenses (e.g. accommodation, transport, etc.) and appropriate rates for payment of field staff. Generally these estimates can be sought from in-country collaborators or research organisations in the study country. Figure 2.4 lists the range of budget items for a typical focus group project. While some of these expenses will be for single payments, others will be

---

> - Travel and associated costs to study site or country (e.g. transport, visa, insurance)
> - Accommodation and subsistence in study sites (for research investigators and field team)
> - Equipment (e.g. tape recorders, tapes, batteries, stationery)
> - Recruitment of field team (e.g. office rental, advertisement, assistant)
> - Training of field team (e.g. room rental, payment, refreshments, training materials)
> - Translation of the discussion guide (if commissioned)
> - In-country travel to/between study sites (e.g. van rental, fuel, driver etc.)
> - Payment of field staff (e.g. moderators, note-takers, recruiters)
> - Transport of participants to venue (if appropriate)
> - Focus group refreshments, participants fee (if appropriate), incentives
> - Transcription and translation of discussion
> - Purchase of data analysis software
> - Data cleaning, analysis and interpretation
> - Report preparation (e.g. research assistants, photocopy costs)
> - Dissemination materials and activities (e.g. preparation of research briefs, posters, reports, room hire and equipment rental, travel and per diem costs)
> - In-country dissemination (may require additional budget)
> - Additional costs, if necessary (e.g. childcare, venue rental, incidentals)

Figure 2.4   Budget items for focus group discussion fieldwork

multiplied by the number of focus groups conducted, to determine the total cost (e.g. cassette tapes, transcription, incentives, and refreshments). In some situations a research agency may be employed to conduct some activities, such as participant recruitment or transcription and translation, in which case the agency fees will apply.

Seeking research permissions

Conducting international research involves seeking permission from various sources, both formal and informal. Research that is developed in collaboration with in-country organisations may seek guidance from these organisations on the procedures and permissions required to conduct research in the country. Where research is not collaborative, it is advisable to begin establishing contacts in the study country as early as possible. Meeting with various stakeholders can gauge their interest in the research proposal, and provide an opportunity for reciprocity (i.e. including stakeholder issues on the research instrument). Research partnerships with in-country organisations or research institutions can be mutually beneficial; such partnerships can assist the research team in seeking research permissions, navigating local protocols and becoming aware of cultural issues. Collaboration can also be beneficial for the in-country organisation to collect information on an area of interest to them. The nature of research collaboration with in-country contacts may vary from the joint development of the research proposal, to sponsoring the research activities, or simply acting as a host institution to advise and support the research team. Similarly, various stakeholders may contribute to the research in an advisory capacity through inclusion on a research committee, which meets periodically to review progress, interpret or disseminate key research findings.

Often two types of permission are needed to conduct international research: formal permission to conduct research in the country and permission from district officials to work in the study area. First, researchers need to follow official procedures for conducting research in the study country. This may be as clear-cut as completing a form to apply for a research visa for the study country, or may involve longer procedures to gain research clearance from relevant institutional bodies in that country (see the following section, Ethical considerations). If researchers are working in collaboration with in-country organisations, such as particular government ministries, then the research proposal may also need to receive 'research clearance' from the relevant committee within that institution. Often such research clearance includes ethical approval for the research. In some cases, aspects of the proposal may need to be revised as recommended by a review committee. These procedures are likely to differ in each country; therefore, it is advisable to check the requirements and procedures with in-country contacts. In some instances gaining research permission involves a sponsor or host institution providing a letter of support for a visa application or for the ethical review committee. Having these documents may influence whether permission for the research is granted (Scheyvens and Storey 2003). The procedures for seeking research permission take time and need to be taken into consideration in the research timetable.

A second tier of official permission may be required from district officials in the area where the research will be conducted. This may involve meeting a range of regional officials, such as the district commissioner, medical directors or regional government officials, or involve attending committee meetings to present the research protocol. District officials may have a vested interest in the research topic or concerns about the research findings, so it is advisable to discuss the research purpose, implementation and anticipated outcomes with regional stakeholders. Informing district officials of the research activities not only shows respect for local protocol, but can also facilitate the smooth implementation of the research activities in the study area. Liaison with district officials can also prove invaluable in understanding local customs and identifying prominent local figures who may be helpful or problematic to the study.

Even though the research team may have been granted official permission to conduct the research, this may have little impact on individuals in the communities where the study will be conducted. Therefore, perhaps the most important of all permissions (in terms of data collection) are the informal endorsements from local gatekeepers in the actual study sites. These individuals often have the power to influence or control access to the study site and to participants, therefore their co-operation is essential. Local gatekeepers may be community and religious leaders, the village chief, the chairmen of a residents' committee, influential local spokespersons or community service providers, all of whom may influence whether others participate in the study. The manner in which these gatekeepers are approached may determine the success of the research project (Ulin *et al.* 2002). Most often the research team will conduct a meeting with local gatekeepers prior to conducting the data collection, to introduce the research, seek endorsements, discuss any concerns and request local assistance. Although this is an informal process, local gatekeepers need to be satisfied before a study can commence, therefore conducting this process is essential. In most instances the research will be welcomed if the local protocols are observed, the study has been endorsed by the district officials and the research is being presented in a culturally appropriate manner.

Gaining both formal and informal permission from various sources is a time consuming exercise that needs to be considered in the research timetable. However, these permissions, endorsements and activities are an essential part of the early stages of fieldwork; they reflect respect for local protocols and provide an opportunity for the research team to become familiar with the culture and context of the study. Contacts made with local gatekeepers in seeking permissions can also lead to mutually beneficial partnerships that can be invaluable throughout the research process and beyond it.

Recruiting a field team

Research investigators may be trained in research methods but often have little understanding of the cultural norms, languages or the socio-economic context of the study country. This can be true of those conducting research internationally or within areas of their own country. Therefore, researchers need to recruit a local field team to assist with conducting the study. Often the recruitment of the field team not only provides a workforce with appropriate skills for the data collection, but the field team can also bridge the gap between the research investigators and the study participants, to assist researchers in understanding socio-cultural issues that arise during the field-work. In addition to the actual data collection tasks, the field team may also be called upon to assist in meetings with local community leaders, translate the study objectives to local officials, and work with community assistants to recruit participants in the field sites. The presence of a local field team can also improve local rapport in the study sites and be invaluable in negotiating cultural issues and protocols throughout the fieldwork process.

Typically the field team will comprise of focus group moderators, note-takers and assistants. The size and characteristics of the field team will be somewhat dependent on how the group discussions will be stratified. For example, male and female moderators may be required, younger and older and so on. Each project will require different criteria for the field team. The most common criteria are language requirements, to ensure that the field team can effectively communicate with the study participants, and demo-graphic characteristics, so that a moderator's characteristics match those of the group participants. Although it is preferable if members of the field team have prior experience in qualitative methods, particularly group facilitation, this is often a difficult criterion to fulfil. If the field team are proficient in the required languages and have suitable interpersonal skills they can often be trained to become effective moderators (see Chapter 4 on Training the focus group team). The research team also needs to be informed of ethical prac-tices in data collection and to be encouraged to respect the confidentiality of participants by not sharing what was discussed in the focus groups with others in the community. Training local assistants on focus group method-ology can also build local capacity and provide individuals with key skills that they can use to gain similar work in the future. It is therefore particularly valuable for the field team to receive a letter stating their participation in the training and field activities (Ulin *et al.* 2002).

A focus group team is often recruited by advertising for specific skills and characteristics, conducting interviews, selecting individuals and providing training. In some situations in-country collaborators may recommend suit-able individuals with field experience. Figure 2.5 describes a typical experi-ence in recruiting a field team for focus group research. This case study highlights the need to remain flexible in the planning process and to be willing to revise the recruitment of field staff in response to the realities of the study context. In recruiting the field team the research investigators not only need to ensure that individuals have the required skills, such as language or literacy, but that they have a broad understanding of the research topic and are able to

A research study in Zambia needed to recruit a field team to conduct focus group discussions in two regions of the country with different cultural and linguistic traditions. The field team therefore needed to comprise of individuals who were competent in four local languages spoken in the different study sites. In addition, the principle researcher hoped that the field assistants would have experience in health research. These were the initial criteria for recruiting the field team.

One month prior to the fieldwork the researcher e-mailed the in-country link person to advertise for field assistants with the required criteria. *'Because of my limited budget I couldn't afford to hire field assistants who were just competent in one or two languages, I needed people who could speak all four, and that was nearly impossible!'* The initial recruitment attracted thirty applicants, only three of whom could speak all four languages; however, ten assistants were required. The recruitment strategy was then revised, with the assistance of the in-country link person, advertising more widely and focussing specifically on the language skills required. Thirty-five more applications were received and another day was spent interviewing. Although language skills were a criterion, the research team need to ensure competence in each of the languages required. *'It occurred to me that I was just asking these people 'can you speak this language?' . . . I had no way of telling if they were telling the truth and I know jobs are hard to come by . . . so I then needed to do a language test of those we recruited.'* Finally, eight suitable assistants were recruited for the field team. On reflection of the recruitment process, the researcher stated, *'At first I had this very ambitious daily planner, I was supposed to do recruitment day one and two, day three I was supposed to start the training . . . it was not going to plan! So that is something to remember, be flexible, and allow room for such hic-ups . . . The whole process of recruitment took one week, which I was hoping would take two days, but it was worth it in the end. I had to compromise on the research experience because I just couldn't get people who could speak the languages and also had the research experience. So I rather got people with the language experience and trained them (on the research).'*

Research Student, Zambia

Figure 2.5   Recruiting a field team in Zambia

travel with the field team to the study sites, as cultural norms may restrict some individuals from travel or staying overnight in research sites away from their home. It is also advisable to avoid the recruitment of people who are known to have controversial views, or strong community and authoritarian positions (e.g. traditional leaders, political figures, etc.) as these individuals may be renowned in the community and influence the dynamics of the group discussions. Local collaborators can advise on these issues.

Selecting a moderator

Selecting a moderator requires identifying individuals with suitable socio-demographic characteristics, language fluency and appropriate interpersonal skills to facilitate the discussion. The ideal qualities of a moderator are summarised in Figure 2.6. A research project may require several moderators with differing socio-demographic characteristics, so that they can be matched with those of the group participants. It is also preferable to select a moderator who is familiar with the cultural traditions of participants and so likely to make participants feel at ease (Vasquez and Han 1995; Fern 2001). A lack of sensitivity to the social values and cultural norms of the target population can

- Well developed interpersonal skills
- Effective communicator
- Empathetic and encouraging
- Cultural sensitivity
- Fluent in language of discussion
- Confidence in controlling discussion
- Non-judgemental
- Aware of own biases
- Confidential
- Flexible and spontaneous
- Experience with group dynamics
- Clearly express thoughts
- Interested in others' opinions
- Sense of humour
- Active listener
- Good memory

Figure 2.6   Ideal characteristics of a moderator

impact on the validity and reliability of the data collected. It is also important that a moderator is conscious of the subtle messages portrayed by their style of dress, which can easily portray social status and power. Participants need to feel comfortable with the moderator; therefore, a moderator's style of dress should not be overly status laden or too casual so as not to be taken seriously. Clearly the moderator needs to be fluent in the language of the study participants; this may require the recruitment of moderators who are fluent in several different languages if the study is conducted in several regions of a country with different linguistic traditions. Language issues are not only a consideration in international research, but also in research amongst ethnic minority groups in the researcher's own country, who may prefer to communicate in their natal language. Research amongst Hispanic communities in the US found that seventy percent of participants preferred to respond in Spanish, despite knowledge of the English language and their level of acculturation (Marin and Marin 1991).

Many texts also highlight a range of desired personal qualities of a successful moderator, which are summarised in Figure 2.6 (Greenbaum 2000; Krueger and Casey 2000; Fern 2001; Ulin *et al.* 2002). A successful moderator needs to have well-developed interpersonal and communication skills, to make participants feel at ease in the group situation, develop good rapport within the group and encourage participation. Good listening and communication skills are also vital in clearly framing questions and being able to quickly tailor follow-up questions to the issues raised. A moderator needs to be flexible and spontaneous to be able to diverge from the prepared discussion guide and follow the natural flow of the discussion while still covering the key issues of the research. Experience with group moderation and group dynamics will also enable a moderator to manage a discussion with confidence. Above all else, a moderator needs to be empathetic and respectful towards participants, showing a genuine interest in the views and feelings of participants on the topics discussed. Smiling generates warmth and empathy and a sense of humour can promote easy and enjoyable discussion. A lack of respect or disinterest will quickly discourage meaningful discussion. A moderator also needs to be non-judgemental and 'neutral' by not contributing their own opinions and possibly biasing the discussion. This involves the moderator being aware of their own biases and separating these from what occurs in the group discussion. The moderator has the difficult task of 'balancing the requirements of sensitivity and empathy on the one hand and objectivity and detachment on the other' (Stewart and Shamdasani 1990). A moderator also needs to be aware of ethical issues, in particular to retain confidentiality of the information discussed in the group.

Payment and incentives

One of the early decisions that the research team needs to make is whether focus group participants will be given a payment or any other incentive for their participation in the group discussions. The convention of paying a fee to participants possibly originates from the use of focus groups in market research, where the fee is a considerable inducement to aid recruitment and retention of participants (Bloor *et al.* 2001). It is usual to provide refreshments for participants during a focus group discussion; this is a positive social gesture that helps to create a relaxed, informal atmosphere. Also, where participants need to travel some distance to attend the group discussion, they may be given a 'participant fee' which is intended to cover any expenses incurred as a result of attending the group discussion (e.g. transport, parking, childcare, etc.) or as compensation for time lost in earnings. Such compensation may be necessary in developing country contexts where high unemployment means that participation would be unlikely if it were to compete with income-generating activities. Aside from these provisions, any additional incentives or payments are an area of debate amongst researchers because of the effect that it may have on participants' contributions to the research.

Many social science researchers believe that participants should not be paid for their involvement in focus group discussions as this creates an atmosphere of commercialisation of research and may lead to an expectation amongst study participants of 'payment for information'. This is seen as unethical and inappropriate as payment may influence the information received or the behaviour of participants. There is a related concern about 'poisoning the well', in that the provision of monetary incentives by one research team may cause difficulties for future researchers who are unable to provide any incentives and therefore encounter difficulties in recruiting study participants. However, in some contexts, payment for participation has become expected and it is therefore necessary to pay according to the local rate (Ulin *et al.* 2002). For most small research budgets, payment for participants is simply not possible. Other researchers feel that recruiting certain types of participants is difficult (e.g. executives, professionals) and therefore payments are a necessary incentive to recruit participants (Morgan and Scannell 1998). Researchers also vary in their opinions on the provision of non-monetary incentives. Some research teams will provide a small gift to participants as a token of thanks for their time in contributing to the research, while other researchers may find this inappropriate. Any inducement may persuade an individual to participate in the research, but this is not in itself inappropriate. However, incentives are generally considered to be inappropriate where participants may feel that the benefits offered by an inducement outweigh the risks in participation. The greater the inducement the more likely that this situation may arise. In considering the provision of incentives for participants, researchers should seek guidance from local collaborators to ensure that incentives are appropriate to the local cultural context of the research. If gifts are provided to participants, they may be small household or food items such as soap, washing powder, salt or maize for each participant; vouchers or any small items of interest to the participants can also be provided. Alternatively, if the study is focussed in a particular community, some research teams may give a donation of items to the community (e.g. school books); this may be appropriate if returning to the community on several occasions to collect information.

In general, participants do not contribute to research studies to receive incentives, but are motivated to participate because they value the opportunity to give voice to the research issues which may have important outcomes for themselves or their community. However, without any benefits, either for themselves or others, individuals would be unlikely to participate in any research. In some situations participants may expect a lot from their contributions, such as money, gifts, jobs, immediate changes in their community and so on. However, it should always be stressed that research on health and social issues is being conducted to improve the circumstances of the community in the long term and that this is an important motivation for participation, while the incentives given are small tokens or compensations for costs incurred as a result of participation.

Ethical considerations

All research should be conducted with respect to ethical principles and practices. Gaining ethical approval at the beginning of a study does not mean that ethical issues can subsequently be ignored. Instead ethical considerations should inform each stage of the research process. Focus group research, in particular, requires continual assessment of ethical issues due to the evolving nature of data collection, the group context of the discussion, and the type of issues discussed. The dynamic and flexible nature of focus group research, as with other qualitative methods, often means that a discussion can change direction, unanticipated topics may be raised and participants may share more intimate or personal experiences with the group than expected by the researchers. This may raise ethical dilemmas, in that the discussion diverges from the issues indicated by the moderator at the outset. Focus group research also involves asking people to discuss issues openly in the presence of a moderator and other participants. The group nature of data collection poses additional risks to the confidentiality of the information discussed, in that some participants may share the content of the discussion with others outside the group. This situation puts the onus on the research team to reinforce issues of confidentiality amongst the group. These characteristics of focus group research mean that the research team needs to continually assess ethical issues throughout the research process, from the study design to data collection and in the dissemination of findings, and to remain aware that changes in the research process may lead to new and unexpected ethical dilemmas. Ethical principles should inform all stages of focus group research and in international settings the research should be conducted in a manner that is sensitive to cultural issues and respectful of the community in which the research is being conducted.

Institutional review committees

Institutional review committees are mandated by governments and research institutions to assess proposed research studies for scientific validity, ethical acceptability and relevance to the advancement of knowledge. Scientific evaluation of the research is essential, as research which is poorly designed will be unable to meet the research objectives and therefore have little benefit. The ethical acceptability of a research study will typically be assessed in terms of the risks and benefits to participants, the provisions made in the research design to protect participants from harm, and appropriate procedures for gaining consent from participants and protecting confidentiality. Each professional body has established codes of practice and ethical guidelines to assist in the design and conduct of ethical research. Research proposals involving human participants are required to be submitted to an institutional review board for approval before any fieldwork can be undertaken.

The Nuffield Council on Bioethics (2002: 107) recommends that '...externally-sponsored research projects should be subject to independent ethical review in the sponsor's country(ies) in addition to the country(ies) in which the research is to be conducted.' However, they also note that there exists wide variation between countries in the existence of institutional review committees and, if established, in their capacity to conduct effective ethical reviews. The Nuffield Council highlights that in some developing countries there exists no formal internal ethical review process (e.g. Myanmar, Laos), although there may be mechanisms to review research by Ministry of Health officials. Other countries request that research be reviewed by a research ethics committee of a neighbouring country. For example, research in Guinea Bissau is reviewed by the ethics committee in The Gambia. Some developing countries do have national guidance for the review of the ethics of research (e.g. India, Thailand, Nepal, Uganda, South Africa and Brazil) and may have implemented national, local or institutional review committees, although the quality of the assessment may vary. In some countries ethical approval is an essential pre-requisite for the research to proceed, in others it is simply viewed as a formality that is granted without effective procedure, and in other situations the decisions of a research ethics committee may be ignored or overridden by government officials (Nuffield Council on Bioethics 2002).

If effective and enforced, ethical review committees can govern the ethical standards and practice in research, and compel researchers to consider systematically the ethical issues throughout the study. Researchers have a responsibility to become informed of the ethical review process in their home and study country and to follow appropriate procedure. Due to the great variability between the protocols in each country no specific guidelines can be given here. Navigating the ethical review procedures in a study country can be time-consuming, especially if procedures are unclear or committees only meet at specified times during the year, so adequate prior planning and close liaison with in-country collaborators is advised.

Informed consent

All research should begin with the informed consent of participants to be part of the study. To be ethically acceptable, a research project should provide participants with sufficient, relevant and accurate information, in a comprehensible format, so that participants can make an informed and voluntary decision on whether or not to participate. Without appropriate information about the research and their expected contribution to it, participants may be exposed to harm that they would prefer to avoid. Informed consent may be described as follows:

Informed consent is when a potential participant freely and with full understanding of the research agrees to be part of the project. It is premised on the notion that the person has a complete and thorough understanding of the aims and processes of the research project, what the research will be used for . . . and who will have access to the information gathered. (Scheyvens and Storey 2003: 142)

Schinke and Gilchrist (1993: 83) state that '. . . all informed-consent procedures must meet three criteria: participants must be competent to give consent; sufficient information must be provided to allow for a reasoned decision; and consent must be voluntary and uncoerced.' (Cited in Kumar 2005: 213.)

The Declaration of Helsinki (World Medical Association 2000) sets out the information that should be provided to participants in seeking informed consent. Participants should be provided with information about the research project, the research organisation and what their contribution to the research will involve (i.e. group discussion, topic, duration of participation). An essential part of informed consent is people's freedom to decline participation at the outset or at any stage during the research process without any negative impact, and that their information will be removed from the pool of collected data (Scheyvens and Storey 2003). Researchers should also inform participants of any potential harm or benefit that may result from their participation in the research. It is important to remember that harm can be any type of negative impact, such as physical, social, economic or psychological harm. Participants also need to be informed on how confidentiality will be maintained in the storage and use of the information, who will have access to the information provided and how participants' identities will be

Basic information for participants:
- Purpose of the research
- Description of research procedures and type of involvement requested
- Identification of research organisation(s)
- Sources of funding and possible conflicts of interest
- How individuals were selected to participate
- Duration of participant's involvement
- What will be expected of participants
- Possible risks, discomfort or inconvenience of participation
- How risk will be minimised and compensation (if appropriate)
- Possible benefits to participant or population in general
- Costs incurred from participation (transportation, childcare, time lost)
- Participation is voluntary
- Right to withdraw from the study at any time
- No negative impact on participants if they decline participation
- Seek consent for audio, video or photographic recordings of participants
- Procedures to protect confidentiality
- Who will have access to the information
- How the information will be used (by whom and for whom)
- Identify payment for participation (if appropriate)
- Who to contact with any concerns

Basic rights of participants:
- To participate voluntarily
- To decline participation
- To have consent documents translated or conveyed verbally
- To withdraw from the study
- To ask questions about the study
- To have privacy and confidentiality protected
- To refuse audio recording
- To receive information about the study findings
- To receive copy of consent documents

Figure 2.7   Basic information for potential participants

protected in reports of the study findings. In addition to seeking informed consent for participation in the group discussion, the research team also need to request permission to tape record the discussion and, if appropriate, to take photographs of the group session. These requests may be included in the informed consent procedure or as a separate permission. Participants should be advised that they can request the audio equipment be turned off at any time during the discussion. The information to be provided to participants in seeking consent for participation is summarised in Figure 2.7. It is advisable to pre-test the informed consent form and information sheet to check that the language and information can be clearly understood; this is particularly critical if the documents are translated.

In many developing countries individuals often seek permission for certain actions, including the participation in research, from others in their household or community. In these contexts it would be considered culturally inappropriate for researchers to approach individuals to participate in research without first consulting the community as a whole or gaining the endorsement of community leaders. For example, local protocol often dictates that a community leader or village chief endorse any activities that are undertaken in their community. In addition, certain individuals may require the permission of others in their household to contribute to research, for example, young women may need the permission of a mother-in-law, husband or household elder. Researchers need to respect these cultural hierarchies in seeking consent for participation in the research, even if this complicates the research process. At the centre of informed consent is the requirement that participation in a study is voluntary and not coerced. In some contexts community leaders or household elders may imply or authorise consent for individuals to participate in research, particularly in communities where strong power dynamics exist (Mauthner *et al.* 2002). Researchers should be careful not to assume an individual has consented to participate in the research, simply because community leaders have endorsed their participation. Individual consent is always required. The Nuffield Council on Bioethics (2002: 15) states that '... in some cultural contexts it may be appropriate to obtain agreement from the particular community or assent from a senior family member, before any prospective participant in research is approached. However, genuine consent to participate in research must also be obtained from each participant.'

Providing potential participants with written information about the research and seeking signature of a written consent form may not be appropriate in some contexts. Seeking written consent is particularly difficult when conducting research in communities who are largely illiterate, where written documents have little meaning, or in socially repressed societies where signing formal documents is particularly feared. It would be disrespectful to insist that a consent form is signed when individuals are unable to read the contents or fear the reprisals of signing an official document. Ulin *et al.* (2005) state that written consent may also be inappropriate in studies where a breech in confidentiality may have serious repercussions for the participant, such as clandestine contraceptive users, women who have undergone unsafe abortion or unmarried adolescent contraceptive users. In these situations the written consent form is the only document linking the participant to the study and may jeopardise participant confidentiality.

Ethics committees now recognise that in specific circumstances seeking written consent may be culturally inappropriate or may put participants at risk. In these situations written consent may be obtained by providing verbal information and gaining oral consent from participants, but there is usually a requirement that this consent is documented in some way. The Nuffield Council on Bioethics (2002: 83) states that 'where it is inappropriate for consent to be recorded in writing, genuine consent must be obtained verbally. The process of obtaining consent and the accompanying documentation must be approved by a research ethics committee and, where only verbal consent to research is contemplated, include consideration of an appropriate process for witnessing the consent.' Gaining oral consent and documenting such consent typically involves reading the consent document to potential participants in a language understandable to them and then seeking their verbal consent to participate in the study. This process also requires a witness to observe that consent was gained appropriately. Both the participant and the witness need to sign, or make a thumb imprint on, the consent document. In addition, the oral consent statement may be read to the focus group prior to the discussion and participants' consent tape recorded.

The informed consent document should be written in lay terms and at a level of understanding appropriate for the study participants. A sample informed consent script for focus group discussions conducted in Rwanda and Zambia is shown in Figure 2.8.

Harm to participants

It is important that participants are not at risk of harm through their participation in the focus group discussions. Researchers need to continually weight the potential social benefits of the information sought against the potential risk of harm to participants. Harm to participants can be evident in many ways; it can be physical harm, such as evidence of clandestine contraceptive use that may put a woman at risk of physical harm from her husband; psychological harm, in terms of personal embarrassment or shame; social harm, such as impacting a family reputation; or economic harm such as loss of employment, promotion opportunities or programme funding. Researchers have a responsibility to identify and inform participants of the potential risks that may arise from their participation in the study and to minimise these risks as far as possible. This may be done by carefully considering which issues will be discussed in the group, by reinforcing confidentiality of the discussion and by protecting respondents' identity in the documentation and reporting of the study findings (Miles and Huberman 1994; Ulin et al. 2005).

Confidentiality and anonymity

Participants' contributions to the group discussions should remain confidential and their identity concealed in the use of research data. Participants

INFORMED CONSENT

Formative Focus Group and Interviews in Two African Capitals

Names of Principle Investigators   _____

Institutions of Principle Investigators   _____

Name of Research Sponsor   _____

Explanation of Procedures

You are being invited to participate in an interview or discussion group being conducted as a collaboration between (research organisations). This research is funded by (funding organisations) and executed in collaboration with the Ministries of Health (MOH) in Rwanda and Zambia and their hospitals and clinics.

This interview or discussion group is designed to help us understand your knowledge and beliefs concerning many issues relating to HIV infection and AIDS. You are one of many people being asked to participate in this group discussion or individual interview. Participants represent all segments of local populations, and will include housewives as well as health care providers, educators, government bureaucrats, and others. (Research organisation names) conduct many different types of HIV/AIDS research. Your counselor will notify you if you are eligible for participation in any of the studies, or any other services offered by this project.

Risks and Discomforts

Discussing and answering questions about HIV may be uncomfortable for some people. You are always free to not answer a question if you do not want to.

Benefits

You may not personally benefit from your participation in this research. However, your answers may provide us with information that will be used to develop programmes to reduce HIV/AIDS in adults and children.

Alternative Procedures

Your participation in this study is entirely voluntary and there is no expectation on the part of your doctors, the study directors, or the Ministry of Health that you participate. Your decision on whether or not to participate will not affect the care you receive from your doctors, and will not affect your participation in other studies at (research organisations). Whether or not you decide to enter the study, you will receive the best available general health education information on ways to avoid receiving or transmitting the HIV/AIDS virus. This will include advice that you should limit your sexual partners and use condoms while having intercourse.

Confidentiality

All information collected during the interview and/or focus group will be kept confidential to the extent permitted by law. The session will be tape recorded and converted into written format. Your participation means that you agree to allow the information to be used for scientific purposes, but your name will not be identified in any way in reports or publications. This research team has over 18 years of HIV/AIDS and STD research experience in Africa. Procedures for maintaining confidentiality have been well tested and are successful. However, your doctor, representatives of the sponsor, the (university name) Institutional Review Board, and US and international regulatory agencies who monitor research to ensure that the work is done correctly and that the safety, confidentiality and well-being of participants is protected, may have access to information which identifies you by name. Any publication of the data will not identify you.

Rwanda Ethics Committee

Approval Date: _____

Expiration Date: _____

Cont'd...

Withdrawal Without Prejudice

You are free to withdraw your consent and to discontinue your participation in this study at any time without prejudice against future medical care or study participation at (research organisations). Participation in this study will have no effect on your availability of access to current or future studies at (research organisations) or at MOH facilities.

Significant New Findings

You will be told by Dr. _____ or their staff of any new information learned during the course of the study that might cause you to change your mind about staying in the study. If we discover any important information during the study that might affect your health, we will tell you right away. Care or appropriate referral will be provided, if necessary.

Costs for Participation in Research

There are no costs to you for taking part in this discussion group or interview. Every effort will be made to arrange for provision of necessary assistance, but any services other than those routinely provided in the study will be the financial responsibility of the study participant.

Payment for Research Participation

You will be reimbursed for your time and if appropriate, your transport, based on current costs (amount in local currency). The exact amount and nature of the reimbursements may be modified in light of changes in bus fares, exchange rates, or cost of living.

Payment for Research Related Injuries

In the event of an injury resulting directly from participation in the research, outpatient treatment will be provided at the (name of clinic), with referral to government health clinics or hospitals (names of hospitals) as needed. The costs of treatment related directly to the injury resulting from participation in the research will be paid by (names of organisations), which are registered respectively with the Zambian Medical Council and the MOH.

Questions

You have the opportunity to ask any questions you may have, and to discuss your answers fully. You are urged to contact the principal investigators at any time if you have any questions. (Names and contact details.) For questions concerning your rights as a research participant, you may contact the following persons (Names and contact details).

Legal Rights

You are not waiving any legal rights by signing this form.

Statement of Agreement to Participate in Research Study

You have read this consent form or had it read to you in a language that you can speak, and its contents explained to you. All of your questions have been answered. Your rights and privacy will be maintained. You freely and voluntarily choose to participate in this study. You will be given a copy of this consent form. If you do not wish to keep a copy, the study clinic will keep it for you in a safe and secure place. By signing your name or making your mark in the space below you voluntarily agree to join the study.

_____

Signature/Thumb Print   Printed Name   Date

_____

Witness/Authorised Personnel   Printed Name   Date

Source: Allen (2006)

Figure 2.8   Example Informed Consent script

need to be assured of the confidentiality and anonymity of their comments. Typically these assurances are given when seeking informed consent for participation and in the introduction to the group discussion. Researchers must then implement measures to ensure confidentiality and anonymity throughout the research process. As the data are collected in a group setting (rather than in individual interviews), there may be a greater risk to the confidentiality of information by another participant sharing the issues discussed with those outside of the focus group. Therefore a moderator should take additional time to reinforce to participants the importance of keeping the discussion confidential. Participants should also be informed about how confidentiality will be maintained and who will have access to the information. Researchers also have a responsibility to maintain participant's anonymity in the storage of the data, during analysis and in reporting the information. If the names of respondents are recorded, these should be kept separate from the data transcripts, the transcripts should be anonymised before data analysis and any other information which may reveal the identity of a participant should also be removed from the transcripts (see section in Chapter 11 on Data preparation). In the presentation of focus group findings the data used in the report should be reviewed carefully to identify whether there is any information that may enable any participant to be identified. In many focus group studies, the names of participants may not be known or recorded by the researchers. However, there may be other details which link the information to a specific individual. These details should be removed to ensure participant's anonymity.

Ethics in data analysis and dissemination

Ethical data analysis involves following accepted procedures for data analysis that minimise bias and subjectivity in the analysis procedures and in the interpretation of the information. Researchers have an obligation to remain objective in the data analysis and to be transparent in the procedures used and the conclusions drawn from the data. Part of ethical data analysis involves honesty in reporting the conclusions of the research, by indicating all results both positive and negative, and reflecting on those aspects of the research process which may have impacted on negative results. For a detailed discussion of ethical issues in the analysis of qualitative data see Miles and Huberman (1994).

Ethical research must not only ensure that no harm comes to participants through their participation in the discussion groups, but also that no harm arises as a result of the publication or dissemination of their views. Researchers must ensure anonymity in reporting participants' views or experiences in published reports of the study; even if the information does not contain participants' names there may remain other information that could reveal the identity of a participant or their family (see Chapter 11 on how to anonymise data). Once research findings are published they may be used for various purposes, perhaps unintended by the research team. It is therefore critical that researchers are particularly careful about ethical reporting of the study findings to protect the study participants from harm once the information is in the public domain.

Ethical research also needs to consider reciprocity in considering what researchers can give back to the study communities that provided information for the research (Miles and Huberman 1994; Ulin *et al.* 2002; Scheyvens and Storey 2003). One of the fundamental activities is to ensure that the research findings are disseminated in the study country and back to the study communities (see Chapter 12 on community dissemination of results). Disseminating the study findings to a broad audience may mean that they are available to be used to improve the social situation of the study participants, while returning to the study community to share insights of the research will contribute towards encouraging community members to participate in future research projects.

Key terms

Research permission refers to the formal authorisation and informal endorsements that need to be gained before fieldwork activities can begin (e.g. research visa, research clearance, endorsement of community gatekeepers).

Informed consent involves providing potential participants with sufficient and relevant information about the research project and what will be expected of them, so that they can make an informed choice about whether to contribute to the research. Often two documents need to be developed for informed consent, an information sheet and a consent form.

A *consent form* is a document to be signed by participants to indicate that they have agreed to participate in the research study. In some instances signing a consent form may be waived and oral consent to participate in the study may be given.

Oral consent is where participants give verbal consent to take part in the study, in place of signing a consent form. Oral consent is usually documented by tape recording the consent or through a proxy signature by the researcher.

An *institutional review board (IRB)* is a committee that reviews research proposals to assess whether the research complies with ethical principles and practices.

Ethical approval for the study involves submitting the proposal to an ethical review board within the researcher's institution and in the study country. The proposal is then assessed

to identify whether the research will be conducted according to recognised ethical protocols of the professional body.

Incentives are monetary or non-monetary items provided to participants to encourage
their participation in the study.

Anonymity means that the identity of participants is not revealed during the research
process in the data storage, analysis or in the research reports.

Confidentiality means that a participant's contribution to the discussion is not revealed to
others outside the group discussion or the research team.

Summary of key issues

- Careful planning is fundamental to the successful implementation of focus group
  research, particularly when it is conducted in another country.
- Researchers need to be clear about the purpose of the study, the target population and
  how the information from the group discussions will be used.
- Developing an accurate fieldwork timetable and budget are necessary for inclusion in the
  research proposal.
- Conducting international research involves seeking permission and endorsements for the
  research from various sources, both formal and informal.
- Collaboration with in-country institutions can be mutually beneficial in facilitating the
  smooth implementation of the research activities, understanding local customs and
  protocols and jointly identifying study recommendations.
- Recruitment of a local field team not only provides assistance with data collection, but can
  also assist researchers in understanding socio-cultural issues that arise during the
  fieldwork.
- The research team needs to identify whether payment or incentives for study participants
  are appropriate.
- Ethical issues need to be continually assessed throughout the research process, from the
  study design to data collection and in the dissemination of findings. The evolving nature of
  qualitative research means that new and unexpected ethical dilemmas may arise.
- When written consent from participants is not possible or appropriate, researchers need to
  assess the feasibility of seeking oral consent.
- Researchers need to respect cultural hierarchies when asking individuals for consent to
  participate in research.
- It is important that participants are not at risk of harm through their participation in the
  group discussions. Researchers need to continually weigh the potential social benefits of
  the information sought against the potential risk of harm to participants.
- Participants' contributions to the group discussions should remain confidential and their
  identity concealed in the use of research data.
- Ethical data analysis involves following accepted procedures for data analysis that
  minimise bias and subjectivity in the analysis procedures and in the interpretation of the
  information.

Preparing the discussion guide

Introduction

The main data collection tool in focus group research is the discussion guide. If well developed, this research tool can elicit the type of information from a group discussion to meet the research objectives. The quality of the information received will be a direct reflection of the forethought given to the design of the discussion guide and the question strategy, therefore sufficient time and careful attention need to be given to developing the discussion guide. The development of the discussion guide is one of the crucial tasks in focus group research. This chapter outlines the purpose of a discussion guide, the different types of discussion guides, the structure and function of each part of the instrument, and effective questioning strategies. For international focus group research, it is often necessary to translate the discussion guide into the language of the study population. This chapter also discusses language and translation issues as well as sensitivity to the development of culturally appropriate questioning strategies. A checklist of issues for designing the discussion guide is given at the end of the chapter.

Purpose of the discussion guide

A discussion guide is a pre-prepared list of discussion topics or actual questions used by a moderator to facilitate the group discussion. The main function of the discussion guide is to act as a memory aid for the moderator to assist in managing the discussion around a range of key topics. Although the discussion guide is designed to lead the discussion through a logical sequence of topics, often the issues will be raised in a much more haphazard manner, and the moderator will therefore rely on the discussion guide as a checklist to ensure that all issues of importance were raised in the discussion. Morgan (1997: 48) describes the discussion guide in the following way: 'In essence, the moderator uses the guide as a resource to maintain the balance between the researchers' focus and the group's discussion.' In this way, the moderator will use the discussion guide to simultaneously navigate the discussion through the issues on the discussion guide as well as allowing new issues to be explored, so that by the close of the discussion all the critical issues have been discussed. Ideally, the moderator should use the discussion guide as a prompt to pursue the key issues to their natural conclusion, while not neglecting to explore new issues or prompt the discussion with new questions.

Although the primary purpose of the discussion guide is as a memory aid, the discussion guide also has a range of other functions. First, using a discussion guide can introduce some consistency in the data collection across all group discussions within the study, in terms of similar topics being raised or similar questioning strategies used. The need for consistency in the discussion topics becomes important during data analysis when comparing responses to the discussion issues across different group discussions in the study. It is through the comparison of the issues between group discussions that patterns and themes in the data emerge which illuminate the research problem. The need for consistency is also important when several moderators are used in a study, so that each will use similar phrasing of the discussion questions and the responses from each group can then be compared. If the discussion questions are phrased differently by each moderator they may also be interpreted differently by participants and evoke different types of responses in each group discussion, thereby making comparison of issues across groups difficult. The need for consistency is particularly apparent when the discussion guide has been translated into the language of the study participants. Translating a discussion guide often involves much debate on the most appropriate terminology and phrasing of the issues, as in some languages a slight alteration in the words or phrases used can significantly alter the meaning or the emphasis of a question and elicit a different type of response than intended. Therefore, the translated discussion guide provides each moderator with a consistent set of translated questions and terms to use in the discussion. Although one function of the discussion guide is to introduce some consistency in the discussion questions, this does not suggest that moderators need to use each question as in a formal survey interview; it is consistency in the meaning of the questions which is of key importance.

Second, Greenbaum (2000) states that the discussion guide is a useful document to show others the intended nature of the discussion, the type of information that may be collected, and to seek input on the issues included. It can be used in discussions between the researcher and research collaborators, donor agencies or doctoral supervisors. A written discussion guide provides an opportunity for others to comment on the issues selected, suggest additional topics, or review the cultural appropriateness of certain questions or approaches. In addition, the discussion guide may need to be submitted with the research proposal to an ethical review board. A fully developed discussion guide provides a clear indication of the issues to be discussed and the way in which participants will be asked about the issues; thereby enabling a clearer assessment of any potential ethical issues.

Third, the discussion guide can assist the moderator to achieve closure on the discussion. Greenbaum (2000) suggests that the presence of a discussion guide can be used to convince participants that all the intended discussion issues have been covered and then draw the group to a close. This is particularly useful when the participants would like to continue the discussion on unrelated topics once the core issues have been covered. It also acts to reinforce to the commissioning agency that all the agreed discussion topics were covered in the group discussion. Finally, the discussion guide is a useful document to include in the appendix of the research report, as it indicates what was (and was not) discussed in the group discussions. The delineation of topics on the discussion guide may also be used to structure a preliminary report, as the discussion topics are often designed to directly respond to the key research questions.

Developing the discussion guide

There are a number of influences on the development of the discussion guide which are shown in Figure 3.1 and highlighted below. First, a comprehensive review of the literature on the study topic will provide an indication of the potential issues to explore in the group discussion. It may also indicate appropriate terminology to use amongst a particular study population. Second, the context of the study will determine the types of issues that may be appropriate, the language of the discussion and culturally appropriate questioning strategies. Third, the research purpose is the key influence on the design of the discussion guide and will determine the selection of discussion topics and the focus of the discussion. Fourth, the research methodology will determine how the information from the group discussions will be used and will indicate the level of detail required on the discussion guide. For example, a less detailed discussion guide would be required if the findings of the group discussions will be used to design a survey questionnaire, compared with a study that will analyse the substantive results of the group discussions. Finally, the characteristics of the target population will influence the language, terminology, topics and question strategies used.

The discussion guide is often developed with input from a range of sources. Some studies are conducted in collaboration with government or non-government agencies in the study country, who may suggest issues to be discussed in the focus groups. A funding agency may also contribute to the design of the research instrument. In smaller studies or for doctoral research the discussion

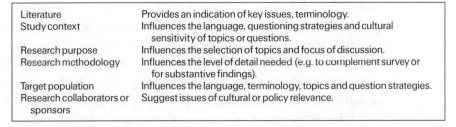

Literature	Provides an indication of key issues, terminology.
Study context	Influences the language, questioning strategies and cultural sensitivity of topics or questions.
Research purpose	Influences the selection of topics and focus of discussion.
Research methodology	Influences the level of detail needed (e.g. to complement survey or for substantive findings).
Target population	Influences the language, terminology, topics and question strategies.
Research collaborators or sponsors	Suggest issues of cultural or policy relevance.

Figure 3.1   Influences on developing the discussion guide

guide may be designed by the research team alone. However, in international focus group research it can be extremely beneficial to receive input from in-country collaborators or research organisations, particularly to assist with language use and to comment on any pertinent cultural issues of the research topic.

Types of discussion guides

A discussion guide may take several formats. The two most common types of discussion guides are a topic guide or a questioning route (Krueger 1998a). A *topic guide* consists of a list of topics or key words that act as memory prompts for the moderator. The main advantages of the topic guide are the speed in developing the research instrument, as only key topics or phrases are listed rather than fully developed questions; and the greater conversational style in the delivery of questions, as the questions are being formed by the moderator as the group progresses. However, this type of discussion guide puts a great deal of pressure on the moderator to spontaneously phrase the list of topics into single coherent questions as the group discussion progresses, and it is therefore not recommended for inexperienced moderators. One of the key drawbacks of using a topic guide is the difficulty in data analysis, as the actual questions asked of participants are variable and likely to have a different emphasis in each group discussion. This makes comparative analysis between focus group discussions more difficult or not feasible, as slight changes in the wording of questions may lead to significant changes in their meaning and hence the responses given may vary considerably. This disadvantage is multi-plied with numerous moderators in a research project, who may each interpret the listed topics differently or assume a different emphasis. A further drawback is the difficulty in pilot testing a topic guide, as the actual development of questions will be done spontaneously as the discussion progresses.

Alternatively, a discussion guide may take the form of a *questioning route*, whereby the actual questions and prompts are included on the discussion guide. This overcomes the need for a moderator to formulate impromptu questions during the discussion. This approach is generally preferred in academic research. An important benefit of this type of discussion guide is the greater consistency in the way that questions are used, which improves the comparability of information between focus groups. This benefit is particularly important in academic research where the study population is often divided into sub-groups and their responses compared in data analysis. It is also beneficial to retain consistency when using a variety of moderators and when using a translated discussion guide, as consistent translations and colloquial phrases can be used by all moderators. The main drawback of the question-route approach is the amount of time required to develop and phrase the questions and prompts. There may also be a reduction in spontaneity in the delivery of the questions, although experienced moderators will easily deliver questions with spontaneity using a question route. A more detailed comparison of the two types of discussion guide can be found in Krueger (1998a).

Some moderators prefer not to use any form of discussion guide as they feel it may impose unwanted rigidity into the discussion and impede the natural flow of a discussion (Greenbaum 2000). However, experienced moderators understand the benefits of using a discussion guide in providing structure and focus to the group discussion, while at the same time not feeling constrained by the guide when following new or interesting issues in the discussion.

It is important that any type of discussion guide is seen as a guide and not a rigid format for the group discussion. The moderator should use the discussion guide to manage the group discussion around the key topics, yet remain flexible to explore new issues as they arise or change the order of topics as they are spontaneously raised by participants. For some research issues, particularly exploratory research, a discussion guide may evolve during the data collection process. This is sometimes referred to as a *rolling discussion guide* (Stewart and Shamdasani 1990). This involves the design of a basic discussion guide, which is then revised after each group discussion when the issues become more tangible. This process continues until the discussion guide satisfactorily covers the key issues around the research topic. This method of refining a discussion guide enables the researchers to identify previously unknown issues around a research topic. However, there will be considerable variability in the types of issues discussed in each group, which may be problematic during data analysis if the research requires comparison of issues between groups. Even though there may be disadvantages in using the rolling discussion guide, for some research topics there may be no other method of identifying the issues. It must also be remembered that in most focus group research the discussion guide will be modified during the process of data collection as new issues are identified or issues refined. Focus group research is an iterative and interactive method which evolves during data collection. It would be expected that new information from a previous group is incorporated into the discussion guide for the next group; this is the essence of exploratory research and a component of the grounded theory methodology.

Structure of the discussion guide

A discussion guide should have a clear structure and a logical sequence of topics, even if this does not eventuate in the discussion. Similar issues should be grouped together and the discussion topics should move from general to more specific issues. It is important to remember that the questions or topics need to be placed in an order that will make sense for the participants and the flow of the discussion, which may be different to how they appear in the research proposal or in the final report. A well-structured discussion guide will help the moderator to manage the logical flow of the discussion and avoid unnecessary repetition in the discussion topics.

A discussion guide should follow a *funnel design*, whereby the discussion flows from broad, general issues to more specific and focussed issues, as shown in Figure 3.2. The basic principle of the funnel design is that the initial questions are broad and general to put participants at ease in the discussion by asking them to respond to simple questions at first. It also enables the researchers to gain broad information on the study topic. The discussion questions should then proceed to more specific issues, which are central to the objectives of the research. These should be placed in the middle of the discussion guide and take up the largest portion of the research instrument. As the discussion reaches these central topics the participants will be more comfortable in the group setting and the moderator can begin to focus the attention towards the key issues for the study. In the final part of the discussion guide the discussion questions should proceed to broader summary and concluding questions to complete the discussion.

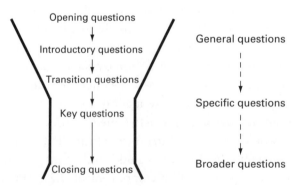

Figure 3.2   Funnel design of the discussion guide

The structure of a typical discussion guide will include various types of questions. Each type of question has a different purpose and level of importance. Krueger and Casey (2000) identify five different types of questions that are used in the various stages of the discussion; these are opening, introductory, transition, key and closing questions. These are shown in Figure 3.2 and discussed below after a discussion of the introduction to the group discussion.

Introduction

The focus group session begins with an introduction by the moderator. A number of issues need to be covered in the moderator's introductory remarks; therefore, the introduction is often included on the discussion guide, to assist the moderator in covering all the necessary points. It may be a written statement or a series of points, but should not be read as a formal statement, instead the main points should be covered in a friendly, conversational manner. The moderator's introduction is important as it sets the tone for the group discussion and helps to develop an environment where participants feel comfortable to share their views and experiences. It is important to remember that some participants may have been informally recruited and will not have any background information about the research or what is expected of their participation, so these issues need to be addressed in the introduction. It is easy to overlook this task once the group is assembled. The key points to be included in the introduction are shown in Figure 3.3 and discussed below.

The moderator should first welcome and thank participants for attending the discussion. All members of the research team present in the discussion should be introduced, for example the note-taker and observer. Participants should be informed on why they were selected for participation in the group discussions, so that they do not feel they have been targeted for any particular

---

- Welcome and thank participants for their attendance
- Introduce the note-taker and observer (if appropriate)
- Explain the general purpose of the research
- Identify the research organisation and sponsor (if appropriate)
- Reinforce why participants were chosen and importance of their contribution
- Explain the 'guidelines' for conduct of the group discussion
- Briefly outline how information will be used and by whom
- Explain the purpose of tape recording and seek permission
- Assure participants of confidentiality
- Indicate the expected duration of the discussion

Figure 3.3   Points for introductory statement

reason. For example, participants may have been invited to the discussion because they are parents of young children or they may have been selected from phone listings as residents of a specific area. Knowledge of their selection characteristics will help to put participants at ease and will reinforce the group homogeneity. The moderator needs to introduce the research topic, the funding agency (if appropriate) and indicate how the research results will be used. The purpose of the research should be given in general terms, without revealing the central research questions or hypothesis, as this may pre-empt the direction of the discussion. Any specific terminology should also be clarified to provide a common knowledge base for all participants.

Participants should then be told about the conduct of the group discussion and what will be expected of them. This will give participants *cognition*, a necessary condition to enable participants to know the type of information that is required and what is expected of their participation (Hennink and Diamond 1999). The moderator needs to state that they are most interested to hear participants' own views and opinions and encourage participants to say what they really feel about each of the discussion topics. The moderator should then briefly explain a number of guidelines for the conduct of the group discussion. First, participants should be told that they do not need to speak in any particular order. However, they need to ensure that only one person speaks at a time to ensure a clear tape-recording. Second, it should be stated that there are no right or wrong answers to the discussion questions and it is the views of each participant which are sought. Third, the moderator needs to reinforce that they are interested in a range of views on each topic, so it is acceptable to disagree with others in the group if they have a different opinion. Fourth, the moderator should emphasise that their role is to facilitate the discussion, and they are not an expert on the issues of discussion. This will dispel any expectation by participants that their knowledge or contribution is being tested or judged by the moderator in any way. Fifth, participants should be told to share their comments with the whole group rather than the person seated next to them. This will discourage fragmentation within the group discussion. Finally, participants should be informed of the expected length of the discussion.

The moderator's introduction should also review ethical issues. They should emphasise that participation is voluntary and ensure that each participant has willingly consented to participate. It is particularly important that the moderator assures participants of the confidentiality of their responses, seeks permission to tape record the discussion and briefly explains how the information will be used and stored to maintain confidentiality. See

---

Improving family planning services in Nepal

I would like to thank you all for coming to this goup. My name is _____ from _____ organisation and I am conducting these discussion groups as part of a research project on family planning services in Nepal. We are conducting this research in partnership with the Family Health Division to identify your views about the family planning services provided in your community, whether you feel that these services are suitable for you and how the services could be improved.

Family planning is a very important part of health care for both men and women and we would like to focus this discussion on your opinions of the family planning services provided in this area. We feel that the best way to improve family planning services is to talk to men and women in this area about your own experiences, and gather your views on how these services could be improved. Even if you have never used family planning services your views are still very valuable to us. During the next few weeks our research team will be talking to groups of women and men like you about family planning services so we can find out as much as possible about your views and experiences.

Your participation in this discussion group is completely voluntary. So if you prefer not to be a part of this discussion, you are completely free to leave. However, we value everyone's views on the topic and hope that you will stay and share your opinions. The information that we discuss today will remain confidential and will be used only for research purposes. It will be securely stored so that it is not accessible to anyone outside the research team.

I would like to say that there are no right or wrong answers in this discussion, we will simply be discussing your views, opinions and experiences on a range of topics, so please feel comfortable to say what you honestly feel. During the discussion _____ will be taking notes and reminding me if I forgot to ask something. However, so that s/he does not have to worry about getting every word down on paper, we would also like to tape record the whole session. Please do not be concerned about this, the recording will remain completely confidential and will only be used for this research project. Is everyone comfortable with recording this discussion? (Ensure that everyone consents to recording.)

We don't want to miss anything that is said so it's important that only one person talks at a time. Remember we want to hear as many different points of view as possible, so feel free to disagree with someone else and share your own opinions. We would like you all to have the chance to express your opinions, so please let everyone have their say. We would like to spend about 60–90 minutes with you. Please also help yourselves to the refreshments we have provided during our discussion. Are there any questions before we start? Let us begin ....

Introduction question: As an introduction, let us go around the group and perhaps each person could give their first name and tell us if you have any children, and how many you have . . .

Figure 3.4   Example introductory statement

Chapter 2 on Ethical considerations for a more detailed discussion of ethical issues. Figure 3.4 shows an example introductory statement for focus group research conducted in Nepal.

Opening questions

The opening question(s) act as 'ice-breakers' to make participants feel at ease in the group situation. The first question is usually a brief factual question about the respondent themselves, as the purpose is to gain a short response from each participant. Opening questions are not discussion questions and are not seeking long responses. Often an opening question may involve asking participants to respond to the first question in turn around the group. This ensures that each respondent has said something from the start of the discussion. Enabling people to talk early in the group discussion is important as the longer one remains silent in a group the more reluctant they will be to contribute later in the discussion. Another reason for asking participants to respond in turn around the group for the first question is to enable the transcriber to become familiar with the different voices in the group when the discussion is transcribed.

It is important that the opening questions do not highlight power or status differences among participants, for example by asking about education level or occupation rank where these may differ between participants. Instead an opening question should try to reinforce the similarities within the group by asking something that will highlight common characteristics of participants. An example of an opening question amongst adolescent boys may be: '*Let's start by going around the table and telling us your name, age and your favourite football player*' or amongst women from rural villages: '*Let us begin by introducing ourselves around the group, please tell us your first name and how many people live in your house?*' The information from these questions is rarely analysed.

Introductory questions

The introductory questions begin with general 'warm-up' questions followed by questions that introduce participants to the broad area of the research topic. The purpose of these questions is to make participants feel at ease in the group setting and begin to focus participants' attention on the research issues in a broad sense. Introductory questions are typically open-ended questions, with probing and follow-up by the moderator to gain detailed responses and to encourage participants to respond to the comments of others. It is useful for a moderator to use a lot of probing early in the discussion to demonstrate a high level of interest in their responses. An appropriate series of introductory questions for a study on young people and relationships may be:

Q1 *What type of leisure activities do young people enjoy in this area?*
Q2 *Where do young people generally go to socialise?*
Q3 *Do young people socialise with the opposite sex?*
Q4 *Do many young people have relationships?*

This sequence of questions begins with a very general question about leisure activities, then begins to refine the focus towards mixed-sex socialising and then relationships, which is the key area of interest for the research. Another introduction strategy may be to ask participants to clarify a specific term or phrase which is central to the research study. For example, '*We often hear the* term "going out together", but what does this actually mean to you?' or 'What do you understand by the term "disability"?' These types of introductory questions begin the discussion by identifying a common knowledge base about the term or phrase from which the moderator can then build the discussion.

Transition questions

Transition questions move the discussion from the introductory stage towards the key issues of central interest to the research. Transition questions may act as links between the various topics on the discussion guide and may take the form of a question or a brief statement before a new series of questions. For example, 'I would now like to discuss the transport facilities for the local health services. Could you tell me your experiences in using . . .?' Such transition questions may be used numerous times in the discussion guide.

Key questions

Key questions are those that are directly related to the research problem. They are the most critical part of the discussion guide and contain the essential questions which must be asked of participants in order to answer the research questions. The information gained from the key questions will be analysed in the greatest depth. The key questions may be a series of individual questions or two to three topic areas each containing a series of questions. Key questions are usually placed about one-third to half-way into the discussion guide, as it can take some time for the discussion to 'warm-up' and for participants to feel comfortable in the group discussion. Asking the key questions too early in the discussion will risk receiving too superficial responses if a group discussion is not yet well developed. It is during the key questions that the moderator will use the greatest amount of probing to elicit depth and detail in the discussion. The most discussion time should be spent on the key questions; in some instances, ten to fifteen minutes may be taken with certain issues or questions to ensure the issues are fully explored and all participants have had an opportunity to highlight their views. Approximately half of the group discussion time is usually taken up in discussing the key questions.

Ending questions

Ending questions begin to bring the discussion to a close. Although the most critical issues will have been covered in the key questions, ending questions are also important as they can provide the moderator with a sense of the relative importance of issues raised (Greenbaum 2000; Krueger and Casey 2000). For these reasons ending questions are also critical in the data analysis.

A number of different types of ending questions are commonly used; these include the 'all things considered' question, 'advice to a Minister' question, and the summary question. The *all things considered* question asks participants to identify the most important aspects or issues related to the topics discussed. For example, '*Considering all the issues discussed this afternoon, which do you feel are the most important influences on . . .?*' This type of ending question allows participants to reflect on the comments throughout the discussion and identify what they perceive to be the most important components. This approach is useful as it provides an indication of the importance of the issues discussed and overcomes an assumption that the issues which received the most discussion time were the most important.

Another common ending question is to ask participants which key issues they would like to highlight to a prominent person (e.g. minister, president, policy-maker, director) about the issues discussed. For example, '*Our discussion is now almost over, but there is one final input which would be helpful. If you had one minute with the Minister of Health which key issues from our discussion would you highlight?*' The purpose of this question is to identify the most critical issues for participants and identify their justifications for these. These types of ending questions can reveal some of the most fruitful information from the discussion and help to put all issues discussed into some perspective.

The 'summary question' involves the moderator making a short (two to three minute) summary of the major themes discussed in the group, and then asking participants whether this was an adequate summary of the issues, and if any issues were missed or misinterpreted. This ensures that nothing has been overlooked and allows participants to have a final input, clarify or expand on the issues. It is worth leaving this question ten minutes before the group closure as it may stimulate further discussion. The responses from these ending questions can also be critical in the data analysis.

Number of questions

It is tempting for less experienced focus group researchers to include too many questions in the discussion guide. It must always be remembered that each question is being asked of a *group* of people, therefore sufficient time should be given for all participants to express their views, to disagree and to raise new or related issues; so the discussion of even a single question may take some time. Consider that a discussion guide of twenty-five questions, with ten participants over a ninety minute period, would allow three and a half minutes to discuss each question which gives each participant about twenty seconds to respond to each question. The discussion element of focus group research will lengthen the time required to gain responses for each question. Therefore, it is advisable to limit the questions on the discussion guide to two or three main areas, to allow sufficient time to explore each area in depth. Too many questions will put enormous pressure on the moderator to cover all the issues within the discussion time. It will also lead to superficial coverage of the issues as the moderator will be unable to follow up on new issues raised or probe the discussion fully. In addition, participants may not feel they have had sufficient opportunity to fully discuss the issues.

Most discussion guides have approximately twelve to fifteen questions. This number of questions allows for follow-up questions to be added spon- taneously and for some deviation from the issues on the discussion guide. A focus group discussion is a dynamic exercise and time should be allowed to explore new topics raised or deviate from the prepared discussion guide; this process is critical to the success of a group discussion. The nature of the discussion topic and the composition of the participants will also determine the number of questions to include on the discussion guide. Generally fewer questions will be required if a topic is complex or emotional, as one would expect the discussion to proceed in greater depth with participants taking time to describe issues or experiences; while for general topics there will be less detailed discussion so more questions may be needed. Also, a group of participants with quite homogenous characteristics may move more quickly through the discussion questions, than a group of more heterogeneous individuals who may contribute different perspectives to a discussion and therefore take longer to cover the same issues (Stewart and Shamdasani 1990).

The discussion guide should be designed for a group discussion of one to two hours. Typically a group discussion would last between sixty and ninety minutes. A group discussion should not go longer than two hours, as after this time participants become tired and lose interest in the discussion and the value of the information declines.

Group activities

For some research topics it is beneficial to introduce an activity for partici- pants to conduct as a group. Group activities will improve the group cohesion and enrich the discussion. The types of activities will vary by the research project, but may include writing a list of key terms about a topic on a large sheet of paper, ranking a pre-prepared list according to certain criteria (e.g. cost, quality), or commenting on the design of educational material (e.g. posters, packaging of health products, etc.). The discussion between participants during such exercises can provide valuable information on the justification for participants' views or the reasons for the final ranking of a list. For example, a study in India (Kauser 2001) used a 'pile-sorting' activity where participants were given a pile of cards with an illness written on each and asked to put the cards in different piles according to their views on the severity of the illness. If group activities are included as part of the discussion, sufficient time must be allocated to complete these tasks, which will mean a reduction in the number of discussion questions.

Question design

The questions on a discussion guide often appear to be deceptively simple and spontaneous, but in reality they are carefully considered, constructed and pilot-tested. Questions for a group discussion are distinct from those used on other types of research instrument. The questions on a focus group discussion guide differ from those on a quantitative survey. Survey questions are designed to gain short, precise and often factual information, while questions for a group discussion are designed to explore people's attitudes, opinions or experiences and seek to gain a variety of responses. Although there are some similarities between the questions used in an in-depth interview and a focus group discussion, there are three essential differences. First, in-depth interview questions will typically include more questions than those in a focus group discussion. This is because the focus group questions are being asked of a group of people and there needs to be time for all participants to respond and discuss the issues. Second, questions for in-depth interviews are typically more personal, individual and seek sensitive information, while the group nature of a focus group discussion means that such questions are not always appropriate. The questions for a group discussion also seek more general or community views, although participants often volunteer personal information it should not be asked directly. Third, questions for a group discussion should be designed to encourage a discussion of issues between participants, while an in-depth interview essentially seeks individual responses. For further distinctions between focus group discussion and in-depth interviews see Chapter 1.

- Phrased as discussion questions not *research* questions
- Short and simple
- Clear
- Use familiar phrases or terminology
- Informal and conversational
- Non-technical language
- Non-judgemental
- Uni-dimensional
- Open and non-directive
- Avoid dichotomous questions
- Promote discussion

Figure 3.5   Key characteristics of question design

Well-constructed discussion questions will elicit information from participants that can be used to meet the research objectives. There are a number of question design issues that can assist in developing effective questions for group discussions, these are listed in Figure 3.5 and are described below. A fundamental task in designing questions for focus group discussions is to distinguish between the *research* question and the *discussion* questions. The research question reflects the overall purpose of the study and is typically written in academic, technical language. This is designed for the researchers and not for the participants in the focus group discussion. The discussion questions are those questions asked of participants in the group. An example of a research question may be, '*What are the key influences on post-partum abstinence?*' Asking this question in a discussion group would be inappropriate as participants would not know how to respond and may be alienated by the terminology. This research question needs to be rephrased so that it becomes an appropriate question for the group discussion, which involves taking the essential issue and wording the question so that participants can clearly comprehend the issue and respond. The same issue may be rephrased into a question suitable for the group discussion, as such: '*Why do you think it is important to stay apart from your husband after your baby is born?*' (Probe: '*Who told you about this?*'). Redesigning the research questions into discussion questions involves considering how participants will understand the questions and designing the questions from their perspective. This issue is highlighted below by a research student in Zambia.

I think you do your question route with your supervisors and your exam in mind, instead of having your respondent in mind, so you are thinking at a much higher level, when in fact you should think of the respondent.

Questions for a group discussion should be clear, short and simple. A simple question does not necessarily mean a simple answer will be given;

often the most successful questions are those which are brief and simple. Participants can only respond to questions they understand, so it is important to keep questions clear and simple by using terminology and language that respondents can relate to. To achieve this, questions may be phrased in the participants' colloquial language to improve their comprehension of the questions. As a general rule the longer the question the more the clarity is reduced. It is useful to consider the shortest way to ask a question to achieve the greatest clarity. Questions should be free of difficult language and jargon terminology. If questions are simply worded, clear and short, participants will also remember the question during the discussion and keep their responses focussed. Questions should also sound informal and conversational to create a non-threatening environment in the group discussion and make respondents feel confident to contribute to the discussion. The wording of the questions should not be judgemental or loaded with social morals so that participants feel guilty or embarrassed to admit to particular behaviour or attitudes (Hennink and Diamond 1999).

To improve comprehension of the questions and elicit specific responses, questions need to be uni-dimensional, asking about only one issue at a time. Double-barrelled questions or questions with several parts should be avoided as various participants may respond to different parts of the question which leads to confused discussion. For example, '*How much should the health clinic charge for consultations and vaccinations?*' This is a multi-dimensional question, which should be broken into several short, precise, questions asking about each of the specific components in turn (i.e. consultation cost and vaccination cost).

Questions should be open and non-directive. An open question is one where no response categories are given and the participants can respond from many different perspectives. A non-directive question gives respondents no indication of the type of response the researcher may expect. Open, non-directive questions are important in focus group discussions as they allow the respondents to answer a question from a variety of dimensions, and to identify and discuss the issues which are important to them rather than to the researchers. An example of an open, non-directive question is: '*What is your opinion of the new local health clinic?*' This question allows participants to comment on a range of aspects, both positive and negative, and enables participants to share their experiences of using the service. No type of response is implied in the question and what participants choose to discuss indicates what is important to them.

Avoid dichotomous questions. A dichotomous question is one which elicits a yes/no response and as such will not promote a discussion.

Essentially dichotomous questions are avoided as they do not allow participants to respond in the level of depth and detail which is ideal for a focus group
discussion. An example of a dichotomous question is, '*Have you used the
health service?*' This could be replaced by a question which seeks more detailed
responses and promotes discussion such as, '*Tell me about your experiences
of using the health service.*' In some cases a dichotomous question may be
used to clarify the existence of a phenomenon, but it should then be followed
up by a question that promotes discussion. For example, '*Does this community
have a leisure centre?*' followed by '*What is your opinion of this facility?*'

It is sometimes useful to initiate a discussion by using a statement and
asking for participants' reactions or experiences. This can provide a clear
focus for participants to respond and can be a useful way to frame potentially
sensitive or uncomfortable questions into a less personal context. For example, '*We are told that men are not using the clinic for family planning services.
Do you have any views on this?*' or '*A woman in another village told us she had
been beaten several times by her husband. Are you familiar with this in your
community?*' (Ulin *et al.* 2002). This indirect question may gain a more open
response or elicit spontaneous examples of the issues.

It has been stated that 'why' questions should be avoided in focus group
discussions. This may seem contradictory, as focus groups are often conducted to explain why certain phenomena occur or to explain patterns
of behaviour, attitudes or events. However, this issue is related to the wording
of questions rather than to avoid seeking explanations of issues. Questions
which directly ask participants why something occurred may sound threatening to participants and carry a tone of interrogation, which may cause
discomfort. 'Why' questions also imply that there is a rational answer to
explain the issue, however, people's behaviour or decisions may not be
entirely rational. Participants may not have given any thought to their
motivations for certain behaviour and may therefore feel pressured to provide instant rationalisations to respond to the question. Lazarfeld (1986)
states that 'why' questions are typically answered on two levels, according
to a) what influences behaviour and b) desirable attributes. For example, the
question '*Why did you select this hospital for childbirth?*' may receive the
response, '*Because my sister went there.*' or '*Because the maternity facilities
are the most advanced.*' Lazarfeld suggests that it is better to break 'why'
questions into their attributes and to ask, '*What influenced you to go to the
hospital?*' and '*What features of the hospital attracted you?*' These questions
seek the two types of responses to 'why' questions without the direct style
of questioning that may cause discomfort.

Gaining depth in the discussion

Achieving a detailed discussion around the research issues is one of the objectives of focus group research. Gaining depth in the discussion is usually achieved in two ways: first, through the structure of the discussion guide, and second, through the use of probing and follow-up questioning. Firstly, designing the discussion guide to move from general issues to more specific issues can be one strategy to focus the discussion on gaining detailed responses on very specific areas of the topic. In this case the discussion would begin with general questions that are followed by more focussed questions on specific aspects of the topic. In this way greater detail on each of the specific issues can be gathered in turn. For example:

General question: *What is your opinion of the new mobile health clinic?*
General question: *Are people satisfied with the new service?*
Specific question: *What is your opinion of the opening times of this clinic?*
Specific question: *How do you feel about the cost of consultations at this clinic?*
Specific question: *Are the staff in the mobile unit always able to serve your needs?*

In developing more specific questions, one needs to be careful not to change a neutral question into a leading or bias question by refining the focus. For example, '*What is your opinion of the **limited** opening times of this clinic?*' This question suggests that there may be a problem with the opening times, while participants may not think so themselves.

The second strategy to achieve depth in the discussion is through probing and follow-up questioning by the moderator. Typically a discussion guide includes the questions plus a range of probes, which prompt the moderator to ask on specific issues if they were not raised spontaneously in the discussion. The questions on the discussion guide will generally elicit a broad response from participants, while the probing of participants will achieve more detailed responses. It is good practice to include probes on the discussion guide directly after the relevant question to prompt the moderator to raise these issues and gain depth in the discussion. For example:

Question: *Why do people in this community believe that four children make an ideal family size?*
Probes: (child mortality, workforce, marriage practices, sex preference, family income)
Question: *How do people in this community learn about HIV?*
Probes: (friends, school, media, billboards, medical sources)

It is important to include sufficient probes on the discussion guide, particularly if the group discussion will not be moderated by the researchers themselves. For the researcher, the issues on which to probe would be instinctive as they are most familiar with the research objectives, however, another moderator may need to be reminded of issues worthy of further exploration. It is not necessary to include probes for each question, as too many probes will clutter the discussion guide. Typically probes are included alongside issues that are central to the research question and for which the most detailed exploration is required.

Follow-up questions may also be used to encourage detailed responses. A follow-up question is typically a spontaneous question from the moderator which is asked when greater detail is needed on the issue raised. Follow-up questions move the discussion to a deeper level by asking participants for more detail or further experiences. Follow-up questions also confirm to the group that their issues are important and that further information is required. They also suggest to participants the level of detail that is desired in the discussion. However, care needs to be paid to the amount of follow-up questioning used by the moderator, as insufficient follow-ups could suggest disinterest in an issue, while aggressive follow-up questioning may be intrusive and threatening (Rubin and Rubin 1995).

Figure 3.6 provides an example of a discussion guide on young people's sexual health awareness in Pakistan. The example includes the introductory statement, introduction questions, three key areas of discussion and the concluding questions. The key questions in each sub-section also include question probes.

Young people's sexual health awareness: Pakistan

I would like to thank you all for coming to this meeting. My name is _____ from _____. I am conducting discussion groups as part of a research project on health issues for young people in Pakistan. Our research team is going to speak to lots of groups of young people in the Punjab about young people's health issues, because we feel it is important to hear the views of young people like yourselves. Young people's health care covers a range of topics including personal development, relationships and using health care services. We would like to cover these issues in the discussion. Even if you are unsure about any of these health issues your views are still very valuable to us, so please do not feel shy during the discussion. I would like to say that there are no right or wrong answers, we will simply be discussing your views, opinions and experiences; so please feel comfortable to say what you really think.

As we have already told you, your participation in this group is voluntary. Whatever we discuss today will be confidential and used only for this research project. During the discussion _____ will be taking notes and reminding me if I forgot to ask something. However, so that s/he does not have to worry about getting every word down on paper we will also be tape recording the whole session. The reason for tape recording is so that we don't miss anything that is said and so that the rest of the research team who are not here can also hear your views exactly. Please do not be concerned about this, our discussion will remain completely confidential; we will use only first names in the discussion and the information will only be used for this research project to improve the health services for young people. Is it OK with everyone to tape-record this discussion? It is also important that only one person talks at a time. We will not be going around the room; just join in when you have something to say. Remember we want to hear all your views, so it's OK to disagree with everyone else if you have a different opinion, but please also respect the views of the others here as well. This discussion will probably last about an hour or so. Are there any questions before we start? Let's start. . . . .

Introduction questions

As an introduction, let's go around so that you can introduce yourselves, and perhaps tell us your favourite Pakistani film star.
What are the popular leisure time activities for young people of your age in this area?
In your opinion, what are the main health issues of young people your age?

A. **Learning about personal/sexual development**
    An important part of young people's health care is personal and sexual development. Much of our discussion today will focus on these topics.
    1. Do young people learn anything about <u>personal development</u> – that means the physical changes to boys/girls during adolescent years? (Probe: what is learnt; sources of information)
    2. At what age/stage in life do young people learn about personal development topics? (probe: for example, menstruation/wet dreams)
    3. Do young people learn anything about <u>sexual behaviour</u>? (Probe: what is learnt; sources of information)
    4. When do young people learn about sexual behaviour? (probe: what age or life stage)
    5. Do young people of your age openly talk to anyone about sexual development or sexual behaviour? (Probe: who, topics, why prefer them)
    6. Is there anyone that young people don't feel comfortable to talk to about these matters? (Probe: reasons)

B. **Information delivery**
    7. Do you think that the information that young people receive about personal and sexual health is adequate? (Probe: reasons)
    8. What type of information should be given to young people – which topics should be covered?
    9. What is the best way for young people to receive information about personal and sexual health matters?

C. **Health services**
    I would now like to discuss the places young people can get advice and services for health.
    10. Can you tell me any places that young people can visit to find out about sexual health matters?
    11. Is there anything that would stop young people from attending these services for sexual health matters? (Probe: privacy, staff, cost, services offered, etc.)
    12. What do you think should be the most important features of a sexual health service for young people?

Conclusion

We are now reaching the end of the discussion. Does anyone have any further comments to add before we conclude this session? I would like to thank you all very much for your participation in this discussion, your experiences and opinions are very valuable to assist in improving young people's health care in Pakistan.

Figure 3.6   Example discussion guide

Discussion guides for international focus group research

For international focus group research it is often necessary to translate the discussion guide into the language(s) of the study population. A range of key decisions need to be made in the process of translating the discussion guide, including the most appropriate language for the discussion, who should translate the discussion guide, terminology to use and how to check the translations. The process of translating the discussion guide is summarised

1. Draft the discussion guide in the language of research investigators.
2. Identify the language (s) of the discussion.
3. Identify an appropriate translator.
4. Translate the guide into the required language (s).
5. Ensure that question strategies are culturally appropriate.
6. Use colloquial phrases and terminology for key issues.
7. Check the quality of translations.
8. Pilot-test the translated discussion guide and modify, if necessary.
9. Conduct the first group discussion.
10. Revise the discussion guide again, if necessary.

Figure 3.7   Process of translating the discussion guide

in Figure 3.7, and the following sections discuss language and translation issues, and developing culturally sensitive discussion questions.

Using a translated discussion guide

Translating the discussion guide into another language may be necessary when conducting focus group discussions in another country or equally when conducting research among sub-groups of the population in the researcher's own country who speak a different language to that of the research investigators, for example, focus group discussions with migrant groups or ethnic minorities. There are several reasons why it is preferable to use a translated discussion guide, even if the moderator is bi-lingual in the languages of the research team and the study participants. First, a translated discussion guide will be beneficial for the moderator in that they are able to refer to translated questions rather than having to spontaneously translate the questions during the discussion. A moderator has a challenging task simply managing the group discussion, so to also translate the discussion questions would be extremely demanding. Second, it is often valuable to use colloquial expressions in the discussion guide which reflect the language used by participants and more clearly relate the concepts under discussion. The use of colloquial language also improves the quality of the information received and increases rapport within the group. Developing the appropriate colloquial phrasing of questions often takes time and considerable discussion of various alternative phrases. However, if the translation of questions is left to the moderator during the discussion then appropriate colloquial terms may not be used, as little forethought is able to be given to the translation of issues while conducting the group discussion. As a result important information may be lost through participants not fully understanding the key issues for discussion. Third, if a moderator translates the questions during the discussion, they may inadvertently place a different emphasis on the question than was intended by the research team. This may elicit responses which are not central to the research questions and may therefore create difficulties in meeting the research objectives. A moderator may also translate questions in a long, wordy format to explain what is meant and so reduce the clarity of the questions. Finally, if several moderators are used in the project there may be little consistency in the translation of questions, which may lead to important variations in the responses, as slight differences in translated wording can significantly alter the meaning of a question.

The extract below highlights the importance of translating the discussion guide even when the researchers are bi-lingual:

> I did the question guide originally in English, and that's one thing I overlooked. I thought I am competent in the language of my country and I can read a question in English and directly translate it, no problem. But it proved very, very difficult. Translating it correctly from the English to the local language, right there and then, was very, very difficult. The easier way was to translate the whole instrument into the local language and use the local language. I think that is the best way of all . . . It takes an awfully long time to do [the translation], it's a tedious task, but it's inevitable that you have to do that. (Research Student, Zambia)

Which language to use?

The research team needs to identify the most appropriate language in which to translate the discussion guide and decide whether it should be translated into more than one language. The most important consideration is to identify the language in which participants will feel most comfortable to converse; this may be the national language or a regional language of the country.

Identifying the most appropriate language into which to translate the discussion guide may seem like a straightforward decision. However, whereas in some countries there is one common language spoken throughout the country, in others the linguistic traditions vary between regions and it is common for different languages to be prominent in different regions. Prior identification of the language(s) spoken in the study areas is critical. Where focus group research is conducted in several regions of a country, the discussion guide may need to be translated into a number of different languages. For example, a study on contraceptive use in Zambia was conducted in two regions, the copperbelt province, where the language of Bemba is spoken, and the north-western province, where the languages of Luvale,

Lunda and Kaonde are spoken. It was therefore necessary to translate the discussion guide into four languages in order to effectively communicate with study participants in the various regions of the study (Benaya 2004). Similarly, a study on the affordability of health services in Malawi was conducted in the central and northern regions of the country, which are strongly delineated by language. Therefore, the discussion guide was translated into both Chichewa and Timbuka to conduct effective group discussions in each region (Madise *et al.* 2000). In a minority of situations, regional or tribal languages may exist only as an oral language with no script. Therefore, a written translation of the discussion guide will not be possible. These situations should be identified prior to conducting the fieldwork, so that moderators can be briefed and given sufficient time to consider how to convey the questions in the group discussion.

In some countries there exists a large number of regional or tribal languages, but also a national *lingua franca*, which is the common language of communication between people from different regions. The *lingua franca* may be the language of a former colonial power (e.g. English, French, Spanish), or it may be a common national language in addition to the regional languages, such as Urdu in Pakistan. In these situations it may be appropriate to translate the discussion guide into the *lingua franca*, particularly if the group discussion will comprise participants who speak different regional languages. It will be necessary to identify whether this is feasible as certain population groups, such as the uneducated or elderly, may not be familiar with the national *lingua franca*. Participants may not be fully conversant or confident in the *lingua franca*; however, in some situations this may be the only way to conduct the discussion. Generally, when participants speak a range of languages it is advisable to conduct different group discussions according to the common language of participants; however, there will be situations when this is not possible.

In some international focus group studies it may be appropriate to use a discussion guide in the language of the research investigators. This may be appropriate when the study participants are well-educated or professionals. It is also possible that some of the discussion groups are conducted in the language of research investigators, (e.g. focus groups in urban areas), while others are conducted in regional languages (e.g. rural villages). The characteristics of the study population will determine the most appropriate language(s) to use. Even when the discussion guide has been translated into various languages it is useful to keep a copy in the language of the research team for inclusion in the study report.

Translating the discussion guide

It is necessary to identify an appropriate person to translate the discussion guide. It may seem logical to seek a professional translator for this task; however, there are a number of reasons why this may not be suitable. Firstly, it may be costly to use professional translating services and out of reach of most research budgets. Second, and much more importantly, a professional translator may not translate the discussion questions into the informal, conversational style of language that is suitable for the focus group discussion. A professional translator may use formal or technical language which is unsuitable for a focus group discussion where informality is desired. Inappropriate language can quickly create an unwanted distance between the moderator and participants. It is necessary to match the language *style* of the discussion guide to that of the participants and the context of the study. Using professional translators may not achieve this objective. In addition, translations done by professionals may result in a literal translation of the *words*, when what is often required is that the translation captures the *meaning* or the concept of the question, which may entail using entirely different words. It is often more appropriate to seek individuals who are native speakers of the required language(s) to translate the discussion guide. For example, teachers or nurses in the study country may assist with translating a discussion guide on health or education issues, similarly bi-lingual researchers may be useful in providing translations into the local languages while understanding the style of research enquiry required. These individuals may be best suited to translate the discussion guide into colloquial language and achieve more ordinary, familiar phrasing of questions. Using such individuals for the translations is particularly useful when translations into regional dialects are required. However, in seeking colloquial translators, care should be taken to avoid inappropriate language, as shown in the extract below:

It was slang Swahili. So even when you have colleagues around you who speak the language, be very sure and certain that the language they speak is rich enough to be taken seriously. It's not being understood, but being taken seriously by the respondents ... (Researcher, Tanzania)

Some of the terms or phrases used in the discussion guide may not translate easily, and it can take time to identify appropriate phrases which capture the intended meaning. A study on sexual risk-taking in Kenya required the translation of the discussion guide into the Kikuyu language. However, the researchers and the translator struggled with appropriate translations for a number of key terms that were central to the research topic. For example, *sexual behaviour* was translated into a specific word which referred to 'when men and women sleep together'; *contraception* could not be translated into a single word but a description equivalent to 'ways in which you could avoid having children' or 'the medicines you use to stop pregnancy'; the concept of *risk* was translated as 'danger' and *sexual risk* as 'negative things that can result from having sex'; no appropriate translation could be found for *safer sex* so the concept had to be described to participants. Also, reference to '*unmarried men and women*' was ambiguous as in the Kikuyu language only those who are married can be termed 'men' or 'women', so this phrase had to be altered to 'boys and girls' (Akwara 2002). The appropriate wording of the translations also needs to be suitable for the type of study participants. In a study on young people's sexual behaviour in Malawi, the direct translation of '*having sex*' in the Chichewa language was too formal for the study participants of young people, so the more colloquial phrase of 'sitting together' or 'sleeping together' was used, which implies the occurrence of sexual activity in the Chichewa language (Chimbwete 2001). In some instances certain concepts may not be recognised in the cultural content of the study and therefore may not translate well. For example, a study on physical exercise and obesity in India referred to the terms *overweight, physical activity* and *exercise*. However, these concepts were not well recognised amongst the study population and were difficult to translate into the regional language, Kanada. As a result, part of the discussion guide was re-phrased to convey the meaning of exercise and obesity, but not necessarily using those terms (Griffiths and Bentley 2005).

There will be times when neither the research team nor the translator will be able to identify the appropriate translations for a particular study topic, for example, the colloquial terminology used by adolescents when discussing relationships. In these situations it may be necessary to conduct some preparatory work amongst the study population or with key informants who work closely with the study population, to identify the translation of issues, phrases or terms that appear on the discussion guide. This may involve developing a draft translation of the discussion guide and conducting informal discussions with members of the target population to identify whether the intended meaning of the translations is conveyed. In this way the discussion guide will reflect the translated terms used by participants themselves, which will help to create an informal, friendly atmosphere during the discussion. For example, a study amongst adolescent boys in the United Kingdom included a discussion on the withdrawal method of contraception. However, the term 'withdrawal' was not used by the study population. After some preliminary discussions with youth workers it was identified that the phrase 'getting off at parkway (station)', meaning the train station before the central station, was the phrase used when discussing withdrawal. This phrase was then included in the discussion guide.

It can take some time to develop a suitable translation of the discussion guide in the language of the study participants. It is important for the research team to work in close collaboration with those conducting the translation, so that they can identify the intent and meaning of each question while the translator can seek the appropriate terminology. Although it is desirable to translate the discussion guide before arriving at the fieldwork location, in some situations fieldwork time may need to be allocated to the translation tasks.

Checking the translation

Back-translation is a common strategy for checking translated text, whereby the translated text is re-translated back into the source language and compared to the original for accuracy. While this strategy may be appropriate in some circumstances, the translation of the research instrument largely relies on the translation of the *concept* or the *meaning* of the discussion questions not necessarily the actual words, so back-translation may not always be an appropriate strategy. Instead, the accuracy of the translated discussion guide may be checked by asking the questions to individuals familiar with the language and identifying how each question is understood. This oral method of checking the quality of the translations is a useful measure to identify whether the intended meaning of the questions has been captured in the translation. This method can be used with a range of individuals familiar with the language of the discussion guide, such as bi-lingual researchers, professionals, key informants, or, if possible, with a selection of the target population.

Culturally appropriate questioning strategies

The questioning strategies on the discussion guide also need to be culturally appropriate. In general, most questioning strategies used on research instruments are acceptable in many contexts. However, in certain settings or amongst particular target populations some questioning approaches may be inappropriate or, at worst, cause offence to participants. The discussion of sensitive issues also needs to be approached with care in settings where certain topics may not be openly discussed or illegal, for example sexual behaviour, sexuality, domestic violence or abortion. The discussion guide needs to be carefully reviewed in order to identify any inappropriate questions. However, some cultural taboos or sensitivities may not be uncovered until the research is underway. For example, a study of maternal health practices in India sought to identify women's health concerns during pregnancy. However, the researcher found that the pregnant women participants were not willing to discuss problems that might occur during pregnancy, as they believed that the fate of the pregnancy may be at risk through such a discussion. This was a well-known taboo amongst the local population, but unknown to the researchers. The researcher was therefore unable to discuss women's concerns about the *potential* problems related to pregnancy with pregnant participants and a different strategy was required to seek the information from other sources (Kauser 2001). This same study found that hypothetical questions were difficult for respondents to comprehend. They found it difficult to discuss certain health problems if they had not actually experienced them. Although this may have been a reflection of the education level of the respondents, the appropriateness of this type of question strategy for the intended participants needs to be given some forethought. Another study in India focussed on the issue of obesity and women's body image (Griffiths and Bentley 2005). The concept of obesity is viewed differently in Indian society to many western nations, as a larger body size is often associated with wealth and status in India. Therefore, careful attention was given to the wording of the discussion questions so as not to imply a negative association between obesity and body image. Culturally appropriate phrases were identified together with local research collaborators to improve the phrasing of the discussion questions.

Pilot-testing the discussion guide

It is often difficult to predict how participants will interpret or respond to the questions on a discussion guide, particularly if the discussion guide has been translated into another language, so pilot testing is critical. The first draft of a discussion guide is rarely problem free and piloting the questions is a critical part of the process of designing a discussion guide. Pilot-testing involves asking the discussion questions to a group of people with similar characteristics to the study population, assessing how the questions are comprehended and considering the responses to discussion questions. In international focus group research it may not be possible to pilot-test the discussion guide prior to the fieldwork due to the unavailability of people speaking the required language. In this situation it is common to conduct the pilot-testing once in the study country, or to use the first focus group discussion as a pilot. If the discussion guide requires extensive revision after the pilot, then the information from the first group will need to be discarded. Using this method to pilot-test the discussion guide is not ideal as it can take up fieldwork time and therefore be costly and time consuming. It is recommended, whenever possible, to pilot-test the research instruments before fieldwork begins.

It is important to pilot-test the discussion guide amongst a group of people unfamiliar with the research objectives to properly test their comprehension of the questions. If it is not possible to identify a suitable group of people, the questions may be piloted with selected individuals, as the essential purpose of the pilot is to identify how the questions are comprehended and whether the questions and their translations capture the issues as intended by the researchers.

After the pilot-test, the research team needs to reflect on the effectiveness of the discussion guide. Typically both the question design and the structure of the discussion guide will be assessed. Figure 3.8 lists the issues to consider in pilot-testing a discussion guide. Pilot testing the discussion guide enables the research team to review the questions for clarity, ambiguity, wording, translations, sequencing, repetition and the type of responses received. The structure of the discussion guide should also be reviewed to assess the logic of the topic order and to identify any repetition in the discussion topics. The pilot-test will also enable the length of responses to specific questions and the length of the overall discussion to be identified. This will indicate if the number of questions needs to be reduced or increased to conduct a discussion

---

Test question design:
- Are questions understood as intended?
- Do questions elicit the expected type of response?
- Do questions encourage discussion?
- Is the terminology appropriate for participants?
- Are the translations clear and appropriate?
- Is the language style sufficiently colloquial?

Test discussion guide structure:
- Is sufficient information given in the introduction?
- Does the discussion flow well between topics?
- Is there any repetition in the issues/questions?
- Is the discussion guide sufficient for a 90-minute discussion?

Figure 3.8   Key issues in piloting the discussion guide

of approximately ninety minutes. The pilot test normally involves focussing on the effectiveness of the questions, phrases and language rather than the actual conduct of the group discussion. As a result of the pilot-test, some questions may be rephrased to clarify the discussion issues, and questions may be reordered or removed altogether. With a well-designed discussion guide and sufficient pilot-testing the discussion guide should be an effective tool to guide the focus group discussion relatively smoothly from one topic to the next. If the moderator has to work to keep the discussion focussed on a topic or the discussion naturally shifts to an alternate topic, this is a strong signal that there is something out of sync between the discussion guide and the participants' perspectives (Morgan 1997).

It should also be remembered that the discussion guide is not a stand-alone instrument and the moderator is an important component in the delivery of questions, clarifications and probing in the discussion. So the combination of the questions and their delivery by the moderator may also be observed in the pilot discussion. Finally, it may be difficult to separate the effectiveness of the discussion guide from the skills of the moderator or the environment of the pilot discussion. If a pilot group is unsuccessful, the research team may need to reflect on whether the poor discussion was a reflection of the discussion guide, the moderator or the participant group.

Key terms

The discussion guide is a pre-prepared series of questions or list of topics used by the moderator to facilitate the focus group discussion.

The funnel design describes the structure of the questions on the discussion guide which should move from broad general questions to more specific, focussed questions.

Open, non-directive questions are where no response categories are given (open), so participants can respond from many different perspectives, and respondents have no indication of the type of response expected (non-directive).

Pilot-testing involves asking the discussion questions to a group or to an individual to test how the questions are comprehended and the types of responses received.

Questioning route is one type of discussion guide which comprises of a series of actual questions and prompts for the moderator.

A topic guide is one type of discussion guide which consists of a list of topics or key words that act as memory prompts for the moderator.

A rolling discussion guide is where the discussion guide evolves during the data collection process. Used mostly in exploratory research, it enables participants to have a greater influence on the shape of the discussion issues.

A research question is the research problem, hypothesis or objectives which the focus group will set out to answer and provides the key focus for the discussion guide.

Checklist in designing the discussion guide

- Is the introduction clear and welcoming?
- Have issues of consent been included in the introduction?
- Is there a clear and logical structure to the question guide?
- Do questions flow from general to specific following a funnel design?
- Does the discussion guide include opening, transition, key and closing questions?
- Are sufficient probes included with the key questions?
- Have questions been reviewed for clarity, simplicity, brevity and informality?
- Is the phrasing and terminology appropriate to the target population?
- Is language in the vernacular?
- Is there any technical language or terminology?
- Does the discussion guide need translation; have appropriate language(s) been identified?
- Does the translation convey the meaning of each question/issue?
- Are the questions culturally appropriate?
- Are the moderators clear about the meaning and focus of each question?
- Has the question guide been piloted?
    Were the questions interpreted as intended?
    Is there any repetition in the questions?
    Is the question guide too long or too short?
- Will the issues discussed answer the research question(s)?

4 Training the focus group team

Introduction

International focus group research is often conducted in contexts where the research investigators do not speak the language of the study participants, for example, research conducted in another country or in regions of the country with different linguistic traditions. In these situations it is necessary to train a field team to conduct the focus group discussions. In many instances those who become part of the field team will have the necessary language skills for the research, but may have limited research experience or exposure to qualitative methods. The ultimate goal of training the field team is to transfer the skills of conducting focus group discussions to individuals with the linguistic proficiency to communicate with the study participants. Training the field team is essential, however it is often a forgotten element when planning focus group fieldwork, and research proposals often neglect to include time and resources for in-country training of field staff. This chapter describes the components of a training schedule for field staff, which includes role-play sessions to enable experiential learning of the various roles of the focus group team.

The importance of training

One thing I really learnt, that I didn't find in any book, was about training . . . I realise now that this is very important. (Researcher, Lesotho)

The importance of providing training to the field team cannot be overstated. In an ideal situation field staff would be proficient in the language(s) of the study participants and have experience in qualitative research and group facilitation. However, it is often difficult to find this combination of skills in many research settings. Typically, those who have the necessary language skills will not be trained in scientific research or have the relevant field experience. Furthermore, those with research experience are most likely to have skills in quantitative data collection, such as interviewing for a population survey, rather than in in-depth interviewing or focus group facilitation. This underscores the need to provide training in the general principles of qualitative data collection, and on the focus group method specifically. Fundamentally, the training involves transferring to the field team the researchers' skills in conducting focus group discussion plus the overall objectives of the research. This transfer of skills needs to be provided in a limited time period and in sufficient detail to provide trainees with the confidence to conduct the group discussions. In some respects it is equivalent to putting the head of the research investigator onto the shoulders of the trainee moderator, as described below:

The moderator really has to get inside [the researcher's] mind to know exactly what they would probe for given that the respondent had just said this or that, so you need to train them. (Researcher, Kenya)

I treat my training like soldiers, you know, because you have to share the 'minefield' with them. (Researcher, Tanzania)

The field team may come from a wide variety of professional backgrounds; they may be health professionals, teachers, students, government employees or university researchers. The diverse backgrounds and experience of trainees underscores the importance of comprehensive training before any data collection begins. The training sessions will ensure that all members of the field team are trained to the same level in the skills required to conduct the group discussions. Some research investigators feel that it is often more difficult to train individuals with significant experience in quantitative data collection to become effective group moderators, than to train those with little research experience. Experienced survey researchers have a tendency to use a qualitative discussion guide as if it were a questionnaire, to deliver questions in a rigid order and wording, move too quickly through the question guide and fail to encourage discussion or probe on issues raised by the participants. Other trainees may have been raised in a relatively authoritarian society and may need considerable guidance in achieving a non-directive, non-judgemental and informal style of group facilitation (Ulin *et al.* 2002). These types of trainees will particularly benefit from role-play activities during the training. For a more detailed discussion of the benefits and drawbacks of training field staff from different backgrounds see Ulin *et al.* (2005).

Training of the field staff improves the quality of the data collected. It provides the field team with the skills to conduct productive group discussions and to manage situations that may jeopardise the quality of the information collected. Without adequate training the group discussions may produce poor quality, biased or incomplete data. An untrained or inexperienced moderator may inadvertently bias the discussion, they may fail to probe on key issues or face difficulties in managing the group dynamics, all of which influence the quality of the information collected. Inadequate training of the note-takers may also lead to a failure to recognise non-verbal cues which indicate participants' level of comfort in discussing certain issues, and may result in biased data or poor interpretation of the data during analysis (Maynard-Tucker 2000). Effective training of the field team is therefore essential to provide the skills to elicit quality information from the group discussions, as reflected below:

There has been a lot of lost information because of the moderator not really understanding the methodology properly and the idea of probing. (Researcher, Lesotho)

Even when skilled moderators can be identified in the study country, there remains a need for training, albeit limited. Often skilled qualitative data collectors will act as consultants for a wide range of national and international organisations, including government departments, market researchers, non-governmental organisations, donor agencies or academic researchers. Each of these organisations will undoubtedly have a different approach to focus group research (see Chapter 1). It is therefore necessary to ascertain the type of focus group research these professionals have conducted previously and whether this is compatible to that expected in the research project. If there are significant differences in approach, then these moderators will need re-training on the requirements and expectations of the research project, as shown below:

Most of my assistants had worked for different non-government organisations before, which were result-oriented. They want the work done fast and are not so careful about the process. So it was important to make the moderators understand about probing – how, why, what – to settle clearly what you expect of them in your project. (Researcher, Kenya)

Finally, training the field team should not be viewed as a one-sided activity. Ideally it will be a two-way exchange, whereby the research investigators provide training in the skills required to conduct focus group discussions, while the trainees provide valuable insights into the cultural context of the research issues, and appropriate language or terminology to use in the discussions. This exchange is an invaluable opportunity for the research investigators to become informed on cultural concepts and practices which will assist in interpreting the results of the study. A training session is shown in Figure 4.1.

Figure 4.1   A focus group training session in Zambia. Photo K. Benaya

Who to train

Training should be provided for all members of the field team, including the moderators, note-takers and those transcribing the tape-recorded discussions. Often the field team will comprise a range of moderators and note-takers with differing characteristics to match those of the focus group participants (i.e. male and female moderators/note-takers). If resources are sufficient, it is worthwhile to train more people than are required in the field team, as there will inevitably be some individuals who are not suitable for the tasks. The trainers can then select those most suitable for the field team from the larger trainee group. It is recommended that all trainees receive instruction on the roles of each member of the field team (moderator, note-taker and transcriber). This will improve their understanding of the research method, and means that the roles of the field team can be interchangeable if required during data collection. It also improves teamwork if each member understands the role of others.

Moderator

All focus group moderators need to be fluent in the language of the study participants in order to conduct the group discussion. The moderator is the central member of the field team, whose task it is to manage the group discussion in such a way that sufficient information is gained to meet the research objectives. Therefore, the moderator needs to develop a clear understanding of the research objectives and how to utilise the focus group method to elicit quality information from participants. Moderators need to be trained on developing rapport, managing group dynamics, impartial group moderation, effective listening and probing, managing timing and pacing of the discussion, and be informed on ethical issues, such as consent and confidentiality. The issues for training moderators are summarised in Figure 4.2. Much of the moderator's role involves managing the discussion, particularly the group dynamics, as described by Maynard-Tucker (2000: 401):

A major challenge for local facilitators is to grasp the role of the moderator, which involves the use of probes at the appropriate time, the self-control of body motion, participating without personal input, the allocation of equal time to each participant, the reviving of the discussion with the formulation of topic questions, the handling of difficult participants and undisciplined participants who cut in, controlling participants who turn the topic into a political issue and keeping track of each participant's answers.

- Check fluency in the language of the discussion
- Check experience in group facilitation
- Provide overview of research objectives
- Observe natural ability for rapport development and stimulating discussion
- Train in introductory tasks for group discussion
- Revise ethical issues (e.g. consent and confidentiality)
- Train on group dynamics and encouraging discussion (see Chapter 9)
- Practice listening, probing and follow-up questioning
- Instruct on focussing the discussion to meet research objectives
- Review timing and pacing of discussion

Figure 4.2   Key issues for training moderators

One of the most effective techniques to train moderators in both managing the group discussion and the group dynamics is to conduct role-play activities, so that trainees can experience the role of moderation. Further discussion on moderation techniques is provided in Chapter 9.

Note-taker

Training of note-takers is often overlooked. The note-taker's role is to develop a written summary of the discussion, so that the main issues discussed can be recalled at a later time. Note-takers need careful instruction on how to recognise and record the essential issues in a fast moving group discussion. Without clear instruction, the note-taker's record may be superficial, incomplete or inadequate, as shown below:

Looking back, the training of the note-takers was not done well ... They didn't take notes very well, they would just write one word for the discussion rather than the actual issue description. So the notes didn't help me to understand what was happening, until the transcripts were done. So if the tape broke we could not rely on the notes at all to recall the discussion. This is an area where I didn't put much emphasis in the training, I didn't realise. (Researcher, Lesotho)

The importance of the note-taker's role must be stressed in the training sessions. It is easy for note-takers to become despondent that their role is redundant if the discussion is being tape-recorded. Three important issues need to be stressed to note-takers. Firstly, note-takers need to understand that their notes will complement the tape recording, in that they will include an indication of the body language and gestures of participants that will not be evident on the tape recording. The note-taker's summary will, therefore, become part of the research data used in the analysis. Secondly, the tape recording may have failed (e.g. if the microphone was not switched on), it may be inaudible or the tape may be lost or damaged after the group discussion. In these situations the note-taker's summary is crucial as it will be the only record of the discussion issues. The experience of one researcher in Zambia highlights this issue.

I had a bad experience when we did a field study for about thirty days. It was so intense and exhausting and during the hot season in Africa and it can get **hot** ... When you expose a tape to too much sunlight it deteriorates ... so half of the tape all you could hear was mmmmmmm ...! So we had to fall back on the notes. (Researcher, Zambia)

Thirdly, the importance of the note-taker's role is most apparent when participants refuse consent for the tape-recorder to be used, so that the note-taker becomes the sole means of recording the discussion issues. Two different experiences of note-taking are shown in the extract below:

One of the problems was that the note-taker in the men's groups knew that there was a tape recorder so he felt there was little point in taking notes. But in the women's groups it was more obvious that the note-taker was important as sometimes the women refused the tape recorder, then we were one hundred percent reliant on the note-taker. (Researcher, Pakistan)

The key training issues for note-takers are summarised in Figure 4.3. The note-taker, like the moderator, must be fluent and literate in the language of the target population to quickly write a summary of the issues as they arise in the discussion. Note-takers also need to develop a clear understanding of the research objectives, to enable them to identify issues of central or marginal relevance to the research objectives. Note-takers need to be instructed on:

- Check literacy and fluency in the language of the discussion
- Provide overview of research objectives
- Develop note-taking guidelines (i.e. brief written document)
- Highlight the importance of note-taker's record of the discussion
- Instruct on identifying and paraphrasing key issues in the discussion
- Train to identify colloquial phrases or terms in local language
- Instruct on objective note-taking (no interpretation or judgement)
- Encourage clearly structured notes, by topic or discussion questions
- Identify the language of notes
- Instruct on translation and transcription issues
- Train on recognition of body language and non-verbal signals of participants
- Conduct role-play to practise note-taking
- Check that the notes reconstruct the main issues of discussion
- Encourage clearly labelled notes
- Instruct on use of the tape recorder

Figure 4.3   Key issues for training note-takers

identifying key issues from the dialogue, paraphrasing the discussion, recognising colloquial phrases or terms to record, identifying body language signals and developing objective note-taking whereby they record the facts of the discussion without judgement or interpretation. Typically, the note-taker's notes are written in the language of the discussion to enable the note-taker to focus on the discussion issues rather than on translation. These notes would then be translated into the language of the research investigators. However, if a note-taker is able to make quick, simultaneous translations, the notes may be written in the language of the research investigators. This has the advantage that the research investigators will have an immediate insight into the issues discussed once the group discussion is completed.

Finally, note-takers need to be instructed on how to structure their notes. The written summary may be structured by each topic in the order that they were raised in the discussion. The summary may also be structured by the main questions or topics on the discussion guide. Whichever structure is used, the written summary needs to clearly highlight the main points raised in each group discussion. The notes from each group discussion need to be clearly labelled to link the summary with the corresponding group discussion in the project. In addition, the note-taker may need to operate the recording equipment, and so needs to be familiar with the operation of each device.

Transcriber

The person responsible for transcribing the tape recording of the discussion into a written document will also need guidance. The type of transcription required will depend on the purpose of the research and how the information will be used. For some research projects the transcription may involve simply developing a list of the issues discussed, while for others a full verbatim transcript is required for detailed textual data analysis. The transcriber will need to be instructed on the requirements of the project. A summary of key issues for training the transcriber is given in Figure 4.4; these training issues relate to projects where a verbatim transcript is required.

For projects that will conduct analysis of the substantive issues in the group discussions, it is critical to obtain a verbatim record of the discussion. This is an exact, word-for-word record of everything that is said on the tape recording. Transcribers need to be carefully instructed on how to develop a verbatim transcript of the group discussion. This involves transcribing everything that is said on the tape recording, exactly as it is spoken. It will include the

---

- Transcribe the discussion *verbatim* (include every word as spoken)
- Transcribe everything said by the participants and moderator without omissions
- Include moderator's questions and comments
- Include pauses, interruptions, laughter, silences, etc. in the transcript
- Include speaker identifiers, where appropriate
- Retain some key terms, phrases and local proverbs *in vivo*
- Decide whether to transcribe colloquial grammar and speech
- Indicate whether simultaneous translation and transcription is preferred
- Provide instruction on translation issues, if relevant
- Clearly label each transcript
- Identify a format for transcripts
- Ensure transcript formatting is compatible with data analysis software, if appropriate

Figure 4.4   Key issues for training transcribers

moderator's questions or comments, and each participant's response exactly as it is said. One of the most common problems with transcription is that the transcriber will summarise the issues in the discussion in their own words, rather than transcribing what the participants actually said. Summarising the discussion not only has a risk of bias, but also loses the richness and context of the information as it is spoken by the participants themselves. Verbatim transcripts will often also include pauses in the discussion, interruptions, laughter, silence, or if a respondent hesitates when making a comment. This level of detail can be valuable when interpreting the information during data analysis. Transcribers need to be instructed if this level of detail is required in the transcript. The transcriber also needs to be instructed on whether to include speaker identifiers that enable the comments of each participant to be identified separately. For example, each speaker may be given a different identifier, such as P1, P2, P3, to denote participant 1, participant 2, and so on which appears before each of their comments in the transcript.

Some participant groups may speak in strong colloquial grammar or in dialect. The transcriber needs to be instructed on how to transcribe this form of spoken language in the transcript. In addition, there may be some local terms, phrases or proverbs used in the discussion that describe a specific cultural concept in the original language. For example, the terms *purdah* (gender segregation) or *lobolo* (bridewealth) describe very specific concepts in some cultural contexts. It is useful to retain these words in the transcript in their original language with a brief translation in brackets. Transcribers will need to be briefed on how to recognise these terms in a discussion.

The task of transcribing and translating the group discussions is often conducted in the study country, as a bi-lingual transcriber may be more easily identified in the country of the research. There are two approaches to translation and transcription of the group discussions. The first, and most common, approach is for the transcriber to conduct simultaneous translation and transcription of the discussion from the tape recording. The second approach is to develop a transcript of the discussion in the original language and then translate this into the language of the research team. The transcriber needs to be informed on which strategy is preferred. As with all other research documents, the transcription needs to be clearly labelled and formatted, particularly if data analysis software is to be used. See Chapter 11 for further discussion on translation and transcription issues.

Field staff

There may be other field staff who need some training, but this will vary for each research project. For example, the field recruiters who will identify participants for the focus group discussions will need to be briefed on the criteria of participants and on recruitment protocol to avoid bias in participant recruitment.

Training manual

A training manual can be prepared for use during the training sessions and as a reference document for trainees. Not all projects develop a training manual, but those that do find it a useful document. The training manual need not be an extensive document. It needs to provide a brief background to the study and highlight the purpose of the research, the research funding agency and the characteristics of the study population. The training manual should also summarise the focus group methodology, particularly the roles of each member of the focus group team. The main part of the training manual will be a guide to each question in the discussion guide, outlining its purpose and clarifying any terminology.

The training manual is particularly useful in that it encourages consistency, within the field team, in the application of the discussion questions. It helps to avoid simple misinterpretation of the discussion questions and can be used as a reference to clarify uncertainty about any questions while in the field. This document is particularly valuable when the research investigators cannot be present during the training or are not available when the group discussions are being conducted.

Components of training

There are several important components to a training schedule for the field team. First, the training should include a general briefing about the research issues and the purpose of the research. Second, much of the training will involve familiarising trainees with the research instrument and a detailed overview of each section or question in the discussion guide. Third, the training needs to provide information on the principles of the focus group method of data collection. One of the most effective strategies to enable trainees to grasp the focus group method and to become familiar with the research instrument is through practical role-play activities. There is little substitute for experiential learning, particularly when training on interactive approaches to data collection, such as focus group discussions. Figure 4.5 summarises the six suggested components of a training schedule, which are discussed in turn below. Each research project will differ in terms of the level of

---

Part 1: Research objectives
- Outline the purpose of the research
- Identify relevant background information on research topic
- Identify why focus group discussions are being used for the study
- Describe how the information will be used and by whom

Part 2: Focus group method
- Describe the essential components of the focus group method
- Distinguish between in-depth interviews and group discussions
- Review the role of each team member (moderator, note-taker, transcriber)
- Outline techniques for moderating a focus group discussion
- Review ethical issues (e.g. consent for participation and tape recording, confidentiality)

Part 3: Discussion guide
- Outline the structure of the discussion guide ('warm-up', key, and closing questions)
- Clarify the purpose of each question
- Review translations and terminology
- Explore areas where probing is most beneficial

Part 4: Role-play sessions
- Conduct role-play of focus group discussions
- Conduct practical sessions for note-takers
- Discuss any difficulties arising from the role-play
- Review areas of the discussion guide, if necessary

Part 5: Research setting and study population
- Identify characteristics of the study population
- Identify the study setting (i.e. location of group discussions)
- Identify potential problems or hindrances

Part 6: Equipment operation
- Review the operation of all equipment (e.g. tape recorder, microphones, etc.)

Figure 4.5   Components of a training schedule

expertise of the field team, the complexity of the research instrument and in the resources available for training activities. It is important to tailor the training schedule described in this chapter to meet the individual needs of each project. Some level of training will always be required; however, there may be variation in the components of training required or the level of detail provided.

Research objectives

The first component of a training schedule involves orienting the trainees to the research topic, the objectives of the research project and how information from the group discussions will meet these objectives. Providing a brief overview of the research topic and summarising the critical issues will familiarise trainees with the types of issues that may arise during the group discussions. It is also necessary to define any terminology that may arise in the discussions and to identify any equivalent terms in the local language. Knowledge of the issues surrounding the research topic and related terminology will assist the moderator in probing the discussion and help a note-taker to recognise key terms and issues in the discussion. Outlining the research objectives is essential. A moderator needs to gain a clear understanding of the purpose of the research and how the information will be used in order to conduct a productive group discussion.

Focus group methodology

The second component of training involves instructing trainees on the focus group method of data collection. Trainers should provide an overview of the characteristics of the method, the roles of each member of the focus group team, guidance on moderation techniques, note-taking and transcription. Training should also include a session on observing non-verbal communication, such as eye contact, gestures, facial expressions and posture. Awareness of non-verbal cues alerts the moderator and note-taker to participants' level of comfort with the discussion issues. It is also important for a moderator to become aware of how to project positive and open body language. If trainees have experience in group facilitation then this component of the training may be a brief session to refresh on the method or to re-orient those who have experience in a different approach to focus group research. An important component of the training is sensitivity to ethical issues in data collection, particularly on issues of confidentiality and seeking consent from participants for their participation and for tape recording the discussion (see Chapter 2 on Ethical considerations).

A common problem with trainee moderators is a lack of understanding of the focus group method and how to apply it effectively. Trainers need to clearly distinguish between the approaches for survey interviewing, in-depth interviews and focus group discussions. The focus group method requires a different approach to elicit information and the presence of a group of participants makes the process more challenging than other approaches. The experiences below illustrate the effect of lack of adequate training on the information collected.

Some moderators had to be called back because after reading through the transcripts, I found it was question and answer, question and answer rather than really discussing an issue, debating this issue and encouraging discussion. (Researcher, Lesotho)

Sometimes the moderators seemed to be happy when people were talking generally about the subject area rather than concentrating on whether participants are discussing the relevant issues and guiding the discussion. (Researcher, Pakistan)

Discussion guide

The central component of the training schedule involves careful review of the discussion guide. The discussion guide is the research tool used to gain information to meet the study objectives and therefore must be clearly understood by each member of the field team. Trainers should allow adequate time for this component of training so that the discussion guide and question strategies can be reviewed in detail.

The structure of the discussion guide should be made clear. This involves identifying the 'warm-up' questions, key discussion questions and the 'closing' questions. The key discussion questions should be clearly identified as this is where the greatest amount of probing and group discussion will be required. It is also where the moderator should focus the discussion if time becomes limited. Each question on the discussion guide should be reviewed in detail to clarify its purpose and meaning, and to review any misunderstanding of the intent of each question. If the discussion guide has been translated, the meanings of the translations or terminology also need to be clarified.

Role-play sessions

One of the most valuable components of the training schedule is the role-play sessions, whereby trainees can experience their roles in the group discussion and trainers can provide valuable feedback. The extracts below highlight the value of role-play during training.

The problem with the training was that the moderators found that it sounds very simple. Only once they did one focus group did they raise questions about problems . . . only after a few practice focus groups did they really grasp what they were supposed to do. (Researcher, Lesotho)

I realise that it is very different to quantitative training, the content of training especially. In quantitative studies we sit in a room and go through the questionnaire and most things will be clear . . . But for qualitative training you spend less time sitting down to chat and more time for them to practise. I would advise anyone to do this, as they learn more when practising, both moderator and note-taker. You can't re-do a focus group, so practice in training is crucial. (Researcher, Lesotho)

It is useful to conduct two role-play sessions; the first in the language of the trainers or research investigators, and the second in the language of the study participants. The first role-play session is a class-room activity where the trainees act the roles of focus group participants, moderator and note-taker. The topic of discussion for this activity is not important, as the purpose of the activity is for trainees to experience the roles of moderator and note-taker. Each trainee should experience introducing a discussion topic, moderating the discussion and managing group dynamics. Trainees should also experience note-taking a discussion, identifying the main issues discussed, highlighting key words or phrases from the discussion, and identifying non-verbal signals of participants. To expose the trainee moderators to managing difficult group dynamics, some participants may be asked to adopt certain personalities, such as a dominant, quiet or argumentative personality. This aspect can help to build trainee moderators' confidence in handling these situations. It is also useful to tape-record the group discussions to illustrate the strengths and weaknesses in the discussions and to demonstrate where recording is unclear when several participants speak at once. Conducting the practical session in the language of the trainer or research investigators enables them to provide feedback on the delivery of questions, the extent of probing and the management of group dynamics. This session is particularly useful for those with little experience in conducting focus group discussions. Figure 4.6 shows trainees conducting role-play of a focus group discussion.

The second practical activity involves conducting focus group discussions in the language of the study participants, using the actual discussion guide for the study. This practical session is intended to familiarise the trainees with a discussion on the actual research topic, in the language of study participants and using the research instrument. The research investigators may not be able to understand the content of the discussion but can observe the conduct of the group discussion and participants' body language. The focus group

Figure 4.6   Trainees conducting a role-play exercise in India. Photo M. Hennink

participants in this activity can be members of the community or volunteers who speak the language of the discussion. For example:

What we did was intensive role-play, and class exercises. We had the advantage of being within the University, so I arranged with different departments to have some volunteers to participate in the focus groups [training] over lunch and I provided refreshments. We had some men, some of the workers and some of the women secretaries . . . it worked very well. (Research Student, Zambia)

Alternatively a focus group discussion can be held with the study participants and the exercise may be used to pre-test the discussion guide. However, using members of the study population for training activities may not be logistically possible.

It is essential to schedule a feedback session after each practical exercise to discuss any issues that arise from the sessions. These may include problems with using the methodology, the discussion guide, the translations, or other issues. As a result of the briefing it may be necessary to provide some additional training focussed on areas causing difficulty, or to review questions, translation or probing strategies.

Research context and study population

Trainees should also be briefed on the context of the research, such as rural or urban locations, and the likely venues for the group discussions (e.g. indoors or outdoors). Trainers need to highlight potential problems or hindrances in the study location and how to manage these situations, such as excessive noise or onlookers, which may affect the group discussion. The field team can then be prepared for these problems if they occur.

It is also valuable to tell trainees about the characteristics of the study population and to describe how participant characteristics may influence contributions to the discussion. For example, Maynard-Tucker (2000) states that the gender and age of participants may influence the nature of group participation. Particular subgroups, such as illiterate participants, may not express their thoughts as easily as other types of participants. Local facilitators are usually aware of any cultural differences in participation; however these issues can also be discussed during the training sessions.

Equipment operation

Finally, the training session should include instruction on the use of any equipment; usually this includes a tape recorder and microphone. Particular attention should be given to the location of switches on both the tape recorder and the microphone, and the need for both to be engaged for recording to commence. The field team should also be reminded to carry any spare components to the study site, such as batteries, cassette tapes or microphones.

Training schedule

Training often requires more time than anticipated and the research proposal should allow sufficient time and resources for training activities. The time required for training the field team is typically influenced by: the scope and complexity of the research project, the skills and experience of trainees, the fieldwork timetable and resources available. A basic training schedule, with inexperienced field staff, on a relatively straightforward research issue will take approximately three to five days. A generic four-day training schedule is shown in Figure 4.7. The most time consuming, yet critical, components of the training schedule are the review of the discussion guide and the role-play activities.

Day 1	Identify the research objectives
	Review focus group methodology
Day 2	Review discussion guide questions
Day 3 and 4	Conduct role-play sessions in classroom
	Review issues arising from role-play
	Conduct practical sessions in field
	(with community members or study participants)
	Review issues arising from practical activity

Figure 4.7   Generic training schedule

When the focus group discussions are conducted in a language not familiar to the research investigators, it is worthwhile to transcribe and translate the first group discussion immediately. This provides an opportunity for the research investigators to assess the quality of the information gained, identify whether effective moderation is occurring and provide feedback to the field team early in the fieldwork process. Further training on specific areas may be required to address any problematic areas. This strategy is worthwhile to avoid uncovering poor quality group discussions and incomplete information collection when the fieldwork is completed, as shown in the example below. However, this strategy may not be feasible in all fieldwork situations.

The first field trip I let the discussions run and did the translation later, the groups were in the local language. It appeared that the groups were going reasonably well, everyone seemed to be talking and the moderator seemed to be interacting with the women in the group. But after translation it was very clear that some of the conversations were not actually related to the topic at all! Also the moderator would get one response from one of the women, then move onto the next question and didn't allow any discussion on the question to develop. (Researcher, Kenya)

Key terms

Transcription is the written record of the focus group discussion as taken from the tape recording.

Verbatim refers to an exact, word-for-word, record of what was said in the focus group discussion.

Summary of key issues

- Lack of adequate training for the field team can result in the collection of poor quality, biased or incomplete data.
- Training should be provided for all members of the focus group team: the moderator, note-taker and transcriber.

- Training is a two-way exchange, whereby research investigators provide key skills to conduct group discussions and trainees provide valuable insights into the cultural context of the research, appropriate language and terminology to use.
- Essential components of a training schedule include: outlining research objectives, focus group methodology, and review of the discussion guide questions.
- Role-play sessions are invaluable in the training schedule. They enable the moderator and note-taker to experience their roles, and receive feedback from research investigators.
- A training manual is a useful reference document for trainees.
- The time required for training the focus group team is influenced by: the scope and complexity of the research project, the skills and experience of trainees, the fieldwork timetable and funding available.

5   Participant recruitment

Introduction

Recruiting participants for the group discussions is one of the fundamental tasks of focus group research. Participants in focus group research are recruited non-randomly (sometimes referred to as 'purposive' recruitment), according to criteria specific to the research objectives. There are a wide variety of participant recruitment strategies for focus group research; the most appropriate strategy to adopt will be influenced by the characteristics of the study population and the context of the research. The process of participant recruitment will be determined by whether the study participants are members of the general community or represent specific sub-groups of the population. The research context will also determine the most appropriate recruitment strategy to adopt. For example, participant recruitment in developing country contexts typically involves following local protocol to seek endorsement for the research and seeking assistance from local 'gatekeepers' in gaining access to community members. Recruitment in developing country contexts also makes use of the often close-knit social structures, which can be beneficial in quickly identifying appropriate participants. This chapter describes a range of strategies to recruit focus group participants and the situations in which each strategy is most applicable.

What is participant recruitment?

Participant recruitment refers to the process of identifying individuals with certain characteristics and inviting them to participate in the group discussion. Careful selection of participants is essential to create an environment suitable for productive discussion. Participants in focus group research are typically selected non-randomly, and according to certain criteria specific to the research objectives. A wide range of strategies are used to select appropriate individuals, which are described throughout this chapter.

It is worthwhile to make clear the distinction between participant recruitment for qualitative and quantitative research. Quantitative studies typically have large samples that are selected randomly. The sample sizes and random selection of respondents enable the findings of quantitative research to be generalised to a larger population. In contrast, qualitative research typically focusses on a smaller number of participants that are selected non-randomly. In qualitative research random sampling is not desired and often not possible for a range of reasons. First, the number of participants in qualitative studies is typically small. This small size would introduce a large sampling error if the purpose was to select a group that was representative of a larger population. Second, true random sampling assumes knowledge of the larger population from which the sample is drawn and that the characteristics of interest are normally distributed in the population. Qualitative studies generally don't have this knowledge of the study population or may be investigating characteristics which are not widespread in a population. It is often the purpose of qualitative research to investigate a certain undefined population or subgroup. Third, some participants will have more information or experience on the research topic than others and random selection may mean missing opportunities for gaining the best information from these individuals.

In addition, the issue of randomisation that is often central to quantitative sampling is not appropriate to the recruitment of participants in qualitative studies, as the aim of qualitative research is not to generalise the findings to a larger population. The aim of focus group research is 'not to infer but to understand, not to generalise but to determine the range and not to make statements about the population but to provide insights about how people perceive a situation' (Krueger 1988: 96). Therefore, participants for qualitative research are deliberately selected for certain characteristics which are of interest to the study (Ritchie and Lewis 2003). In this deliberate or purposive selection of participants researchers need to be aware of the biases in the selection of participants. There are some instances where randomisation may be used in the selection of focus group participants, for example where the required number of participants needs to be selected from a large pool of eligible individuals they may be selected randomly to eliminate any selection bias (Krueger and Casey 2000). For example, in situations where a list of eligible participants has been identified, the selection of names from the list is often achieved through a systematic or random selection procedure. However, in most situations randomisation is not appropriate to the selection of participants in qualitative studies.

Defining the participants

The method of participant recruitment for focus group research will be determined largely by the characteristics of the study population and the purpose of the research. Firstly, the study population will typically be defined by specific characteristics (e.g. 'women of reproductive age', 'young unmarried men', 'adolescent mothers', 'medical students'). Secondly, the purpose of the research may also define the study population; for example, a study may focus on users of a particular health service (e.g. antenatal care or family planning services) whereby the study population will be the service users. Another study may seek community views about an issue, so that the study population will comprise members of the general community. Therefore, both the characteristics of the study population and the research purpose will define who to recruit for the group discussions.

In addition, the recruitment strategy will be determined by whether the study population are members of the general community or comprise specific

Study population		Recruitment strategies
General community	→	Household selection of participants Telephone recruitment Liaise with community 'gatekeepers'
Sub-populations	→	Identify gathering points Identify a list Identify an event Focus on specific services Use social gatherings Place advertisements and notices Initiate a 'snowball' technique Attend meetings of professional groups

Figure 5.1   Selecting an appropriate recruitment strategy

sub-groups of the community, as the recruitment strategies will differ for each. Furthermore, the strategies used to recruit participants from the general community will be influenced by the context of the research. Research in developing country contexts will often necessitate liaising with local 'gate-keepers' and following accepted local protocols before participant recruitment can begin. Recruitment is then often conducted through a community leader or chief. In contrast, recruitment from the general community in developed countries will often directly involve contact with the study population for recruitment to the group discussions. Where the study population comprises a specific sub-group of the population (e.g. 'adolescents', 'pregnant women', 'hospital doctors', 'unemployed people', 'ethnic minorities'), then recruitment from the general community will be inappropriate as it may not identify the individuals of interest in sufficient numbers for the group discussions. Therefore, a range of other recruitment strategies will be more appropriate. These strategies involve identifying locations where the study population gather (e.g. social recreational locations), whether they are members of any organisations (e.g. professional associations) or are likely to be users of specific services or amenities. The different approaches to participant recruitment are summarised in Figure 5.1 and described in detail throughout this chapter.

Screening questionnaire

A screening questionnaire is a tool used during participant recruitment to identify whether individuals are eligible to participate in the group discussions. The screening questionnaire is designed to ask the smallest number of questions to quickly determine an individual's eligibility for the study. For example, a study may seek to recruit unmarried fathers aged below twenty-five years. In this case the screening questionnaire needs to include questions on paternity, gender, marital status and age, to determine eligibility to the study.

There are generally two components to a screening questionnaire. First, the questions to determine eligibility for the study, which are often demographic questions (e.g. age, marital status, place of residence) or questions to identify an individual's experience of the topic under study (e.g. users of a specific service). The narrower the selection criteria the more difficult recruitment will become, as the study population required will be more specific and increasingly difficult to identify. Therefore, the screening questionnaire should focus only on the essential characteristics required of the study population. The second component involves inviting the individual to participate in the group discussion, providing brief information about the study and seeking the person's contact details if they are to be contacted prior to the group discussions. An example screening questionnaire is shown in Figure 5.2. In this example, the study sought to recruit women aged fifteen to twenty-four years and men aged fifteen to thirty years. The listed questions filtered those eligible for participation, who were then asked a few additional questions, invited to take part in the discussion group and asked for their contact details. Using this instrument ensures that only those with the required characteristics are selected for the group discussions.

In addition to using a screening questionnaire for determining eligibility to the study, it can also be used to stratify or segment participants into different discussion groups. For example, if a study was conducted on community perceptions of fitness, the group discussions may be stratified by gender and by age (e.g. young men, older women, etc.). By asking about age on the screening questionnaire individuals can immediately be invited to a specific discussion group relevant to their characteristics.

A screening questionnaire is generally administered verbally and should be designed to be completed in less than five minutes. It may be used when making initial contact with potential participants, or to confirm the eligibility of participants once they have already gathered for the group discussion. For example, the screening questionnaire may be used during household recruitment to determine whether anyone in the household is eligible to be invited to the study. Similarly, the screening questionnaire may be used when a large number of individuals have been assembled for the study, perhaps by a community leader or chief, and there is uncertainty about their eligibility.

Area (Cluster) _____
Hello, I am conducting some interviews as part of a research project on reproductive health and
behaviour of young people. This study is being carried out by researchers at the University of
Malawi. Would you spare me a few minutes to answer a few questions?

1. Sex (fill in) . . . .
2. Would you tell me how old you are?
   a. Under 15   → Thank you very much (terminate interview)
   b. 15–19
   c. 20–24
   d. 25–29 (Male only)
   e. Female over 25/Male over 30 → Thank you very much (terminate interview)
3. How best would you describe your current marital status?
   a. Married and living with partner
   b. Living with partner
   c. In a steady relationship but not living with partner
   d. Not in a steady relationship
   e. Divorced/separated
4. Do you have any children?
   a. Yes   How many? . . . .
   b. No
5. What is your usual occupation?
   a. In school (on holiday)
   b. Employed (including self-employed, farmers)
   c. Unemployed.

That is all I have to ask you for now. The researchers are holding a discussion group at *(venue)* at
(time). This will be a confidential, informal discussion amongst 8–10 young men/women like your-
self and will focus on issues concerning reproductive health and behaviour of young people in your
local area. Participants will be given some refreshments. Would you like to take part in this discussion group? I stress that it will be confidential and that no knowledge is needed. Please do not
feel as though you have nothing to contribute as we are interested in your experiences and opinions.

If respondent agrees:

Would you tell me your name? . . . .
Contact details . . . .

Source: Hennink and Diamond (1999: 121)

Figure 5.2   Example screening questionnaire

The research team would then administer the screening questionnaire to each
person. The screening questionnaire may also be used if recruiting participants from a specific location, for example by screening individuals exiting
the outpatient clinic of a hospital to determine their eligibility, before they are
invited to participate in the study.

Recruitment strategies

There are a wide range of strategies to recruit participants for focus group
discussions. The main distinction between the strategies is whether they

involve recruitment from the general community or from specific sub-groups of the population. In addition, some strategies may vary by the context of the research, for example community recruitment in developing country contexts will likely differ from that in industrialised countries.

It is also important to note that no method of participant recruitment will be completely ideal, and it may be necessary to adapt certain recruitment procedures or to combine several strategies in order to recruit a specific study population. It is also possible that entirely different recruitment strategies are used in various study locations, in particular recruitment in urban and rural areas often differs (see example on Young people in Malawi, Figure 5.4). Researchers also need to be mindful of the limitations of the recruitment strategy used and whether this may bias the selection of participants included in the study. A range of strategies to recruit focus group participants and the situations in which they are most applicable are described below.

Using a list

It may be possible to recruit participants from a list of individuals with the required criteria for the study. The type of list will be determined by the required characteristics of the study population. Examples of various types of lists include the following:

- Government data bases (e.g. social service recipients)
- Client registers (e.g. health care, community services)
- Service users (e.g. recreation or commercial services)
- Employee registers
- Consumer data bases
- Members of professional organisations (e.g. rotary clubs, small business associations, teachers unions, doctor's associations)
- Service users (e.g. domiciliary services, antenatal care, physiotherapy)

Where a suitable list can be identified, the selection of potential participants often involves a process of systematic or random sampling from the list. Systematic selection involves dividing the number of participants required by the number of people on the list and then selecting every n^{th} name on the list to select the required number of individuals. For example, if ten participants are required from a list of 250 names every twenty-fifth name would be selected (i.e. $250/10 = 25$). Alternatively, names may be selected randomly from the list, using random number tables or placing numbers in a bowl and making the required number of selections from the bowl that correspond to names on the list. Once the individuals have been selected from the list, they need to be contacted and invited to participate in the study. If this strategy is used it is wise to over-recruit to compensate for those unwilling to participate in the study.

If focus group discussions form part of a mixed-method research design, for example a quantitative survey and focus group discussions, then focus group participants may be selected from the sample of survey respondents. This may be achieved by employing a systematic random sampling from the list of survey respondents to select a required number of participants for the group discussion or may involve the selection of individuals with certain characteristics (e.g. socio-demographic) that can be determined from the survey data. For example, a study may have conducted a community survey on contraceptive use. From the survey sample the researchers may select eight contraceptive users for a focus group discussion and a further eight non-users of contraception for a second group discussion.

A range of considerations need to be reviewed if using a list from which to recruit participants for focus group research. First, gaining consent from the list holder is critical. Not all lists are available for use in research, and their use may be restricted for ethical reasons. However, some lists are published in the public domain and readily accessible (e.g. business registers, members of professional groups). Second, the list used must be up-to-date and include sufficient detail about individuals for researchers to determine their eligibility to the study. Some lists may simply comprise names and contact details, which may be sufficient, while other lists may include demographic or other information. In some cases only minimum information is given on a list and it may be necessary to further screen the list to identify those of interest to the study. For example, a study may wish to recruit newly appointed male nurses, and identify a list of recently appointed nurses but the list may need further screening to identify those who are male. Second, it is critical that the list provides the contact details of individuals. Third, researchers need to consider whether the list contains a complete coverage of the study population, and whether there may be any bias in selecting participants from a particular list. It may be necessary to use the list in conjunction with other recruitment strategies. Fourth, it is necessary to consider the geographic coverage of the list, as those with national coverage will not be feasible for recruiting focus group participants. Fifth, the list needs to be sufficiently large to provide enough participants for the study, given that not all individuals will agree to participate. If the lists include only a limited number of people then researchers need to consider whether individuals will be familiar to one another and whether this may affect the group dynamics and the information shared. For large lists, it is useful to be able to manipulate the data by certain selection criteria or region.

Telephone recruitment

Focus group participants may be recruited by telephone. This method is most appropriate when recruiting participants from the general population, particularly if the study is being conducted in a geographically defined area. It can also be useful if the participant characteristics are broad and easily found in the general population, such as married women or employed people. The process involves selecting names from the telephone directory through random or systematic sampling; this can be achieved using computer software for random digit dialling (Morgan 1997). Individuals are then asked the questions on the screening questionnaire to determine their eligibility before being invited to participate in the study. This method also requires reminder calls the day prior to the group discussion to further encourage attendance.

When using telephone recruitment it is important to carefully consider the information conveyed to potential participants and the manner in which the information is delivered (Krueger and Casey 2000). Potential participants need to be convinced that attending the group discussion will be worthwhile, either because they are interested in the discussion topic or the incentive given to attend is attractive. The high refusal rate of such 'cold calls' and the time required for the process are significant disadvantages to using this method of recruitment. For example, a study in Britain on the impact of aircraft noise on residents who lived close to an international airport used telephone screening to recruit residents from suburbs adjoining a major airport (Diamond *et al.* 2000). The telephone directory of the suburbs adjoining the airport was used to select the name of every fiftieth resident. The researchers found that an average of sixty telephone calls was needed to recruit sufficient people for each focus group discussion. In addition, even though individuals agreed to participate there was often a significant attrition rate in attendance on the day of the group discussion, so significant over-recruitment was necessary. The low attendance occurred even though participants were offered a financial incentive for their time and travel and the issue was one of common concern to many local residents.

Events or professional organisations

The recruitment of focus group participants may also be scheduled to coincide with an event, meeting or conference which will be attended by members of the study population, for example, the annual meeting of professional associations (e.g. British Medical Association, British Sociological Association,

Public Health Associations). The concentration of the study population at a particular location provides an ideal opportunity to recruit participants for the discussion groups. This will require prior knowledge of the events and some information on the attendees. Researchers may be able to seek the assistance of event organisers to distribute invitation letters for the study prior to the meeting. Alternatively participants may be recruited at the event itself. It is important to carefully schedule the group discussions so that they have the least interruption to the meeting event, such as in the evening or during long breaks in the programme. For example, a study among international professionals in the field of population research used the membership list of the Population Association of America to identify potential participants. They were then invited by email to attend a focus group discussion during the Association's annual meeting. The conference attracts international specialists in population research and provided a valuable opportunity to recruit participants who would normally be globally dispersed (Blanc and Tsui 2005).

Social gathering points

Participant recruitment may involve identifying recreational locations where the study population are likely to gather. Often a study population will be associated with particular social events, clubs, recreational activities or entertainment venues. For example, young people may be found at particular sporting venues, at shopping centres or specific nightclubs; people with young children may be found at playgrounds, children's entertainment venues, and so on. For example, a study on middle-class women in India recruited participants from a local Rotary Club. Another study on retired medical doctors in India recruited participants from the medical profession's social club.

Services

The study participants may attend particular types of services or organisations from which they may be recruited. For example, pregnant women are likely to have contact with health centres, particularly antenatal facilities; some types of migrants may be found at community language centres; unemployed people will be present at job centres; community organisations may conduct social or educational activities that may attract the study population. It is also possible to recruit participants from occasional gatherings, which may attract the study population. For example, a presentation about a specific illness or condition may attract suffers or their families;

parents evening at secondary schools may attract parents of adolescents. Researchers would need to intercept individuals at these locations, ask the questions on a screening questionnaire to determine eligibility to the study, and invite their participation in the group discussion. At some venues there may be little opportunity to describe the study in detail to potential participants, so it may be more feasible to give a brief description of the research, gauge their interest and contact them later by telephone to provide further information. It is important to consider that individuals recruited from services or community organisations will likely be familiar with each other, which may affect the group dynamics during the focus group discussion.

'Snowball' recruitment

A study population with very specific characteristics may be difficult to identify through the range of recruitment strategies outlined above. For study participants with very specific characteristics it is useful to conduct 'snowball' recruitment. This involves initially asking key informants (e.g. community leaders, health or educational professionals) to identify an individual who meets the study criteria, then asking that person if they know of others with similar characteristics to themselves who could be recruited for the study. This method takes advantage of social networks and key informant's knowledge of the local population to identify individuals with specific characteristics. The number of eligible contacts is likely to increase as the technique is used, akin to a growing snowball. Once a sufficient number of eligible individuals are identified they can be invited to a group discussion.

As this method of recruitment utilises social and community networks, it is likely that many recruited individuals may be acquainted, which may affect their contribution to the group discussion. However, this effect can be minimised by using a range of different key informants to begin the snowball process, thereby tapping into different social networks. It may take longer to identify participants through a snowball technique than through other types of recruitment, therefore adequate time is needed to identify participants and arrange a group discussion (see example on Urban migrants in Mumbai, Figure 5.3).

Advertisements and notices

Placing an advertisement or notice in locations that may catch the attention of the study population may be used to recruit focus group participants. This may involve placing an advertisement in a paper or newsletter read by the study population to describe the study and invite participation. Notices about the study and eligibility criteria may also be placed in prominent locations likely to be seen by the study population. For example, a notice may be placed on university notice boards or electronic notice boards. Often a substantial incentive is required to attract participants in this way and one of the drawbacks of this method of recruitment is that those who are motivated by the incentive may be more likely to respond.

Professional screening agencies

In some countries professional recruitment agencies can be employed to select focus group participants from the agency databases. These agencies hold databases of individuals with a range of socio-demographic character-istics by location from which the participants can be selected. Some agencies also conduct telephone recruitment. In general these services are conducted by professional market research organisations.

Community recruitment

Focus group participants may comprise members of the general community, such as residents of an urban slum or a rural village, or residents who live near an airport or health centre. In these situations participant recruitment will focus on the selection of individuals from the general community in these areas. The strategies for recruiting participants from the community will likely differ by the context of the research; the most notable differences are evident between research conducted in developed or developing country settings. When con-ducting community recruitment in many developed country contexts the recruitment process is often technology-based. For example, participants may be recruited using electronic registers of residents, by sending written invita-tions, through telephone recruitment using random digit dialling, or by placing advertisements in local print media. Therefore, community recruitment involves access to appropriate lists of residents, assumes a literate population and universal access to telephones. This implicit assumption is reinforced by the traditional three-step strategy for participant recruitment described by Morgan (1998), which involves making initial contact with participants by telephone two weeks prior to the group discussion, sending a confirmation letter one week before the group and making follow-up telephone calls one day before the group. The recruitment of participants in developed country contexts is also conducted by making contact directly with community members themselves.

In contrast, when recruiting participants from the general community in many developing country settings an entirely different approach is used. There are three main differences in community recruitment in developing country contexts. First, community recruitment often involves following local protocol to seek endorsement for the study from local gatekeepers, and recruitment of participants often utilises the social structures of the community to identify appropriate participants. Community members are therefore approached indirectly, through community gatekeepers. Second, there is a short time between recruitment and conduct of the group discussion, often recruitment will be on the same day or one day prior to the group discussion. Third, participant recruitment is typically achieved through verbal communication with gatekeepers and community members. Written invitations or telephone recruitment may not be appropriate, particularly if working in resource-poor settings or in rural villages. Written correspondence would not be appropriate for informal gatherings and meetings, such as group discussions. Low literacy levels in many communities make written communication unfeasible and it requires seeking the names and addresses of potential respondents, which may be difficult. However, there are some situations where letters of introduction may be useful in community recruitment. Letters of introduction are more appropriate if sent to a community leader or chief, however this is not essential. Alternatively, researchers may carry a letter of introduction during participant recruitment, which outlines the research project and sponsoring agency. This may be requested by some individuals to validate the study. Below are some examples of the use of letters of introduction:

If I sent letters in advance they may forget about it. Letters are appropriate for chiefs but not participants, it's just a formality though as you will meet them anyway. Letters to participants are not applicable, it's not in our culture, it looks too formal, as things work verbally. Even for literate people this would be formal, only the water board writes letters to inform that they will disconnect you! So it is not an appropriate approach in the Malawi context. (Researcher, Malawi)

I did write letters to the principle chief who covers a large area. The principle chief will talk to his sub-chiefs informing them of this work. So the letter just introduced the research and the researchers. This was a helpful system, as we followed the natural hierarchy in the Kingdom, which is quite good for a researcher as people can be instructed at any time – if the chief is calling, you must go. (Researcher, Lesotho)

In the urban areas the researchers carried a letter, 'to whom it may concern'. Some participants were insistent to see this. This is closer to how it is conducted in the UK. In villages it was quite different than in the UK. (Researcher, Lesotho)

A case study example of community recruitment in urban slums in Pakistan is shown in Figure 5.3. The typical process of recruiting participants from the general community in developing country contexts is shown in Figure 5.4 and described below. The recruitment process described in the remainder of this chapter is most suitable for focus group research conducted in rural areas and high density urban settlements. Where the study seeks to recruit participants from low density urban neighbourhoods, different recruitment strategies may need to be adopted. An example of this situation is described below:

Community recruitment

Residents in urban slums in Pakistan

A study was conducted to identify attitudes towards contraceptive use among residents in urban slum areas of Pakistan (Hennink *et al.* 2000). The target population for the study was married men and women of reproductive age (fifteen to forty-five years). The focus group research was being conducted in conjunction with a quantitative household survey in the same locations. The survey identified the prevalence of contraceptive use while the focus group discussions explored attitudes towards fertility and contraception.

Focus group participants were recruited from the community in each of the urban slum areas. Initially a meeting was held with the community leader of each area, whose permission was sought to conduct the research in each area. The research was valued by the community leader, who provided assistants to help with participant recruitment. The community leaders also identified suitable venues for the group discussions, which were vacant school-rooms, courtyards of community facilities, or the community leader's meeting room. The community leaders also suggested suitable times for the group discussions to be conducted, which led to the discussions with women being conducted in mid-morning, while those with men were conducted in the evenings.

The local assistants worked with the research team to recruit men and women from their homes. A screening questionnaire was used to identify the eligibility of residents within each household. Every tenth household was approached to identify eligible participants for the group discussions. Given the very close-knit community in the study area, additional criteria for the composition of each discussion group were stipulated. It was stressed that no group discussion should comprise of participants who were neighbours or relatives, and no discussion groups should include relatives of the community leader. Recruitment of participants took place the day before the focus groups were scheduled. Participants were asked to gather at a pre-arranged venue, and their eligibility was confirmed again before the group discussion began.

Recruitment of sub-populations

Young people in Malawi

A study in Malawi focussed on young people's reproductive health (Chimbwete 2001). The target population for the study was women aged fifteen to twenty-four years and men aged fifteen to thirty years, in both rural and urban areas of Malawi.

Participant recruitment for the focus group discussions in rural areas was initiated by a meeting with the village chief to discuss the feasibility of conducting research in the village. Once the chief's endorsement was granted, the research team outlined the selection criteria for the focus group participants. The chief offered his assistance to gather eligible villagers the next morning to participate in the study. A large number of people gathered the following day, many of whom were older than required for the study. The research team introduced the study to the waiting group in the local language, and stated the criteria for the young people required. The research team then used the screening questionnaire to identify from the large group those eligible for the study and organised these people into different groups by age and gender. Each person was given a time and location for their group, which was conducted the following day. The researchers noted the first names of those in each group. A local church building was used as a venue for most groups, which offered the necessary privacy for the discussion without onlookers. This was particularly important for the study topic of sexual health, where participants may have felt inhibited if older observers were present. After the focus group discussions were completed the research team conducted a brief meeting with the chief to report on the general progress of the groups, but not on the actual issues discussed. The chief was provided with a small gift in appreciation of his support and assistance.

In the urban areas a different recruitment strategy was adopted to identify young people. The researchers first reported to the district commissioner in the urban area to seek their endorsement to conduct research in the area. There was no clear community leader in the urban area from whom to seek assistance with recruitment, unlike the rural villages. Participants were recruited using two techniques. First, by identifying the places that young people gathered, such as shopping areas, music stalls and market places where youths tend to linger. Young people were approached, informed of the study and invited to participate. If they agreed, the screening questionnaire was administered to confirm eligibility and they were told the time and location of the group discussion. Further participants were identified using the 'snowballing' technique, by asking those recruited if they knew other young people who may be willing to participate, and the recruitment continued in a 'snowball' manner. These two recruitment strategies were more successful in recruiting young men than young women. The groups were conducted at a venue near to the recruitment areas.

Urban migrants in Mumbai, India

A study in India focussed on the health-seeking behaviour of migrant families in Mumbai (Stephenson 2000). The target group for the study was rural residents aged eighteen to fifty-five years who had recently migrated to Mumbai.

In the large urban metropolis of Mumbai, identifying recently arrived migrants from rural areas was a challenging task. The researcher learnt that recent migrants to Mumbai tended to concentrate in a relatively small number of poor, high-density settlements. Recruitment began by visiting these areas and asking local residents if there were any recently arrived families in the area. Assistance was also sought from community leaders and from health professionals who may have been aware of recently arrived migrants seeking health care. After some time several migrant families were identified. A 'snowball' technique was then used to identify further migrant families in the same or neighbouring areas. In order to be eligible for the study individuals needed to be migrants from a rural area, who had migrated within the last six months and where the household head was in the economically active age group of eighteen to fifty-five years.

The process of migration often involves a migrant joining relatives or former neighbours from the rural area who assisted them to settle in Mumbai and find employment. These close social networks were invaluable to identify other migrants. The head of each migrant family was interviewed in an in-depth interview to discuss the family's individual migration circumstances. During the in-depth interview respondents were asked if they were willing to participate in a group discussion on a similar topic at a later date. Once sufficient numbers of families were located in the same area, respondents were contacted again and invited to a focus group discussion to discuss more general issues related to the migration experience and their experiences of seeking health care in the new location. The focus groups were stratified by gender and were conducted in a local schoolroom, which had been identified by a community leader who was a health professional.

Figure 5.3 Participant recruitment strategies in developing countries

1. Identify community gatekeeper(s).
2. Meet with gatekeeper(s) to endorse the study.
3. Discuss a location and suitable times for the group discussion.
4. Request assistance with participant recruitment.
5. Brief the recruiters.
6. Screen participants.
7. Conduct the group discussion(s).
8. Debrief the gatekeeper(s) prior to departure.

Figure 5.4 Stages of community recruitment

In the residential areas, the upper class areas, how do we get people together with their high-walled security houses? And educated people are very complicated. You knock on the gate, first the dog would greet you and then the guard, oh! ... the district officer said best to get them through their workplace, so that's what I did, she gave me a list of different workplaces that have employment-based health programmes ... I contacted these places, and the human resources manager said 'I'll do a call out, they have to ask permission from their bosses'. So they did that, it was over a lunch break. (Research Student, Zambia).

Identify community 'gatekeepers'

The first task of the research team is to meet with the community leaders and seek their endorsement for the study. In many developing countries there exists a social hierarchy which should be acknowledged in conducting the research activities. Often communities will recognise a community leader or a chief. This social structure is often more prominent in rural areas, however in close-knit urban communities residents are also recognised as community leaders. In many situations it is not appropriate to access community members without first seeking the endorsement of the community leader and doing so may cause offence to the local community and refusal to participate in the research. Acknowledging the social hierarchies in many developing country settings not only shows respect for local protocol, but can also lead to valuable assistance with participant recruitment. If the community leaders are unknown to the research team, they can easily be identified by asking a local resident to escort the team to their house.

The first task involves meeting the community leaders to introduce the research and seek their endorsement to conduct the study in the area. Even if a study has been pre-arranged it is respectful to notify the community leader that the researchers have arrived in the study area, before commencing with recruitment. Often no prior notice is required for meeting with community leaders, and if they are not available a representative may be willing to assist or an appointment can be made for the following day. Researchers will typically discuss the following issues when meeting a community leader:

- Describe the purpose of the study
- Identify the research sponsor
- State why the study site was selected
- Identify how the study will benefit the community
- Describe how the information will be collected and used
- Seek endorsement for the study

- Seek assistance with participant recruitment
- Identify the required characteristics of participants
- Discuss a location for the group discussions

It is important that the research team gain the endorsement of the community leader before the study commences. The purpose of meeting community leaders is not only to share information about the study but also to gain their approval and support for the activities. The permission of gatekeepers can also be critical in accessing the study population. When the research has the support of the community leader it can be much easier to mobilise community members to participate in the discussion groups, particularly as community leaders will often nominate a person to assist the research team. Community members are likely to be more responsive to recruitment if the research has been endorsed by the chief or community leader. In most instances the researchers will be welcomed by community leaders if it is being conducted in a culturally appropriate manner and has the appropriate permissions from district officials.

It is recommended that the meeting with community leaders is conducted at least one day prior to the focus group discussion. It can take considerable time to conduct the meetings, recruit participants, screen their eligibility, arrange the various groups and then conduct the group discussions. Although it is possible to conduct all activities on the same day, this is usually only done if time is extremely limited or if the study is in a remote location where it is not feasible to return the following day. Researchers' experience on this issue are shown below:

Making the first entry [into the community] should not be done on the same day as the focus group, as you waste too much time. It can take hours to meet the chief, then gather people and run the group. You become tired, it is hot and the group has not yet even begun. When prior arrangements had been made we could start the group at 9.30am and leave the area by lunch. (Researcher, Kenya)

The first time, recruitment was a problem ... we ended up with groups which were too big, a room that was too small, too much to organise. Partly because we just turned up on the day, recruited and had the discussion. It was because we had to travel four hours to reach that rural area. But the next time we did it differently! (Researcher, India)

Identify a group location

Community leaders can also suggest appropriate locations for the group discussions and make available community facilities. The researchers need to highlight the preferred requirements for a private and quiet space, however in some communities there may be no suitable building and the group will need to be conducted outdoors (see Chapter 8 on Group location). The discussion with community leaders is also a good opportunity to identify when to conduct the group discussion and the most suitable time of day to schedule the discussions. Researchers should remember that the primary consideration should be identifying a suitable time for the participants to attend a group discussion, not what is most convenient for the research team. For example:

One of the reasons for going to the community leader the day before was to establish times when women were available, aside from working and family responsibilities. Then find the hour during the day when they were free, it was between 2–3pm for the community women and the groups with upper class women were held on a Saturday. (Researcher, India)

Some warning is important but not too much, one day was enough. An example from a rural area, there was a funeral in the village the day we arrived, it involved the whole village. Then there was another funeral, then another. The chief said 'If you wait you will never get your work done.' So you can't plan too far ahead as long as it is OK with the participants and some warning is given. (Researcher, Malawi)

Seek assistance with recruitment

The research team may also seek assistance from community leaders with the recruitment of focus group participants. It is desirable for the research team to be aided by a local assistant familiar with the characteristics of community members. The community assistant can then identify individuals with the required characteristics for the study, while the researcher's familiarity with the research method can ensure that bias in participant selection is minimised. The type of assistance given by community leaders may vary; for example, community leaders may:

- grant permission for the study to proceed and leave recruitment to researchers
- provide an assistant to recruit participants and make logistical arrangements
- arrange for all individuals with specified characteristics to assemble at a given time, from which the researchers can then recruit participants (as shown in Figure 5.5)
- recruit the required number of participants for a specified time for the group discussion.

Examples of assistance by community leaders are highlighted below:

Figure 5.5   Recruitment of participants in rural village, Zambia. Photo K. Benaya

We were working nearby so made contact in the study village. We spoke to the chief's wife, left a detailed note of the requirements and discussed these with one representative. We explained our intentions and they asked about the number and type of people required, the research assistant went out with the chief's assistants to identify appropriate people using our screening questionnaire. We returned in the morning to find the males we asked for already waiting. (Researcher, Malawi)

Sometimes the chief will select the participants according to the selection criteria, in my case all parents with adolescent children. We carefully explained to the chief the type of people that we wanted and very lightly the type of methodology that we are using and that we need a private place, no intruders, etc. so he could help to discipline the people. (Researcher, Lesotho)

We talked with the woman who ran the anganwadi [nursery school] and explained the selection criteria to her. She did the screening and selected women from the community. (Researcher, India)

Wherever possible it is desirable to recruit participants in collaboration with a local assistant. However, there may be situations when participant recruitment is conducted without a local assistant. If members of the research team are recruiting participants themselves, more time may be required to introduce the study to potential participants, identify the endorsement of community leaders and explain the value of their participation in the study. Participants may be recruited from households and the introduction given by someone familiar with the local language. This process of recruitment may be more time-consuming and achieve lower attendance than if conducted by a familiar community member.

Recruitment of participants

In community recruitment, participants will typically be recruited from their homes and screened for eligibility to the study, with a screening questionnaire. Participants will be provided with information about the study and invited to a group discussion at a specified time, or they may be asked to gather at a certain location to meet the researchers. As the recruitment of participants is often conducted by familiar community members, residents will feel less threatened or suspicious of recruiters compared with recruitment by an outsider to the community. When making contact with community members, researchers need to consider that participants may ask the following questions:

- What is the purpose of the study?
- Who is funding the study?
- Why is the study important?
- Who will benefit from the study?
- Why is the study conducted in this area?
- Who is taking part in the study?
- How were the respondents selected?
- Are there any incentives for participants?
- How long will participation take?

Potential respondents are more likely to agree to participate in research that they feel is worthwhile to them or their community, and if the reasons for undertaking the study are sound. So outlining these areas is important. Face-to-face recruitment also provides an opportunity to have a dialogue with potential participants to address their concerns, to stress ethical issues and to respond to any additional information requested. This contact may overcome doubts about participation and improve attendance at the group discussions.

It is important that participants are screened for eligibility to the study during the recruitment process. This may be done at different stages in the recruitment process, depending on the process of recruitment adopted. For example, screening of potential participants may occur:

- at a participant's home or the place or recruitment (e.g. fields, community venues)
- when participants are assembled by a community leader
- as people arrive at the venue for the group discussion
- when a group of people are assembled for the discussion.

The screening of potential participants is most needed when community leaders have arranged for residents to gather at a certain location to meet the researchers. Often a larger number of people than required will be at the location and it may attract curious onlookers and passers-by. The screening questionnaire is essential to determine which individuals in the gathering will be eligible for participation in the study. Using a screening questionnaire also provides a clear justification for turning away those who do not meet the required criteria. In addition, when participants have been pre-selected from their homes and asked to meet at a location for the group discussion, they may bring friends or companions to the group and other individuals may simply drift into the venue. It is therefore important to screen individuals for eligibility before the group discussion begins. In some situations all those gathered will be eligible for the study. Researchers then need to select only the required number of individuals for each group discussion. (See Chapter 7 on Group size.)

Conduct the group discussion

Once participant recruitment is complete, the research teams can then conduct the group discussions (see Chapter 9 on Conducting the group discussion).

Debrief gatekeeper(s)

Once the focus group discussions have concluded it is protocol to conduct a debriefing meeting with the chief or community leader. At this meeting the general progress of the discussion should be reported, their assistance should be acknowledged and, if appropriate, community leaders offered a gift for their assistance (see Chapter 2 on Ethical considerations). It is not usual to discuss the exact nature of the information discussed in the groups, as this would breach the promise of confidentiality given to participants, however a few general issues are usually summarised for the community leaders. It is also worthwhile to identify how the research will be used and whether there will be any opportunity for community leaders to learn of the study results. For example, through receiving a report or attending research dissemination meetings. It is imperative that researchers do not make overstated promises as to what may be achieved through the research, as this will cause disappointment if these activities do not eventuate and reduce participation in future research activities.

Key terms

Participant recruitment refers to the process of identifying individuals with certain characteristics and inviting them to participate in a focus group discussion.

Purposive recruitment refers to the non-random selection of participants according to certain criteria specific to the research objectives.

Random selection is a method of sampling based on each individual having an equal likelihood of being selected. This is more usually used in selecting samples in quantitative research.

Systematic selection is where individuals are selected in a systematic manner from a list. It involves dividing the number of participants required by the number on the list and then selecting every *nth* name on the list to achieve the required selection.

A *screening questionnaire* is a tool used during participant recruitment to identify whether individuals are eligible to participate in the group discussions.

Summary of key issues

- Participant recruitment refers to the process of identifying individuals with certain characteristics and inviting them to participate in a focus group discussion.
- Participants in focus group research are selected non-randomly according to certain criteria specific to the research objectives. The recruitment of participants aims to seek information richness through detailed discussions around the research topic, and seeks a range of views from different types of participants.
- The method of participant recruitment for focus group research will largely be determined by the characteristics of the study population, the purpose of the research and whether participants are sought from the general community or population sub-groups.
- A screening questionnaire is a tool used during participant recruitment to identify whether individuals are eligible to participate in the group discussions.
- Strategies for participant selection will be determined by whether the target population are members of the general population or a sub-population group.
- Participant recruitment in developing country settings is typically conducted *indirectly* (through a community leader or chief); by *verbal invitation* from a familiar community member; and there is a *short lead-time* between recruitment and the group discussion.
- In developing country contexts, letters of invitation may not be appropriate, given the reliance on face-to-face communication, levels of illiteracy and the formality of this type of communication.
- Participants may be recruited from a list, services or professional organisations, social gatherings, 'snowballing', by telephone, through advertisements or by using professional recruitment agencies.
- Recruitment of participants from the general community will differ by the context of the research, most notably between research conducted in developed or developing countries.

6 Group composition

Introduction

Group composition refers to the characteristics of participants in the group discussion, and how these characteristics may affect group cohesion and productive group discussion. The composition of individuals in a focus group discussion has a significant effect on the group dynamics and can therefore aid or inhibit productive discussion. Group interaction is vital in focus group research, therefore careful attention to the composition of the group is important (Bloor *et al.* 2001; Fern 2001). Good group composition will generate a productive discussion with useful data to meet the research objectives, while poor group composition may lead to little or irrelevant discussion or at worst conflict between participants.

There are two aspects of group composition which are likely to impact on the group dynamics: the level of acquaintance between participants and the level of homogeneity in participant characteristics. This chapter discusses how each of these issues influence the group discussion for research in both developed and developing country contexts. The key issues for consideration are highlighted as well as strategies to achieve the optimum group composition. It is important to highlight that there is no rigid formula for group composition, and the most effective group composition will differ by the research context and the type of study participants. The primary influence on group composition will be creating an environment which fosters an effective discussion, the components of which are likely to vary by the context of the research. A checklist for all aspects of group composition is provided at the end of this chapter.

Stranger groups vs. acquaintance groups

It is vital to create a 'permissive' environment in a group discussion, whereby participants feel comfortable to discuss their opinions, feelings and experiences without fear of judgement by the moderator or other participants. The importance of a permissive environment needs to be stressed, as without it participants may not disclose their true feelings and hence compromise the quality and validity of the information provided. One of the components of a permissive environment is the level of acquaintance between participants.

A debate that has attracted much attention is whether focus group participants need to be strangers to one another and whether familiarity between participants has an impact on the information shared in the group discussion. It has often been assumed that participants must be strangers for the group discussion to work most effectively. This notion is thought to arise from the use of focus groups in market research, which traditionally advocates that participants should be strangers (Morgan and Krueger 1993). Groups of strangers are generally favoured by market researchers as it is felt that they are less likely to express taken-for-granted attitudes and opinions than those participants who are more familiar with the attitudes of others in the group. However, in health and social science research there may be instances where a group of strangers is preferable and other situations where acquaintance between participants is beneficial. The decision as to which type of group composition is most applicable will depend on the research topic, characteristics of the study population and the context of the research. The central concern should be to use the type of group composition that will make participants feel most at ease in the group discussion without compromising the validity of the information received. The discussion below identifies the practical and theoretical issues associated with the use of each type of group composition; these issues are also summarised in Figure 6.1.

```
┌─────────────────────────────────────────────────────────────────────────┐
│                         Acquaintance groups                               │
│   Advantages                              Disadvantages                   │
│                                                                           │
│   Observe naturally-occurring debate      Familiarity may inhibit disclosure│
│   Shared knowledge provides greater detail Existing hierarchy remains     │
│   Group memory leads to greater accuracy and Taken-for-granted information│
│      group reminding of experiences       Information may lack depth      │
│   Familiarity enriches the discussion     Risk of over-disclosure         │
│   Secure discussion of stigmatising issues Confidentiality difficult to enforce│
│   Easier recruitment                      More challenging to moderate    │
│   Lower attendance attrition                                              │
│   Less threatening for participants                                       │
│   Shorter 'warm-up' time                                                  │
│                            Stranger groups                                │
│   Advantages                              Disadvantages                   │
│                                                                           │
│   Confidential and anonymous              Longer 'warm-up' time           │
│   Participants speak freely               More complex recruitment        │
│   Avoids taken-for-granted assumptions    Attendance failure              │
│   Detailed information                                                    │
│      (descriptions, justifications, explanations, etc.)                   │
│   Ethical issues controlled by researchers                                │
└─────────────────────────────────────────────────────────────────────────┘
```

Figure 6.1   Acquaintance groups vs. stranger groups

Pre-existing or acquaintance groups

Groups of acquaintances may comprise individuals who are professional colleagues, social acquaintances, members of a recreational or support group, family members or familiar individuals within a community. The familiarity between such individuals in a focus group discussion may reduce participants' level of comfort to openly discuss the issues and contribute their experiences; but there can also be numerous benefits in recruiting acquaintance groups. One of the benefits of utilising such pre-existing groups for focus group research is that they have an existing group dynamic which may enable researchers to identify 'naturally occurring' data, as the group reflects an existing context in which conversations occur and debate and discussion is natural (Kitzinger 1994; Morgan 1997). Therefore, if the research aims to observe how decisions are reached or discussed, using pre-existing groups would be entirely appropriate. Bloor *et al.* (2001) argue that another advantage of using acquaintance groups is the level of detail brought to the discussion. Within pre-existing groups there exists a great deal of shared knowledge about other members in the group. This can be advantageous in that group members can remind a speaker about additional events or experiences relevant to the discussion which that person may have overlooked or forgotten. This can enrich a discussion by providing a greater level of detail in the experiences of individuals than if there was no familiarity between group members. In addition, familiarity between participants can also lead to group members challenging the statements of others or identifying discrepancies between what is said and actual behaviour, due to shared knowledge of the same events or experiences. This situation can generally promote debate amongst group members and enrich the discussion.

Using pre-existing groups, such as support groups, can also be advantageous when the topic of discussion may involve disclosure of a stigmatising condition or experience, such as HIV or abortion. Participants may be unwilling to discuss or disclose their condition amongst a group of unknown individuals. However, if participants have been recruited from within a pre-existing group where their experience is known or is the basis of group membership, then the issue of disclosure can be overcome and knowledge of the condition amongst the group can aid discussion and encourage group cohesion (Jarrett 1993; Farquar and Das 1999).

From a practical perspective, it may be easier to recruit participants from pre-existing groups as they are already part of an established network of individuals that may have communication links. It may be possible to contact the group through a single individual, both for recruitment and reminders about group arrangements (i.e. venue, time). There may also be a lower attrition in attendance due to the shared obligation to attend the group and the knowledge that familiar individuals will also attend the group discussion. The moderator may also spend less time in the 'warm-up' part of the discussion with a pre-existing group and therefore more time in discussing the central issues.

Although there are numerous benefits in using pre-existing groups, researchers do need to exercise some caution with this type of group composition. When a group comprises of well-acquainted individuals who may also share social or professional contact, there exists a level of familiarity which in some circumstances can aid discussion and the comfort of participants, but in other situations may inhibit the disclosure of information and opinions. Participants who are acquainted may not feel comfortable to disclose their opinions or experiences with those familiar to them, as they will continue to interact with these people after the group has ended. If participants are reluctant to reveal their feelings, this will jeopardise the quality of the information collected. The researcher will be unable to determine whether the comments made were influenced by the composition of the group and participant's fears of disclosure, or if they were the actual views of participants. Familiarity can also limit the level of disagreement between participants as individuals may revert to the type of interaction that they conduct outside of the focus group discussion, such that work colleagues may interact as if in the employment setting and may not wish to challenge the views of certain individuals. This situation may mean that the information discussed in the group remains limited to the shared knowledge within the group, rather than uncovering more detailed perspectives and experiences from each individual (Meyers 1998).

A further drawback of pre-existing groups is that there exists a level of taken-for-granted information which is not shared in the group discussion. A well-acquainted group will have a great deal of common information about each other, which they overlook in the group discussion. For example, one person may voice an opinion but not feel the need to expand or justify their views to others in the group who are familiar with the reasons for that person's view; while amongst a group of strangers the same contribution may be explained or justified in greater detail. Therefore, one danger of focus group discussions with well-acquainted individuals is that the information gained may be superficial and without the level of clarification or justification that may be evident where individuals are not acquainted (David and Sutton 2004). Researchers need to be aware of this lack of disclosure or depth in the information received, as this will influence the quality of the data collected.

The greatest drawback in using pre-existing groups is the risk of over-disclosure by participants and the related difficulty in controlling confidentiality of the information discussed. Over-disclosure is 'where respondents impart more information, express views or declare experiences in the group setting that they subsequently may feel uncomfortable about revealing' (Bloor *et al.* 2001: 25). This may occur where an individual discloses information about themselves, perhaps in the excitement of a debate or to demonstrate a critical point on the topic of discussion. Over-disclosure can also be exacerbated in a group discussion amongst acquaintances as there is the additional risk that one group member may refer to the personal views or experiences of another, and inadvertently reveal information or experiences that the individual does not feel comfortable divulging within that particular group setting (Bloor *et al.* 2001). The researcher has to be aware that, unlike other research methods, focus group discussions involve individuals revealing information not only to the moderator but also to other group members. Even though the moderator can remind participants of the confidentiality of information discussed in the group, they have no control over confidentiality of the information outside the group setting and there exists the risk that sensitive information revealed in the group may be shared through the common social circles associated with the participants. Therefore, there may be ethical considerations in using pre-existing groups, as participation in the group discussion can have consequences for individuals after the group discussion has ended. The moderator's assurances of confidentiality are thus more limited in acquaintance groups. Researchers need to be aware of these ethical issues and carefully consider both the topic and the types of participants before recruiting acquaintance groups. In some circumstances it may be more appropriate to use groups of strangers where individuals can discuss information without the fear of repercussions of information shared once the group is over.

Finally, the group dynamics will inevitably be different amongst a group of acquaintances compared with strangers, which may affect the moderation of the discussion. For example, there may be private conversations amongst friends seated together, glances, muted laughter, which make others feel excluded from the group. Friends may also agree with each other or remain equally silent on certain issues, making discussion difficult. These group dynamics can make moderation more difficult in pre-existing groups (Morgan and Scannell 1998).

Groups of strangers

There are numerous benefits in recruiting focus group participants who are strangers to one another. The main advantage in this type of group composition is the greater anonymity amongst participants and improved confidentiality of the information discussed. These advantages have both ethical and data quality implications.

Focus group participants who are unfamiliar to each other and who are unlikely to see one another after the discussion has ceased, may contribute more freely to the discussion. These participants may feel a greater sense of confidentiality in the group discussion, in that the information they provide is not being shared with familiar individuals and there is a reduced likelihood that disclosure of information will impact on the participants once the group has ended. It is somewhat akin to the notion of confessing one's true feelings to a stranger on the train (Bloor et al. 2001). Therefore, a group who are strangers to one another may contribute more spontaneously to the discussion, provide greater detail about their experiences and opinions and be more 'honest' in the discussion. This is an important advantage of stranger groups as it will impact on the quality of the data collected. Stranger groups also offer greater anonymity, so the information discussed may be more likely to remain confidential, therefore they may be a more ethical means of data collection.

Another important advantage of recruiting a group of strangers is the depth of discussion that may result. A group discussion between strangers means that there is no taken-for-granted information, which is common among acquaintance groups. Therefore, information that may evoke only a nod of agreement amongst well-acquainted participants may require considerably more explanation to a group of strangers. Describing an experience or opinion to a group of strangers typically involves providing a greater amount of detail, justification or context to the issues raised than would be done amongst acquaintances who may be familiar with the circumstances and influences on that person's views. The provision of this level of detail in the discussion can assist the moderator in exploring various beliefs, opinions or views amongst participants to generate productive debate on the issues. The greater level of detail in stranger groups can provide valuable data, especially if the purpose of the study is to understand the reasons for certain behaviour or opinions. Recruiting groups of strangers is particularly valuable when conducting international focus groups when there is a need to understand in detail the socio-cultural influences on certain views or behaviour. In these situations a group of strangers may provide a more productive group discussion than acquaintance groups (David and Sutton 2004).

There also exist some drawbacks in conducting a group discussion amongst strangers, particularly in relation to the group dynamics. Groups of strangers will inevitably take a longer time to 'warm-up' in the discussion as they need to become familiar with others in the group and feel comfortable in the discussion environment before making a contribution. Therefore, it may take a greater effort by the moderator to initiate a discussion amongst strangers. However, this does not suggest that that stranger groups lack effective debate once the discussion is established, as participants who are strangers are equally likely to challenge the opinions and contradictions of other group members and perhaps in a more direct manner than a moderator (Bloor *et al.* 2001).

In addition, attending a group discussion which will be comprised of strangers may be more challenging for a participant than if the group is comprised of familiar individuals. For this reason it is often necessary to over-recruit participants in stranger groups due to the greater likelihood of attendance failures. The recruitment of stranger groups may also be more complex and time consuming than pre-existing groups, as each participant may need to be recruited and contacted individually prior to the group discussion.

Fieldwork challenges

Although researchers may prefer to recruit a group of strangers for the group discussion, in some fieldwork settings this may prove challenging, particularly when working in closely-knit communities, such as in many developing countries.

It may be argued that focus group research in developed country contexts can recruit a group of strangers with relative ease, due to the methods of participant recruitment used (e.g. telephone directories, residents lists) and the relatively dispersed residential living. However, in many developing countries there exist integrated social structures and dense residential living that make it extremely difficult to recruit a group of participants who are truly strangers to one another. This is particularly evident when conducting focus group research in areas such as urban slums and other high density living, or in rural villages, where there exists great familiarity amongst members of the community. Residents may be familiar as neighbours, friends, family members, relatives or prominent individuals (e.g. teachers, shopkeepers and religious leaders). In addition, regular community activities such as residents' meetings or religious activities mean that a wide circle of people are acquainted with one another. Where these close social networks exist it may simply be impossible to recruit a group of strangers for a focus group discussion. In these situations researchers need to determine whether acquaintance between group members is likely to affect their contribution to the group discussion and then determine the appropriate level of familiarity between participants. It is often found that familiarity between participants is beneficial for the group dynamics and fostering discussion between participants. In fact, in some cultural contexts women, and even men, are uncomfortable in sharing their perspectives with people they do not know (Ulin *et al.* 2002). Researchers, therefore, need to consider the local norms of social interaction, in addition to the research topic, in deciding on whether it is appropriate to recruit participants who will be familiar to one another. Some experiences of this issue are shown below:

In a rural situation everybody knows everyone else and what is happening in the next village, therefore composing a group of strangers is not possible. But this was actually good for the discussion as these people already socialise with each other so they are free to discuss things, they're already used to mingling and mixing of information, new ideas, what's going on around. In fact this may have enriched the discussion in some ways. (Research student, Malawi)

If you go to rural areas or a slum community there is no way you can conduct a group where they don't know each other – impossible! Every group had some women who knew each other somehow. This society is structured on communities who know each other and discuss things together. So it is a less artificial situation, as the women can respond to each other in the discussion. Knowing each other may have made it easier to be able to quarrel and disagree over the issues too. (Researcher, India)

Research in some developing country contexts may need to accept that some level of familiarity between participants will be inevitable, and that this may enrich a discussion and be more acceptable in certain cultural contexts than groups with strangers. However, there may be some relationships between participants which will have a negative impact on the group dynamics, the confidentiality of the information and the quality of the data collected. Researchers should therefore avoid conducting group discussions amongst participants with particularly close relationships, such as family members, close relatives, household members or neighbours. Certain measures can be implemented to ensure that these relationships are not evident in the group discussions. During recruitment the research team needs to brief recruiters on the types of relationships to avoid in a discussion group and then check the group composition once the group is assembled. This can be done by asking participants whether they are neighbours, family members or relatives. If these relationships are found within the group, some members can be asked to join another group discussion. Researchers need to continually balance the methodological rigor of focus group research with the reality of the study context. Some common relationships to avoid are highlighted below:

- *Participants from the same immediate family*
  Participants from the same immediate family should not be included together in a group discussion, for example brothers, sisters, cousins or a mother and daughter even though both may meet the selection criteria of the group. Participants from the same family may feel inhibited to openly discuss certain personal issues in the presence of an immediate family member. A moderator often has no idea of the breadth of issues which may be discussed in the group and it is possible that certain issues of relevance may be avoided due to the close relationships between certain participants in the group. In addition, the aim of the group discussions is often to gain diversity in views and including members of the same family may lead to repetitive information. An example from rural Lesotho is shown below:

  It is really difficult indeed to recruit strangers in a village, they **all** know each other. But we didn't have any relatives in the groups. We could identify if there were relations in the groups as in Lesotho they use titles to refer to others rather than names, so if they are sisters you will notice by the way they are addressed. (Researcher, Lesotho)

- *Participants who are closely related*
  There may be similar concerns amongst participants who are closely related, even if not from the same natal family. Particular examples include sisters-in-law or a mother and daughter-in-law. When closely related family members are included in the same group, a hierarchy may develop that reflects the familial relationships (for example, older members may dominate the younger). These relationships can affect the group dynamics and level of contribution to the discussion, and may happen regardless of the topic of discussion.

- *Participants from the same household (even though not related)*
  With extended family living arrangements and the household composition in many developing countries, there may be individuals from the same *household* present in the group, even though not related to one another. There may be several unrelated families living in a single household or a household compound who share some amenities. Avoiding household members in the group discussion is particularly relevant when the discussion will focus on household issues, for example household services, decision-making or financial matters. Members of the same household may feel reluctant to reveal some information in the presence of other household members. It is also difficult to identify whether personal animosity between household members will influence their participation in the group.

- *Participants who are neighbours*
  Excluding neighbours in the same group discussion will help to ensure that participants have only a passing acquaintance with one another. In some situations, it may be relevant to select participants who live in different streets, particularly in very densely populated residential areas. This will enable a greater diversity within the group and further reduce participant familiarity. This can be achieved by asking participants if anyone resides in the same street as others.

Homogenous group composition

The second aspect of group composition that is likely to impact on group dynamics is the level of homogeneity between participants, in terms of their demographic characteristics or experience in the topic of discussion. In this context group homogeneity refers to the homogeneity within individual focus groups, rather than in the study population as a whole. There are two reasons to construct a group discussion amongst participants with homogenous characteristics: to facilitate a productive group discussion and to separate participants with differing characteristics for comparison during data analysis (Krueger and Casey 2000).

The central purpose of homogenous group composition is to facilitate a productive discussion between participants. The greater the similarity between participants in terms of socio-cultural and demographic characteristics, the more likely that group members will identify with others in the group and contribute to a cohesive discussion (Fern 2001). Jourard (1964: 15) states that 'subjects tend to disclose more about themselves to people who resembled them in various ways than to people who differ from them'. In contrast, participants may feel uncomfortable or threatened if they perceive others in the group to have a higher status, greater knowledge of the discussion issues or more influence in the community, which will reduce their willingness to contribute openly to the discussion.

The degree of group homogeneity should not be overlooked as it can make a significant impact on participant's contributions and the degree of cohesiveness in the group. The type of group homogeneity will depend on the purpose of the study, but typically homogeneity is sought in the demographic characteristics of participants (e.g. age, gender, ethnicity, education level, marital status, location of residence or socio-economic status) or in their level of knowledge or experience on the topic of discussion. Researchers should aim to achieve group homogeneity on only a small number of relevant demographic characteristics, as too much specificity in participant characteristics will create difficulties in participant recruitment and result in the need for too many group discussions. Homogeneity on too many variables may also result in a sterile group dynamic with little diversity in experience or opinions. Typically group participants will be homogenous in gender and age group, so that a study may conduct group discussions comprising young women, older women, young men and older men. As a general rule it is not advisable to conduct a group discussion with participants from different socio-economic groups or life stages, as there is likely to be less common ground for discussion. It is also not recommended to mix authority relationships such as managers and employees, as the power relationships in such groups may silence some member's views. To reinforce the homogeneity between participants, the moderator can stress in the introduction that participants were selected because of their *similar* characteristics.

Separating focus group participants by gender is perhaps the most frequently used variable when seeking to achieve group homogeneity. It is common practice not to mix male and female participants in the same group discussion, particularly where the topic of discussion may be viewed differently between the sexes. This gender segmentation is partly so that the views on the research topic can be clearly delineated by gender, but also because mixed sex groups may create a different group dynamic than single sex groups. Even so, relatively little is known about how the gender composition of the group affects the group discussion. Whether men or women interact differently in mixed sex groups is a long-standing debate in focus group research, and for this reason alone some researchers may prefer to segment the discussion groups by gender (Thorne and Henley 1975; Morgan 1997; Krueger and Casey 2000). Krueger and Casey (2000) state that in mixed sex groups men may dominate the discussion, speak more frequently or with more authority than in a single sex group. The dominance of men in mixed sex groups is sometimes referred to the *peacock effect* (Krueger and Casey 2000: 73). It is unclear what effect this behaviour has on female participants' contributions to the group discussion. Due to the uncertainty of the influence of mixed sex groups on the group dynamics, and participants' ability to contribute to the discussion, many researchers choose to separate groups by gender. For a further discussion on the potential influence of gender on group discussion see Fern (2001).

Homogeneity between participants can also be achieved in participants' level of knowledge or experience on the discussion topic. In many cases homogeneity in participants' experience with the research topic will be of greater importance in fostering a dynamic discussion than similarity in demographic characteristics alone. This may be because participants can strongly identify with others who share similar experiences, yet the personal characteristics of each participant provide sufficient diversity to foster a dynamic discussion around the issues. For example, a group of women who have experienced a premature birth may have enough in common to foster a productive dialogue regardless of their demographic characteristics. However, this may not be the case for all discussion topics. Bloor *et al.* (2001) use the example of research on abortion legislation, whereby a group composed by topic alone could include abortion clinicians, pro-life individuals, and those who had experienced an abortion. A group of individuals with opposing views or experiences on the topic may lead to stifled discussion as group members have little common ground for discussion. It may also lead to some members withholding their true feelings about the topic or, at worst, conflict between participants who hold strongly opposing views which will destroy any constructive debate. In these situations it is better to construct group homogeneity through a combination of similar experiences and demographic characteristics. So the same study on abortion legislation may comprise of separate group discussions with adolescents who experienced an abortion, or older women who had an abortion; or separate group discussions are conducted with pro-life groups, abortion clinicians and religious leaders. This type of approach to creating group homogeneity may uncover greater detail of the underlying influences on abortion views amongst different types of individuals. In practice, group homogeneity will be created through the nature of the research topic and the information available about participants prior to recruitment. Researchers should endeavour to balance the homogeneity and heterogeneity of participants, so that there is sufficient homogeneity to promote discussion yet adequate heterogeneity to capture diverse opinions and experiences (Gibbs 1997).

The second reason for homogenous group composition is to separate the responses of particular types of participants for comparison during data analysis. For example, a study population may be broadly defined as 'adolescents in Brazil'; however, it may be beneficial to compare the views of sub-groups of the study population, such as comparing male and female adolescents or those from urban and rural areas. Conducting separate discussion groups comprising participants with specific characteristics enables clear comparisons to be made between these groups during data analysis. If participants with differing characteristics are included in the same group discussion (e.g. urban and rural adolescents), the distinctive issues of each type of participant are difficult to distinguish. The strategy for segmenting the study population in this way is to create a variety of internally homogenous groups that capture a range of potentially distinct perspectives from within each group (Morgan and Scannell 1998).

To achieve effective group segmentation researchers need to identify the sub-categories of the study population whose views are critical to better understand the research problem. For example, if the research objectives require identifying differences in attitudes towards health care by gender or marital status, then group composition needs to reflect these characteristics. Ideally the characteristics used for segmentation will also create group homogeneity, so that segmentation can achieve two goals of promoting discussion and analytical segmentation.

One of the drawbacks of segmenting the group discussions is that it requires the conduct of more group discussions than if segmentation was not used. This is because a range of group discussions need to be conducted with each sub-group of participants in order to clearly identify any distinctive issues within that sub-group. The increased number of groups also has cost and time implications for the study. Segmentation by too many character-istics can also lead to recruitment problems as quite specific participant characteristics need to be sought for each group.

Moderator characteristics

The compatibility between the moderator's characteristics and those of the participants also needs to be considered. The demographic characteristics of the moderator can influence the group dynamics and nature of the discus-sion. It is common practice to match the demographic characteristics of the moderator with those of participants, so that a group discussion amongst young men is led by a young male facilitator. Although some researchers firmly believe that the characteristics of the moderator should mirror those of the group participants to create a fluid discussion, others feel that selecting a moderator with some differing characteristics to participants can in fact be beneficial to the information gained in the discussion. For example, if a western male moderator facilitated a discussion amongst men in China, it is likely that the participants may describe the discussion issues in greater detail to such a moderator than to a similar moderator of Chinese back-ground. This is because participants may perceive the need to describe certain social or cultural issues which influence their opinions, while this justification may be taken for granted with a moderator of the same cultural background as participants. Using a moderator with differing characteristics to group participants also provides some legitimacy in asking for clarifications or explanations which may appear inane if coming from a moderator of the same background as participants. In one sense a moderator with different characteristics takes on the role of a stranger, which may enable a greater depth of information to be drawn from the group. However, this does not suggest that using a moderator with different characteristics from partici-pants will always be advantageous, for example a male moderator of female participants is generally not advised for the same reasons as mixed gender groups are generally avoided. Above all, researchers need to consider the characteristics of the moderator that will make participants feel most com-fortable to contribute to the group discussion. Where there exists uncertainty about how participants will respond to a moderator, it is generally best to match the characteristics of moderator with participants. In much focus group research a number of moderators with varying characteristics will be used to moderate individual groups (e.g. male and female moderators).

Finally, it is preferable that the moderator is unknown to the group partici-pants. Although familiarity between the moderator and participants may make respondents feel at ease, it can also influence the nature of the group discussion, in that a familiar person may be identified with particular beliefs or opinions that influence participants' responses and reactions to topics discussed. For example, a familiar moderator may be known to have strong political, environ-mental or religious views, and participants may feel the need to mirror those views or they may be reluctant to voice their own opinions. With a moderator who is unfamiliar to participants these issues are avoided. It is therefore recommended that moderators are from outside the study community.

Fieldwork challenges

Even though the research team may have given careful consideration to the composition of the group discussions to ensure homogeneity between partici-pants, once the fieldwork commences a range of situations may arise to compromise the group composition. Researchers need to be able to recognise the effect of certain situations on group dynamics and be prepared to imple-ment a range of strategies to maintain the desired group composition. The situations described below are not exhaustive, but highlight common issues and strategies to maintain group composition during focus group discussions.

Demographic characteristics

One of the most common criteria for segmenting discussion groups is by socio-demographic characteristics, particularly age, gender and social class. However, in some circumstances, it may not be easy to determine the demographic characteristics of participants. In some contexts participants may not know their age, particularly if the study participants are poorly educated, and it can be difficult to determine the age of individuals from another culture from their external appearance, particularly in rural or poor communities where people often age prematurely. Some participants may also claim to be a particular age to gain entry into the discussion groups. An example of this problem from a study amongst the urban poor in Pakistan highlights this issue:

She said she didn't know her age, but she was saying that she was in her thirties so that we would allow her to participate in the group. After asking some basic questions and asking the opinion of our local research assistant, it was clear that she had to be in her late forties, she was past childbearing age, so we politely asked her to leave and she agreed. (Researcher, Pakistan)

Determining the social class or caste of individuals may also be important to avoid the formation of hierarchies and power differentials within a discussion group. However, when conducting research in unfamiliar cultural settings it may be difficult to identify the indicators of social class or caste, as is shown by the extract below on research in India:

It is easier in your own culture to know the indicators of social class, but in another country it's difficult. Women's age or number of children are mostly easy to determine, but other cultural things like caste are not. You need to spend a lot of time getting to know your study area before you select participants. Even with the best-trained team it is difficult to identify the differences in the caste groups and to be aware of who you can put together in a group discussion. (Researcher, India)

Researchers need to develop quick strategies to determine the socio-demographic characteristics of participants in contexts where this may present a problem. For example, where participants are not aware of their own age, researchers may ask a number of key questions to determine the likely age of the individual. This may be done by asking about the age they left school, their age at marriage or the number of children they have. It is useful for researchers to have broad knowledge of the demographic patterns within the study population to make a reasonable estimate of a person's age from the information given. So that if a woman is married with four children, and the researcher is aware that the average age of marriage in her community is eighteen years, fertility is high and birth intervals are typically short, then the age of the woman may be estimated to be between twenty-two and twenty-five years. Other characteristics such as caste or social class may be more difficult to determine unless one is very familiar with the cultural setting of the research. In these cases, assistance from local research collaborators is invaluable in identifying the more subtle characteristics which indicate social class or caste (e.g. surname, type of dress).

Personal relationships

When focus group research is conducted in community settings, there may be certain individuals who insist on joining the group or observing the discussion. The presence of individuals with clearly different characteristics from the participants can disturb the group dynamics and make participants feel reluctant to contribute to the discussion; therefore these situations need to be carefully managed by the field team. One of the most common situations, particularly in focus group research in Asia, is where a mother-in-law or family elder will assume participation in the group discussion regardless of the group composition. This may occur when younger participants are accompanied to the group discussion venue by older family members, or when these family members are present in the house or compound where the group discussion is being conducted. When the group discussion is held in the house of a community member, family members will often drift into the room where the discussion is being conducted or quietly join the group once in progress. Clearly the presence of such family members would introduce a hierarchy into the group (even if they are silent) which can influence the group dynamics and stifle the contributions of some members to the discussion. However, in this type of situation researchers are powerless to ask household elders to leave the discussion, as the research team are essentially guests in their house. If this situation is likely to occur researchers may select a more neutral venue or explain the difficulties to the host who may dissuade these individuals from joining the group discussion. When the group discussion is held in a community venue the research team are in a better position to dissuade family elders from joining the discussion. Researchers can explain to those accompanying group participants the purpose of the discussion, the selection criteria and the effect of older members in the group. This may be sufficient to avoid any interruptions. If accompanying elders have travelled some distance or intend to wait until the discussion is completed, they may be offered refreshments or invited to return at a specified time.

In some situations, the insistence of a mother-in-law or family elders to participate in the group discussion is due to their position of authority within the household or social status in the community. Where respect for the family elders has not been adequately shown by the research team they may feel offended or excluded. On most occasions what appears to be an intrusion or insistence by family elders to join the discussion is simply a reaction to their exclusion from the group. To avoid this situation, researchers may conduct a specific meeting with such elders, either an impromptu discussion with those who have accompanied participants to the venue, or by arranging a brief meeting with the mother-in-law and elders of the household where the group is being conducted. This shows respect for the status of the household elders and provides them with an opportunity to contribute their views. They may then be less likely to interrupt a group discussion and feel that they have been overlooked in preference of other household members. The experiences of researchers in various Asian countries are highlighted below:

The group was held in a rural compound. One mother-in-law sat right outside the door where the discussion was held, and kept interrupting! It was disturbing the group and the young women were starting to whisper during the discussion to avoid being overheard. Later we realised that our approach had undermined her authority within the compound and she wanted us to hear her views. As we didn't plan to interview her, the only way she could say her opinion was to keep interrupting the group. (Researcher, Pakistan)

We needed to include the young girls. We discussed the research topics with the guardians, especially the mothers-in-law. We explained that they may not feel comfortable if you are there and asked if they could leave. (Researcher, Bangladesh)

In rural areas of India this was a problem. In the one-room houses of the families the mother-in-law stuck like glue! The only way round this was to say OK we will talk to you next. Then they were fine and would go away for an hour until it was time for them and talk, we had a short interview with the mother-in-law, fifteen minutes or so, and then left. It was not that they were worried that the daughter-in-law would say something they would not like, it was that they felt left out. In India it was a power thing as the mother-in-law was the elder female of the house and wanted to be included. (Researcher, India)

Power relationships

The presence of authority figures in the group discussion can have a strong influence on the group dynamics and participants' willingness to contribute to the discussion. A local community leader, village chief or their assistants may wish to participate in the group discussion. However, this would introduce a clear hierarchy into the group and should therefore be avoided. In every community there are also individuals with strong public or political opinions, these individuals can easily intimidate other participants in the group who may become reluctant to express conflicting views. Such individuals may dominate a group discussion, stifle other opinions or simply cause other members to refrain from contributing their views. Wherever possible it is best to exclude such individuals from the discussion groups. It is important to seek assistance from local residents in the study areas who can easily identify any renowned figures in the community and dissuade them from participating in the discussion. For researchers from outside the community it is impossible to identify those with strong views or political opinions. Examples of strategies to dissuade local authority figures from the group discussion are shown below:

In one village, the chief's councillor [assistant] wanted to be in the focus group and actually had the right to be there. We had problems with taking him away from the group, because he was also curious about the discussion. We were getting to the sensitive discussion about sexual behaviour and finally the participants asked him to leave which was a relief for the researchers. One of the extra researchers took the man for a walk in the village and discussed general issues. This is someone who is important in the community and they feel they should be there to see what is going on, probably that is normal when outsiders come so they are aware what is going on, but in a focus group you don't want these people there. (Researcher, Malawi)

We knew that this man held very particular views and could disturb the group from the topics with his strong opinions. It is so important to try to identify whether there will be any political people in the group. We could do this using a local person as a welcome/resource person at the focus group to screen these types of participants. (Researcher, Bangladesh)

The community leader or chief may also wish to participate in a group discussion to remain informed on the research activities. Typically researchers will conduct a meeting with community leaders to highlight the purpose of the research and the topics of discussion in the focus groups. At this time the community leader may be invited to contribute their views on the research topic in a separate meeting. This acknowledges respect for the views of the local leader and ensures they have an opportunity to contribute to the research. The researchers may also provide a debriefing to the community leader at the conclusion of the group discussions. If the community leaders are kept informed on the research activities and provided with an opportunity to contribute their views, they are often less likely to want to participate in the group itself. However, if community leaders insist on joining the group discussion the research team can re-enforce that their views will be heard in a special meeting or simply explain to them the possible impact of their authority on the contribution of other group members. There may also be additional benefits from conducting a separate meeting with the community leader, in that it provides an opportunity to collect contextual information about the local community, which may provide an additional perspective to the research issues. The meeting may be viewed as a key informant interview or simply as a brief informal discussion. It may be strategic to conduct this meeting concurrent to the group discussion if there is still concern about the leader wanting to join the discussion.

Key terms

Group composition refers to the characteristics of participants in the group discussion, and how these characteristics may affect group cohesion and productive group discussion.

A *permissive environment* is where participants feel comfortable in the group discussion to share their true feelings, behaviours or attitudes without fear of judgement by the moderator or other participants.

> *Group homogeneity* refers to recruiting participants that are homogenous in terms of demographic characteristics or experience in the topic of discussion.
>
> *Group segmentation* involves dividing the study population into sub-groups that are internally homogenous, to assist with comparing the issues of sub-groups during data analysis.
>
> The *peacock effect* refers to the tendency for men to dominate, speak more frequently or with more authority in mixed-sex group discussions.

Checklist for group composition

- Will groups be composed of strangers or acquaintances?
- Will over-recruitment be necessary in stranger groups?
- Will acquaintance between participants encourage or inhibit discussion in the study context?
- What has been done to reduce the acquaintance between participants?
- How has confidentiality been assured in acquaintance groups?
- How will group homogeneity be achieved (i.e. socio-demographic, experience)?
- Are participants likely to have strongly opposing views which may cause conflict?
- Have the possible biases in group composition been identified?
- Will the discussion groups be segmented, if so how?
- Will segmentation assist in data analysis to meet the research objectives?
- Are the characteristics of the moderator likely to aid or inhibit discussion?
- What likely situations may jeopardise group homogeneity in the study context? What strategies have been identified to counter these?

7 Number of groups and group size

Introduction

The optimum size of a focus group discussion is determined by the topic of discussion, the type of participants and the level of detail required in the discussion. The number of group discussions to conduct will vary by research project and is influenced by the nature and scope of the research topic, the level of segmentation of the study population and by the resources available for the research. The number of group discussions will also determine the size of the research project, as it will directly influence the volume of data generated and the complexity of the data analysis, and will determine the resources required for data collection and analysis. Therefore, the number of focus groups to conduct needs to be given careful consideration. Essentially the number of groups to conduct will be a balance between the resources available and gaining the information necessary to adequately address the research question. However, regardless of resources, it is important to make informed and justified decisions about the number of groups to conduct and the group size. This chapter identifies the range of methodological and practical issues which influence decisions on group size and the number of focus groups to conduct in a study. It also highlights common situations that arise during the fieldwork which may compromise the desired group size for the research project, and how to manage these situations.

Group size

Typically a focus group discussion will comprise between six and ten participants, with an average of eight. In general, the size of the group discussion needs to be '. . . small enough for everyone to have an opportunity to share insights and yet large enough to provide diversity of perceptions' (Krueger and Casey 2000: 10). With fewer than six participants, it may be difficult to sustain a discussion, while with more than ten participants there is little opportunity for each participant to actively participate in the discussion and it becomes difficult for the moderator to manage the discussion. However, group size will be dependent on the purpose of the research, topic of discussion, type of participants and the level of detail required of participants (Stewart and Shamdasani 1990; Morgan 1997; Bloor *et al.* 2001).

Small group discussions (i.e. six participants) may be more appropriate for certain types of participants or research topics, and where a greater level of detail is required from each participant. Small groups are desirable when participants are likely to have significant knowledge, experience or motivation on the research topic, as it is anticipated that each participant would contribute more to a discussion on which they have intense involvement or experience (Bloor *et al.* 2001; David and Sutton 2004). Small groups provide more time for each participant to contribute to the discussion, so are suitable when the purpose of the research is to identify detailed experiences from a smaller pool of participants (Morgan 1997). For example, a focus group discussion amongst carers of people with long-term illness would be expected to generate an intense discussion on the topic of long-term care and therefore require only a small group of participants to gain detailed experiences. Small groups may also be more appropriate when the discussion topic is complex or controversial, as it may require fewer participants to generate debate and discussion. There may also be practical motivations for conducting small

> - When high involvement is anticipated from each participant
> - If participants have emotional involvement in the topic
> - Where participants have expertise or detailed knowledge of the topic
> - When the topic is complex or controversial
> - If the research purpose is to identify detailed experiences
> - When participants are few in number or geographically dispersed
>
> Adapted from Morgan and Scannell (1998: 73)

Figure 7.1   Appropriate use of small focus group discussions

focus groups, such as the limited availability of eligible participants or the dispersed geographic location of participants, making a range of smaller groups in various locations more feasible. Situations in which small group discussions are appropriate are shown in Figure 7.1.

Although small groups are advantageous for some circumstances, as a general rule small group discussions are limited in identifying a wide range of issues around the discussion topic. A discussion group of six participants, regardless of how engaged in the discussion, will contribute a smaller pool of experiences than ten participants. The smaller the group discussion the less likely that the information gathered will provide insight into the wider community norms, values or opinions of a study population, and the more likely that it will reflect the experiences of specific individuals in the group (Ulin *et al.* 2002). Unless participants are particularly knowledgeable about the research topic, it may be difficult to maintain an active discussion with a small group of participants. Small discussion groups may also have a greater risk of cancellation if just one or two members fail to attend. They may also be more vulnerable to group dynamics than larger groups. If two members are reticent or dominant the effect will be more pronounced in a small discussion group, which may then be reduced to an in-depth interview with those more willing to contribute (Green and Hart 1999, cited in Bloor *et al.* 2001). Finally, small groups are more challenging for both the participants and the moderator. In a small group discussion, there is greater pressure on each participant to contribute to the discussion; group moderation may require greater effort to encourage contributions (David and Sutton 2004).

Large group discussions (i.e. ten participants) are more appropriate when the discussion topic is of a more general nature, when participants are likely to have less experience in the research topic or when conducting exploratory research to identify the range of issues amongst a target population (see Figure 7.2). In these situations each participant is likely to make only brief contributions to the research issues and a greater number of participants will be required to gather sufficient information and generate a discussion. When

- When the topic is broad or exploratory
- If the research purpose is to identify a range of general issues
- When low involvement is anticipated from each participant
- If participants' knowledge or experience of the topic is low or unknown

Figure 7.2   Appropriate use of large focus group discussions

it is anticipated that participants may have a low level of knowledge or involvement in the research topic it may be difficult to maintain an active discussion amongst a small group of participants, therefore a larger group may be more appropriate. Larger groups are also more effective for identifying broader community views and experiences, simply due to the greater pool of experiences amongst a larger group of people.

Large group discussions also have a range of drawbacks which may limit their productivity and make group moderation more difficult. With a large group of participants, each individual has limited opportunity to contribute to the central discussion and there exists a risk that many participants will speak at once or the discussion may fragment into smaller conversations if participants are unable to contribute to the main discussion. This is a clear sign that the group is too large. Alternatively, if not well moderated some participants in large groups may remain silent throughout the discussion, so that their views of the topic are never heard. These situations make it difficult for the moderator to manage the discussion and for tape-recording the discussion, so a lot of information may be lost. Large groups also require a high level of moderator skill and involvement to manage the discussion and the group dynamics to elicit information which can effectively answer the research questions (Morgan 1997).

An additional factor in determining group size is the desired level of detail required from participants in order to effectively answer the research questions (Morgan 1997). Some research topics require detailed information on participants' behaviour or experiences to respond to the research question; while for other topics, a broader range of ideas or opinions of less detail is sufficient. Researchers need to consider that the greater the number of participants in the group discussion, the less time will be available for each participant to make a contribution. To identify the approximate time available for each participant to contribute to a group discussion, a simple calculation is required comprising of the number of discussion questions, the length of the group discussion and the number of participants. For example, a discussion guide with ten questions over a ninety-minute period with eight participants, will give each participant approximately one minute to respond to each question or approximately ten minutes to contribute during the whole group discussion (Morgan and Scannell 1998). For some discussion topics, this level of contribution by each participant will be entirely adequate to meet the research objectives, while for other topics more time per participant may be needed to elicit greater detail from each participant. If a greater depth of information is required, the number of participants or discussion issues can be reduced to allow greater time to debate the issues and for the moderator to probe for detailed experiences or behaviour. However, it must be remembered that there will inevitably be some participants who will contribute more than others and that participants may simply have less to say on some issues.

Regardless of the group size it is generally advisable to over-recruit participants to compensate for non-attendance by some members. Morgan (1997) suggests over-recruiting by approximately twenty percent, although this proportion will depend on the type of participants and the location of the group discussion, as attrition is more likely amongst participants who have to travel long distances to attend the group and amongst those who are not being paid for their participation.

Managing group size during fieldwork

Even when the size of the group discussion has been determined and suitable recruitment strategies implemented, a range of situations may arise during the fieldwork that compromise the desired group size. These situations need to be carefully managed in order for the field team to maintain the most effective group size for the research topic. The following section describes common situations where the research team may encounter too many or too few participants for a group discussion and highlights a range of strategies to effectively manage these situations.

Managing many participants

In some situations researchers may be faced with the presence of many more participants for a group discussion than required. This problem is less evident in focus group research in developed country settings where the participant recruitment strategies focus on specific individuals (i.e. invitation letters, telephone recruitment). In contrast, participant recruitment for focus group research in developing country contexts is often conducted through social networks and with the assistance of community leaders (see Chapter 5 on Participant recruitment). This may lead to many people arriving at a venue for the group discussion, as some may have been instructed to attend by the community leader, others may bring relatives or companions, some may understand that a community meeting is to be conducted, and still others may simply arrive out of curiosity. This type of situation is most common in rural areas or in close-knit urban settlements. Therefore, despite carefully planned recruitment strategies the research team may be faced with selecting only a few individuals for the group discussion from a large number of people at the focus group venue. For example:

The whole village was there, waiting, and I was faced with the problem of getting only eight participants for the group! (Research Student, Malawi)

These situations can be anticipated in certain study contexts and the research team needs to be prepared with strategies to ensure that only the required number of participants remain in the discussion group, so as not to compromise the quality of the information collected. Some common situations and strategies to manage these are described below.

Use a screening questionnaire

When faced with a large number of individuals for a group discussion, researchers first need to determine whether those present meet the required criteria for participation in the discussion groups. This requires using a *screening questionnaire*, which is designed to ask the least number of questions to quickly determine an individual's eligibility for the study. Individuals who do not meet the study requirements can then be asked to leave (Chapter 5 provides an example of a sift questionnaire and a more detailed discussion on its use). Using a screening questionnaire may be sufficient to reduce the number of people, so that those eligible for the group discussion remain. However, if there is a large crowd of potential participants, it can be too time-consuming to ask the screening questions to each person individually; therefore, a community representative may announce the criteria to the group and ask that only those eligible for the study remain. It is then possible to recruit the required number of participants for the discussion group from those eligible. Some examples of this situation are described in Figure 7.3. The selection of individuals may then be conducted using the following strategies:
- take a random selection from the eligible group
- make a list of those eligible and select every nth name
- conduct several group discussions concurrently, if this meets the research design

> In rural areas we had a problem, even after making arrangements with the chief we had an over-whelming number turn up. We estimate about 100 people turned up. We put them into male and female groups, then quickly sifted them. But there were so many with our required characteristics. We did some random selection to get the right number and let the rest go. (Researcher, Malawi)
>
> We returned in the morning to find twenty-five males, which was too many, so we did a sift, but all were eligible. Looked at the age distribution and let go some who were from a dominant age (i.e. lots of one particular age). Listed all names and ages then selected them randomly. But the problem was how to tell them to go when they had been waiting for us. So the facilitator explained in the local language and they walked away without fuss. They told them that we only needed a few and sorry but it is not that you people lack certain skills and so on. (Researcher, Kenya)

Figure 7.3   Selection strategies when too many participants arrive

- divide those eligible into subgroups (e.g. young men, older men, etc) and select the required number of participants from each sub-group.
- identify the time and duration of the discussion group and ask only those available to remain.

Conduct simultaneous group discussions

If the research design requires the conduct of several group discussions from the same study site, then participants for all the group discussions may be selected from the waiting group and several discussion groups conducted simultaneously. This will only be feasible if there are sufficient moderators and note-takers to conduct simultaneous groups. Alternatively the groups can be conducted sequentially or scheduled for the following day. For any later group discussions it is worthwhile to note the names of those selected so that only the required number of people attend; it also becomes easier to turn away additional members if the group has been pre-selected.

Prior selection of participants

To avoid the problem of too many participants in a group discussion, researchers may pre-select participants. This may be conducted with the assistance of community leaders, whereby only the required number of participants are selected and asked to report to the venue for the group discussion. A list of those selected is then held by the researchers, so that only those on the list will be accepted into the group discussion. For example:

We went with the DASCO (District AIDS and STD Co-ordinator) to recruit people earlier, so only the exact number came. A good way is to go and select ten and select the location, then the next day only those ten will come. If you just send word through the chief they will send out the assistant who will tell all their relatives and others and you end up with a too large group. (Researcher, Kenya)

Use a 'door-guard'

A common situation leading to too many participants in the group discussion happens when the discussion group begins with the required number of participants, but individuals continue to arrive at the group venue or drift into the group after it has commenced. In this situation, the number of participants can quickly double if additional people continue to arrive. It can be difficult for a moderator to interrupt the group discussion to identify whether the additional people meet the study criteria, or to explain that there are sufficient participants for the group discussion and turn the person away. It is therefore useful to ask an assistant to remain at the door of the venue to intercept these people before they join the discussion circle. They can then determine the person's eligibility or politely indicate that the group is large enough. Alternatively, these additional people may be invited to a later group discussion, if they meet the eligibility criteria. Using a 'door-guard' in this way is particularly useful when the group discussion is being conducted in an outdoor location where passers-by may join the group out of curiosity. If using a community building, it may be possible to request a staff member to assist in turning away additional participants and latecomers.

Conduct a 'dummy' discussion group

In some situations people may have been instructed to attend the discussion group by a community leader or other community members, and may have walked or travelled some distance to the group venue. However, only some of these individuals may be eligible for the group discussion. Those ineligible for the discussion may remain at the group venue until the discussion is completed so that they can travel back with their companions who participated in the group. Those who do not meet the study requirements may become annoyed at being called from their tasks and travelling some distance only to be refused participation in the group discussion once they have arrived. Others may try to contribute to the group discussion regardless of their eligibility. If the group discussion is being held outdoors, these additional people can disrupt the group discussion. A useful strategy in this situation is to conduct a 'dummy' group discussion to occupy the additional people while the actual group discussion is being conducted. This involves conducting an impromptu discussion with these individuals on the broad topic areas of the research. This discussion is not tape-recorded and the information is not used in the study, although it may uncover some useful contextual information (see the example in Figure 7.4). The intention of the 'dummy' group discussion is not to use the information discussed, but to enable the

> The study population for the research were women of childbearing age in Malawi. In one rural study site nearly a dozen extra women arrived, who were clearly past their childbearing years. These older women did not meet the criteria for the group discussion, but had walked a long way expecting to participate in the research and were going to wait until the younger women had completed the discussion so to travel home together. So a 'dummy' group discussion was held with these older women. For example, '*We conducted another group with the older women at the same time, but it wasn't a real group, it wasn't planned. We just talked informally about their childbearing experiences. It was actually just to occupy them while the younger ones were in the focus group, so we didn't record it. But actually there was some interesting information about childbearing amongst the older generation.*' (Researcher, Malawi)

Figure 7.4   Example of a 'dummy' focus group discussion

extra people to feel that they have contributed to the research and to allow the actual group discussion to proceed undisturbed. If this strategy is to be adopted there needs to be available a member of the research team fluent in the local language, or alternatively the group moderator may conduct a brief discussion after the actual focus group discussion had been completed.

Managing few participants

In some situations the number of participants in the group discussion may be much fewer than anticipated. Even though participants may be well motivated to attend the group discussion, other things may intervene on the day of the discussion so that they are unable to attend. This situation is inevitable and therefore some over-recruitment of participants is advised. However, there may be other factors that are within the researcher's control that contribute to low attendance at the group discussion. Researchers may need to review the recruitment strategy, the timing of the group discussions or consider issues related to the cultural context of the research, which may contribute to few participants at the group discussion. Assuming that appropriate recruitment strategies have been undertaken, there are two common reasons why too few participants arrive for the discussion: practical considerations, such as the timing of the discussion group, or issues related to the types of participants being recruited. Where few participants attend the group discussion, the group may be conducted as planned to provide those who have arrived with an opportunity to contribute to the discussion (Vaughn *et al.* 1996). However, the small group numbers should be noted in case this affects the information collected in any way. The issues of group timing and characteristics of the study population, which may influence low attendance, are discussed below.

Timing of the discussion groups

The timing of the discussion groups can be a critical factor leading to few participants. Poorly scheduled groups will inevitably lead to low attendance, but this detail is easily overlooked when planning the group discussions. In planning group discussions amongst a study population whose culture is unfamiliar, it is important to identify the regular routines and commitments of potential participants to enable the discussion groups to be scheduled at the most convenient times. This can be done most effectively once in the study location through a discussion with community leaders or in-country research collaborators familiar with the study population. For example:

I sat down with the local interviewers and they planned out a typical woman's day. Then we could try to plan when to have the focus groups. I would suggest making a timeframe of your target group's daily activities. If women get up at 5am and have an hour to spare after breakfast then that may be a good time, even though it does not fit in with your normal activities. (Research Student, India)

In addition, the most suitable timing for the discussion groups may differ for each sub-group of the study population. For example, discussion groups with men may be scheduled in the evening, while those with women are conducted in the morning. The research team needs to be sensitive to these issues to avoid too few participants arriving at the group discussion.

Specific sub-groups

Few participants at the group discussion may also be a reflection of the restrictions on a particular study population or the cultural context of the research. In some cultural contexts there may be restrictions on the mobility of certain household members outside the home (e.g. women, unmarried, adolescents), others may require permission from household elders to attend the discussion and concerns about safety may influence attendance at the group discussion. Even though an individual may have agreed to participate in the group discussions these factors may override and lead to few participants attending the group. The research team may need to consider how to accommodate these concerns. For example, by providing arrangements for young or unmarried women to be accompanied to the group discussion by a familiar community member. A study in India focussing on the views of newly married women faced difficulties in recruiting this specific group, as explained below:

I had the biggest problems when I focussed on recruiting one member of the household, like the younger women, as the mother-in-law would become suspicious and may not allow her to participate, or the young women would get questioned by the mother-in-law and feel intimidated. So I started going to the area every morning so I became a familiar person. In the communal areas where women prepared vegetables I could talk to all women informally. I asked the mothers-in-law about when they had kids, so they got to know what I wanted to talk to the young women about. This really helped to develop trust. (Researcher, India)

Although not all research projects will have the luxury of time to become familiar with the study population, it is crucial to collaborate with community leaders to overcome any factors which may lead to the low attendance of participants at the group discussions.

Number of groups

The appropriate number of group discussions to conduct in a research project will be influenced by the objectives of the research, the types of participants and the nature of the information gained in the group discussions. In addition, the number of group discussions will inevitably be influenced by the resources available. Focus group research can become costly, therefore, '. . .the goal is to do only as many groups as are required to provide a trustworthy answer to the research question due to costs involved in conducting more groups' (Morgan 1997: 44). It is important to take informed and justified decisions about the number of groups to conduct which will generally be determined by a combination of the methodological and practical considerations listed below:
- type of research (i.e. exploratory or defined)
- purpose of the research
- resources available (i.e. time, money and skills)
- type of participants
- level of segmentation of the study population
- diversity of information gained to reach *information saturation.*

The first consideration in determining the number of groups to conduct is the type of research conducted. For exploratory research, the specific issues for investigation may be undefined or unknown at the outset, and the initial group discussions will focus on identifying the issues of importance. In addition, if the research topic is complex more groups may be required to fully understand the complexities of each issue. For these types of research issues, the discussion groups may be less structured and require a larger number of groups to gain sufficient information on the topic (Fern 2001). In contrast, when the research issues are clearly defined and focussed, fewer groups will be required to gain the necessary information. Second, the number of discussion groups will also be determined by the purpose of the research and how the information will be used. For example, fewer groups will be required if the group discussions are being conducted to identify the broad issues or specific terminology to include on a quantitative survey; while more groups will be conducted if the purpose of the research is to analyse the substantive information from the group discussions. Third, the decision on the number of groups to conduct will also be determined by the resources available, such as funding and skills. The larger number of groups conducted will inevitably increase the volume of data generated and the time and resources required for analysis. However, even when resources are limited it is important to make justified decisions on the number of groups to conduct. Where resources are extremely limited it is feasible to identify the number of groups that can be achieved and then seek to conduct the group discussions amongst the most 'information rich' participants, who are likely to have the greatest level of experience or knowledge of the research issues. Although this is not an ideal way to plan the number of focus group discussions, it is often necessary to balance the resources available with the information required. Fourth, one practical factor influencing the number of groups to conduct is the location or availability of participants. If there are only limited partici- pants, then few groups will be conducted; and if participants are highly dispersed, then the groups may need to be conducted in various locations and the total number of groups will be increased. The two remaining factors influencing the number of focus groups to conduct are the level of segmenta- tion of the study population and the diversity of the information gained in the group discussions. These two issues will be discussed in detail below.

Segmentation of the study population

In addition to the considerations above, the number of group discussions to conduct will be determined by the level of segmentation of the study popula- tion. It is usual to conduct different group discussions amongst various sub- groups of the study population; for example, separate group discussions with men and women, or with older and younger participants. Segmenting the study population in this way is done to ensure homogeneity amongst participants within each group to encourage effective discussion, and to enable a comparison of the issues raised between various sub-groups of the study population (for further discussion on segmentation see Chapter 6 on Group composition). The greater the segmentation of the study population the more group discussions need to be conducted. It is therefore advisable to segment the study population only by the essential characteristics required for achieving group homogeneity and to meet the analytical requirements. Typical criteria for segmenting the study population may include a selection of the following:

- location (e.g. rural, urban or district)
- gender
- broad age groups (e.g. under 40, 40 plus)
- services users vs. non-users
- broad socio-economic groups
- specific profession (e.g. doctors, nurses, medical aides)
- lifecycle stage (e.g. unmarried, married, people with children, retired).

When identifying the appropriate segmentation of the study population it is advisable to use broad categories, as only significant differences in the information discussed will be evident between the different sub-groups. For example, a study population aged between 18 and 45 years may be effectively segmented into two broad age groups (i.e. under 30 and over 30 years), as the information gained from each group is likely to be more distinct than using the type of narrow age bands that may be appropriate in a quantitative survey (e.g. 18–24, 25–29, 30–34, 35–39, 40–45 years). Such detailed segmentation will necessitate an enormous number of group discussions and any difference in information between these age groups is likely to be undetectable.

Once the criteria for segmentation have been identified, it is usual practice to conduct *at least* two group discussions within each sub-group of the study population (Vaughn *et al.* 1996; Morgan 1997; Greenbaum 2000; Krueger and Casey 2000; Fern 2001). For example, if the study population is segmented by gender, then conducting two male and two female groups would be a minimum. Conducting only one discussion group per sub-group can be risky, as it is difficult to predict what will happen during the group discussion; if the tape recording fails, the group dynamics are problematic or there are external distractions which lead to the information being discarded then there remains no other discussion from the same sub-group. In addition, group discussions are influenced by numerous factors and it may be difficult to determine whether the issues raised in the discussion reflect the characteristics of the sub-group or reflect the group dynamics in a particular group.

Age and gender criteria	Service use criteria	Study location

	Younger	**Older**
Male	2 groups	2 groups
Female	2 groups	2 groups

Service use criteria
1. Users
2. Non-users

Study location
1. City
2. Town
3. Village

8 Groups
(2 x 2 x 2 = 8)

16 Groups
(8 x 2 = 16)

48 Groups
(16 x 3 = 48)

Figure 7.5   Segmentation of focus group discussions

Conducting even two focus groups per sub-group will allow for stronger grounds from which to identify the core issues amongst a particular sub-group of the study population. However, if the discussion issues in both groups from the same sub-category are markedly different, this is a clear sign that more groups need to be conducted within that sub-category to identify all the issues, or that the group dynamics are affecting the content (Morgan 1997).

Once the levels of segmentation have been identified the total number of group discussions within the project can be determined. It is important to remember that if the study population is segmented by numerous characteristics then the number of group discussions required will quickly multiply. Figure 7.5 provides an example where the study population is segmented by four criteria (age, gender, service use and study location). If the study population is segmented by the first two criteria alone (e.g. age and gender) then a minimum of eight focus groups will be required, as two group discussions will be held in each category. If the service use criteria are added (e.g. users and non-users of a health service) then the number of discussion groups required increases to sixteen. If the study is then conducted in three locations (e.g. city, town and village), sixteen groups will need to be conducted in *each* location, leading to a total of forty-eight discussion groups for the entire project. This example demonstrates that using even limited criteria to segment the study population can lead to an escalation in the number of focus group discussions required. The segmentation criteria therefore need to be considered carefully to conduct a manageable number of group discussions in the project. In a national study on the affordability of health services in Malawi (Hennink and Madise 2005), twenty-four focus group discussions were conducted. These were segmented by gender and location (urban and rural), and the study was conducted in three regions of the country (north, central and south). The gender and location categories led to eight group discussions (with two in each category), these eight groups were then conducted in each of the three study locations, making a total of twenty-four group discussions in the project.

Information saturation

The number of group discussions to conduct is also influenced by the diversity in the information gained from the group discussions. The aim of focus group research is often to identify the range of issues around a particular topic, so enough group discussions need to be conducted to uncover the various issues expressed by the study population. Typically, the first one to three groups will provide an enormous amount of new information on the research topic, and subsequent groups will provide only a few new issues each. Much of the methodological literature suggests that approximately seventy to eighty percent of the common issues around a research topic will be captured after the fourth group discussion (Krueger and Casey 2000; Fern 2001). 'From the first interview on an unfamiliar topic, the analyst learns a great deal. The second interview produces much more, but not all of it is new. Usually by the third session, and certainly by the fourth, most of what is said has usually been said several times, and it is obvious that there is little to be gained from continuing' (Wells 1979: 6). At a certain point the information from each group discussion will be repeated in subsequent groups, until the latter groups uncover no more new information. Once this occurs the data collection has reached *saturation* (Glaser and Strauss 1967). This is the point at which the group discussions no longer generate new information or provide any additional understanding of the research issues. Once the data collection has reached the point of *saturation*, this is a clear indication that a sufficient number of group discussions have been conducted. There comes a point of diminishing returns when the cost and effort in conducting additional group discussions will be greater than the amount of new information collected (Fern 2001).

It is difficult to determine when the data collection will reach saturation, as this will be dependent on the diversity of opinions or experiences which are raised in the discussion, and can often only be determined once the study is underway. Where participants have a broad range of experiences on a topic, more groups are needed to capture this diversity, therefore the degree of variability amongst participants both within and between the sub-groups will provide some indication of the number of groups that may be required to reach saturation (Morgan 1997). In addition, if there is significant variability in the characteristics of participants, then a greater number of groups will be required to reach information saturation than if participants share broadly similar characteristics. Similarly, projects that include distinct sub-groups of the study population will also need to conduct more total groups to achieve saturation within each sub-group of participants.

Although the point of *saturation* will determine the appropriate number of group discussions to conduct in a project, few studies will have the time and financial freedom to continue data collection until saturation is reached. Typically researchers will need to estimate the number of group discussions for the study in the research proposal, in order to develop a project timeline and budget. The following questions may assist in pre-determining an appropriate number of group discussions to conduct:

- Is the research topic broad or narrowly defined?
- Is the research exploratory or focussed?
- Are the characteristics of participants variable or similar?
- Are there different sub-groups of the target population?
- How many groups will be conducted for each sub-group?
- Is the research being conducted in different regions?
- What are the resources available?
- How will the information be used (e.g. to design a survey or provide substantive information)?

Key terms

Saturation (Glaser and Strauss 1967) is the point at which group discussions no longer generate new information or provide any additional understanding of the research issues.

Segmentation refers to the division of the study population into specific sub-groups with whom the focus groups will be conducted (e.g. young men, older men).

Summary of key issues

- Group size will be dependent on the purpose of the research, topic of discussion, type of participants and the type of information required.
- Consideration needs to be given to the cultural context of the focus group discussions and researchers should anticipate how to manage situations where too many or too few participants arrive for the group discussion.
- The number of focus groups to conduct is influenced by methodological and practical considerations, including: the type and purpose of the research, resources available, type of participants, number of sub-groups and the diversity of the information to be gained.

- A sufficient number of focus groups need to be conducted to capture the diversity of issues on a research topic.
- The study population may be segmented into different subgroups for methodological or analytical reasons. The degree of segmentation needs to be limited.
- The key to determining the number of groups is to balance the level of segmentation required to answer the research question with the resources available.

8 Focus group location

Introduction

The location of the group discussion is an important consideration in planning focus group research. Both the physical venue and the internal environment are important in fostering a productive group discussion. Many aspects of the location will influence the progress of the discussion and participants' willingness to openly contribute to the discussion (Stewart and Shamdasani 1990; Vaughn *et al.* 1996). The group location needs to set a positive tone for the group discussion, and provide a comfortable, relaxed and informal environment which is conducive to a productive discussion.

Ideally, the location of a focus group discussion should be quiet, private, comfortable, spacious, free from distractions and in a neutral venue. However, in some research contexts, particularly when conducting research in rural areas and in resource-poor communities, these characteristics may be compromised. Therefore, researchers need to strike a balance between the ideal type of location for a group discussion and what is available at the field site. However, it should be remembered that successful focus group discussions can be conducted in a wide variety of locations, ranging from purpose-built rooms for discussion, to improvised locations at the study site and even in outdoor locations. Some compromises will inevitably need to be made when selecting a group location, particularly when holding group discussions in outdoor locations; however, of prime importance is whether and how these compromises will affect the group discussion and the quality of the information received. This chapter discusses important aspects of the location of group discussions.

Physical location

The first consideration in selecting a location for the group discussion is the physical location or the venue. Focus group discussions may be conducted in a variety of locations such as indoor and outdoor venues (see Figures 8.4 and 8.5), or in makeshift environments, as shown in Figures 8.1 and 8.2. Although an indoor venue is preferred, as it will be quiet and private, many group discussions are held in outdoor locations. The key considerations for the physical location of the group discussion are summarised in Figure 8.3.

Access

The first consideration in selecting a venue for the group discussion is the ease of access for participants. It is important to consider how participants will

Figure 8.1   Focus group discussion in Zambia. Photo K. Benaya

Figure 8.2   Focus group discussion in Nepal. Photo CREPHA

Physical location:
- Accessible
- Easy to locate
- Adequate parking

Internal environment:
- Quiet
- Private
- Neutral
- Distraction free
- Spacious
- Comfortable and flexible seating
- Non-public space (if held outdoors)
- Away from pedestrian areas (if held outdoors)

Figure 8.3   Considerations for the location of focus group discussions

travel to the group discussion venue; whether participants are likely to drive a car, take public transport or walk to the venue will influence the selected location for the group discussion. For those who will drive to the venue or use public transport, the venue should be easy to locate, travel time should be minimal and there should be ample parking and compensation for travel, or parking fees should be provided to reduce non-attendance. If the research is being conducted in rural villages or in densely populated urban settlements, participants may walk to the venue. Therefore, the location of the group discussion needs to be in close proximity to participants' homes, and the group discussion scheduled at a time of day when it is safe to walk outside. If the study participants reside in a specific area or in adjacent neighbourhoods, it may be possible to conduct the group discussion in a community venue in that local area. However, if participants' residence is unknown, a central, well-known location in the study area is best, such as a hall, hotel or school building. If the group discussion is scheduled in the evening, the venue needs to be in a safe, well-lit neighbourhood, and it is usual to provide transport to and from the venue. The characteristics of study participants will also determine a range of access issues. For example, if participants are elderly then access issues are critical, particularly distance to the venue and whether any stairs may hinder access to the discussion room. Similarly, if participants are young or are from conservative cultures then it may be necessary to provide transportation and accompaniment by a familiar person to the venue.

Venue

The type of venue used for focus group discussions will vary widely by the context of the research. For international focus group research, group discussions are often held within the study community in a range of community venues such as school rooms or church buildings, community meeting rooms or health centres. In addition, group discussion may be in private venues, such as the home of a participant or a community leader. Additionally, group discussions may be held outdoors. It is worthwhile considering a venue which is regularly used by the study population and therefore offers a familiar, comfortable discussion environment. For example, group discussions with school pupils could be held after hours at the school, or group discussions with new mothers at an antenatal centre, or discussions with business people at a rotary club premises.

Often researchers need to utilise available venues in the study location and may have little control over the type of venue or its condition. However, researchers need to consider the size and condition of any possible venue for the group discussion. The size of the room should be adequate for the number of participants in the discussion, rooms which are too big appear sterile and make it difficult to create an intimate discussion environment, while too small rooms can become cramped and uncomfortable, making participants eager to leave quickly. The conditions of the room also need to be adequate to induce productive discussion amongst participants. Fern (2001) suggests that if a room is noisy, excessively hot or cold or has many distractions, this may create an uncomfortable atmosphere and cause stress amongst participants that makes demands on their attention and information processing capacities. This may mean that group members become less motivated towards the discussion, less able to recall facts, and less tolerant of the views of others. The room should also be free from visual or audio distractions, for example a large window overlooking a pedestrian area or a television screen in the background of the room may cause a visual distraction from the group discussion (Hennink and Diamond 1999). In addition, participants should be asked to silence mobile telephones during the discussion time.

It is important that the room for the discussion is as quiet as possible. A quiet room will not only assist in conducting the discussion, but noisy environments will affect the clarity of the tape-recording. Newer style microphones are very sensitive and will record background street noise even in what appears to be a relatively quiet room. In outdoor groups the sound of the wind may also distort the recording. Finally, the research team may also consider the suitability of the room for the use of any audio or video equipment intended to record the discussion, such as the location of power outlets and unobtrusive placement of microphones.

Outdoor locations

It is often assumed that focus group discussions will be held indoors. However, in some contexts, it is equally appropriate to conduct the group discussion in an outdoor location (as shown in Figures 8.4 and 8.5). Generally, a group discussion is held outdoors when there is no suitable indoor location available or when the group discussion needs to be held in close proximity to the study participants, such as those working in agricultural fields. Even when the group discussion is held outdoors, researchers need to remain aware of important aspects of the discussion location, to assess whether the location will be quiet, relatively distraction free, private and accessible. Some arrangements should also be made for seating, even if only a ground cover is provided. Although there will always be examples of an ideal outdoor location, these are unusual, as shown below:

I did one focus group outside in India, with women who worked in the fields. They all stopped work and we had a focus group there, in the field. They knew I was coming. Even though we were outside, there was no-one else around, so there was no problem. (Research student, India)

Figure 8.4   Focus group discussion held outdoors in Malawi. Photo M. Hennink

Figure 8.5   Focus group discussion held outdoors in Nepal. Photo CREPHA

Typically some compromises will be made when conducting group discussions outdoors and researchers need to consider if, and how, the outdoor location may affect the quality of the information received in the group discussion. Most outdoor discussion groups have problems of excessive noise, distractions, interruptions, lack of privacy and the risk of onlookers affecting the group dynamics. The tape recording of an outdoor discussion group is likely to pick up the sounds of people conducting their daily activities, children playing, vehicles passing or other outdoor noises. It may be very difficult for the person who later transcribes the tape recording to distinguish the voices of the actual group participants from those of people in the background. Therefore, it is very important to find a relatively quiet location if a group is to be held outdoors and to ensure that a note-taker is present to record the discussion in case the tape-recording is of poor quality.

A further problem with conducting discussion groups in outdoor locations is the possibility of continual visual distractions and interruptions from passers-by, which will affect the concentration of group participants to the topic under discussion. To avoid such interruptions it is wise to locate the group away from any central community areas in which there is likely to be significant pedestrian traffic. Even conducting the discussion group behind a wall or hedge will provide a shield from such interruptions. Outdoor locations may also affect participants' willingness to discuss certain issues, due to the lack of privacy. This will have important effects on the validity of the information collected, and particular effort should be made to find a private location, even if this is simply an open field some distance from the edge of the village itself. If researchers anticipate that group discussions may be held outdoors, it is useful to identify a suitable location in advance of the scheduled discussion groups. It is often when discussion groups are unexpectedly arranged outdoors that the location may compromise the quality of the information gathered.

Discouraging onlookers

The presence of onlookers is a particular problem when conducting group discussions in outdoor locations, but can be equally problematic when using an indoor venue. When conducting group discussions in rural areas or in densely populated urban areas, especially in developing country contexts, the group discussion may attract the attention of community members who are curious to observe the proceedings. When the discussion group is held outdoors it is particularly visible and will often attract attention. It is natural for community members to become curious about a gathering, particularly if outsiders or foreigners are present. In these situations, the research team need to be mindful of the fact that onlookers have an equal right to remain in the community space and so will not feel compelled to leave. However, their presence will undoubtedly influence the group dynamics in the discussion and participants may feel reluctant to discuss certain issues fully with the presence of onlookers who can hear the discussion and identify the participants. It is therefore important for the research team to discourage onlookers from the location of the group discussion.

A simple way to discourage onlookers from the group discussion is to locate the group discussion out of sight and away from open community areas. This may involve conducting the group discussion in a courtyard between houses, under a distant tree or behind a building. This strategy signals that the group is not a community meeting and observers may be less likely to approach or remain present. If onlookers remain, often one of the most effective strategies is for the onlookers to realise that the discussion is of little interest and they will leave by themselves. If onlookers are asked to leave directly this may excite their curiosity and they may insist on remaining, however if they realise that the discussion is of little interest they will soon become bored and move on. For this strategy to be effective the group moderator should begin the discussion with very general questions about the local area, village, community and so on. Any controversial topics should be delayed for as long as possible if onlookers are still present. This strategy will often discourage idle onlookers, and when they leave the moderator can then re-focus the discussion onto the key issues of the research. A group discussion conducted outdoors in India illustrates this issue:

We were showing body silhouettes in underwear in the second half of the focus group. For Indian women to be looking at these in front of male onlookers would not be culturally acceptable. If the men had not walked away in the beginning we would not have been able to continue. (Researcher, India)

Another strategy for discouraging onlookers from disturbing group discussions held outdoors is to ask a member of the research team to engage with any onlookers so to distract their attention from the group discussion. Often the research team will attract the interest of onlookers because they are from outside the local area or from another country. The research team may utilise this interest to engage with any onlookers, by entertaining children, making conversation, or perhaps asking for a tour of the village. Any of these activities will be beneficial in taking the attention of onlookers away from the activities in the focus group discussion. A further strategy to avoid the problem of observers at group discussions is for foreign researchers not to attend the group discussions, as these may be the individuals of primary interest to the onlookers. There may be some instances whereby these strategies fail to deter onlookers, who remain for the duration of the group discussion. In these situations, there is little the research team can do but to note the effect that the presence of the onlookers may have had on the group dynamics and the information received in the group discussion.

Internal environment

In addition to the physical venue of the group discussions, researchers also need to consider the internal environment of the focus group location, such as the seating of participants and the selection of a neutral venue. These issues are discussed below.

Neutral location

Most venues within a community will have some associations, whether positive or negative, and these associations may impact on the type of contribution an individual will make to the group discussion (Vaughn *et al.* 1996). Ideally, a focus group discussion should be held in a neutral location, for which there are few associations for the participants and where there is no authority associated with the venue, as this may influence contributions to the group discussion. For example, a group discussion held in the house of a prominent local politician may influence participants to express only the views that align with those of that political figure, rather than expressing their own views. This may occur even though the political figure is not part of the discussion group, but it is the location of the discussion that causes participants to withhold their true opinions. Furthermore, the characteristics of group participants need to be considered when selecting a neutral venue for the group discussion. For example, a group discussion amongst school pupils may be less effective when conducted in the office of the head teacher, compared with one conducted in a regular classroom, as the head teacher's office will have certain associations for pupils. In these situations, a power dynamic has been caused simply through the selected venue for the group discussion. Furthermore, group discussions held at a local health centre to discuss the quality of health services, may lead to participants' reluctance to criticise that particular health service despite what they actually feel. Similar issues may arise when a group discussion is held in the home of one of the participants. In this situation the participant may display the characteristics of a host in their contribution to the discussion, while other participants may contribute as if guests, and be reluctant to challenge the views of the 'host' (Bloor *et al.* 2001). To enable participants to express their true opinions, care is needed to locate the discussion group in a venue with as few associations as possible, to improve the quality of the information collected. Although it is advisable to conduct the group discussion in a neutral location, Bloor *et al.* (2001) argue that there is no such thing as a totally neutral environment due to the many associations people have with their environment. Therefore, whatever location is chosen the research team needs to recognise that the venue itself may impact on the data collected.

In international focus group research it is common to be invited to conduct the group discussion at the house of a community leader. There is debate about the appropriateness of using this venue and the effect that it may have on participants' contributions to the group discussion. Some research-ers feel that accepting the offer of the community leader shows respect for their hospitality and may be the most practical venue for the group discus-sion. They believe that participants will feel at ease in this location as it is the usual venue for holding meetings. This view is reflected in the quotation below:

Most of the time we got a room in the chief's place, as the chief usually has a place for discussing villagers' problems, so it was not a problem to find a place for the discussion. (Researcher, Lesotho)

Other researchers believe that using the house of the community leader may create a power dynamic, whereby participants feel obliged to respect the views of the community leader on the topic of discussion rather than voice their own opinion. Another consideration is that the community leader may join the discussion at any point during the discussion, which can have a clear impact on the hierarchy within the group discussion.

If the venues within the study community are problematic, it may be possible to conduct the discussion at a venue outside of the immediate community, but only a short distance away. This may offer privacy from the local community, reduce distractions and offer a neutral location. It is difficult to predict the effect of using any type of location on the contribu-tions of participants to the group discussion. However, researchers need to be aware of the *possible* influence of certain types of venues for the group discussion. Above all, it is important to assess each situation individually and to note any possible effect of the group location on group dynamics in the field notes.

Seating arrangements

The seating arrangements in the group discussion are critical to foster effective discussion between participants. It is important to identify a venue with flexible seating so that chairs can be arranged to create a comfortable atmosphere conducive to discussion. Focus group participants should always be seated in a circle, with or without a central table. A round table is preferred, as with rectangle tables there exist dominant seating positions at the table ends, while round tables eliminate the suggestion of a more prominent position. More importantly, circular seating enables all group members to face each other, which is crucial for establishing the interactive group dynamics that are central to a focus group discussion. Vaughn *et al.* (1996) state that group members are most likely to communicate with those seated directly across from them, so a circular seating arrangement would allow all group members equal access to each other to foster discussion. Poor seating arrangements can very quickly hamper discussion. If participants are seated as in a classroom set-up with all group members facing forwards, then there is an expectation for the moderator to provide information to the group rather than for participants to interact in a discussion. In addition, if participants cannot see each other they will naturally direct any comments to the moderator who is in view at the front of the group, and not react directly to any other participant's comments. In this type of seating arrangement people often drift out of the venue as their interest in the discussion wanes and they don't feel part of a group. In some locations it will not be possible to re-arrange the seating in the room to suit the discussion purposes. In these situations the moderator must ensure as much as possible that participants can see each other before commencing the discussion. Fern (2001) suggests that attention should also be paid to the crowding of participants in the discussion group, the more people in each group the smaller each person's personal space, and for some cultures losing personal space may have a negative effect on an individual's sense of privacy and behaviour in group discussion.

Even when conducting group discussions in outdoor locations it is important to arrange participant seating so that group members can

Figure 8.6   Circular seating arrangement in outdoor focus group discussion. Photo K. Benaya

effectively interact. It may be necessary to improvise the seating in outdoor locations, but this can be done relatively easily with ground covers, straw mats, or locating benches that can be formed into a circle (as shown in Figure 8.6). It is also important to reflect any cultural norms with regard to seating. For example, if it is usual practice for older people to be seated on chairs and young people to sit on mats, then it is wise to reflect these norms so that participants will feel comfortable and relaxed in the discussion. When participants arrive at an outdoor location there is a natural tendency to sit in a group, however group moderators need to be pro-active to re-arrange participants into a circle before beginning the group discussion. Ideally the seating for an outdoor group can be arranged before participants arrive, by placing benches so they face each other or laying down extra mats so that there is enough room for participants to sit in a circle.

Key terms

A *neutral environment* for the focus group discussion is one in which there are few associations for participants, particularly one that does not hold an association with authority.

Summary of key issues

- Both the physical location and internal environment of a focus group are important in fostering a productive discussion.
- The physical location needs to be accessible, and neutral, while the internal environment should be quiet, comfortable and distraction free.
- A neutral location may also affect the contribution of participants and affect the data quality.
- Researchers often need to strike a balance between the ideal type of location for a group discussion and what is available at the field site.
- Focus groups can be held in outdoor locations, although these may attract a number of unwanted onlookers.
- Seating participants in a circle is critical for conducting an effective discussion.

Conducting the group discussion

Introduction

Conducting the group discussion is the central activity in focus group research. The central figure in the group discussion is the moderator who is responsible for managing the group discussion using a pre-prepared discussion guide. Effective moderation of the group discussion is a challenging but critical task, as the group discussion needs to be carefully managed to provide sufficient information to respond to the research questions. This chapter describes the roles of each member of the focus group team during the group discussion, with particular emphasis on the tasks of the moderator. The process of focus group moderation is described, highlighting the various stages of a discussion and the role of the moderator during each stage. A range of moderation techniques is described in this chapter to assist in promoting an effective and productive group discussion and to identify and manage difficult group dynamics.

Roles of the focus group team

A focus group team typically comprises the moderator, a note-taker and occasionally an assistant. The common role for all team members during the group discussion is to create a friendly and welcoming environment for participants. If participants feel uneasy during the discussion this may affect their contribution to the discussion and therefore the quality of the data. Serving refreshments before or during the group discussion is a common way to promote social cohesion amongst group members. The specific roles of each member of the focus group team are described in turn below.

Note-taker

The primary role of the note-taker during the discussion is to record the key issues raised in the discussion in as much detail as possible. The note-taker should record the facts as they are discussed and refrain from writing any judgements about what is said. The note-taker may also record any significant body language of participants which may be helpful in later interpretation of the data. The note-taker's notes are essential, as they represent the only detailed record of the issues discussed if the recording equipment fails, the recording is inaudible or the tapes are lost. The notes are also critical if the group refuses permission to tape record the session (see Chapter 10 on Recording the focus group discussion). The note-taker sits outside the discussion circle to take notes unobtrusively and should refrain from making eye contact with participants in the group so as not to disturb the group dynamics (see Figure 9.1). This position also helps the note-taker deal with disturbances, latecomers and enables them to control environmental conditions (e.g. heating, lighting). Sometimes the note-taker also operates the

Figure 9.1   Seating of note-taker. Photo M. Hennink

tape-recorder and changes the cassettes, so that the moderator can continue the discussion uninterrupted.

The note-taker also needs to monitor the topics discussed in the group against those on the discussion guide to identify whether the moderator has overlooked any key areas. The note-taker may pass a note to the moderator, or more commonly the moderator will call on the note-taker towards the end of the discussion to ask if there were any areas missed or if there are any additional questions to ask. The most effective focus group team is one where the moderator and note-taker work closely together. The moderator focusses on managing the discussion while the note-taker takes extensive notes on the content of the discussion and manages any interruptions.

Assistant

Occasionally a focus group team will include an assistant who is responsible for attending to organisational matters. The assistant will welcome participants as they arrive, provide name tags (if appropriate), serve refreshments, arrange transport, pay expenses and distribute pre- or post-session questionnaires. This allows the moderator and note-taker to focus on conducting the discussion. Occasionally an assistant may be called upon to look after children for participants. When the group discussion is in progress an assistant is also useful in managing interruptions and discouraging onlookers from the discussion. This may be more of an issue when conducting discussion groups in community settings, rural areas or developing country locations where the venue may be outdoors or in an open courtyard. The assistant's role in these situations is invaluable in managing persistent onlookers, and discouraging people from sitting nearby to observe the group.

Moderator

The essential member of the focus group team is the moderator. The quality of the information gained in the discussion is a direct reflection of the moderator's skills in managing the discussion and the participants. The moderator has a critical and challenging task. The moderator is responsible for creating a comfortable environment within the group to put participants at ease, ensuring that all members share their views, encouraging debate between participants, probing for depth and clarity in the issues, listening to contributions and asking follow-up questions, monitoring the reactions of participants, remembering earlier points, anticipating the next topic of discussion and remaining aware of the timing and pacing of the discussion. All of these roles are vital in managing a discussion so that the information gained is sufficient to respond to the research questions. Managing a group discussion may seem like a simple task but requires a great deal of skill to facilitate the discussion and confidence to negotiate the group dynamics.

One of the primary roles of the moderator is to create an open, 'permissive' environment in the discussion group, whereby the participants feel comfortable to share their genuine opinions and feelings about the issues discussed. This can be achieved in the manner in which the moderator manages the discussion, by reinforcing that the views of all participants are valued, and through managing the group dynamics so that certain participants do not dominate the discussion or criticise the views of others. The moderator may

also state that they are not an expert in the discussion issues and it is participants who are most knowledgeable about the issues. This will dispel any
concerns amongst participants that their contribution is being tested or judged,
and will put participants at ease. Finally the use of familiar colloquial language
by the moderator can create the informal atmosphere sought in the discussion.

The essential role of the moderator is to manage the group discussion so
that the information gained provides a greater understanding of the research
issues. To do this, the moderator needs to have the skills 'to implement the
content of the discussion guide so that the desired information is obtained
from the participants. This includes developing approaches to draw out
people who are reluctant to participate in the groups, handling those who
try to dominate the sessions, and ensuring a reasonably equitable distribution
of discussion among all participants in each of the groups' (Greenbaum
2000: 27). A discussion flows effectively around the main research topics
with careful nurturing by the moderator. The moderator needs to be familiar
with the objectives of the research to be able to prioritise the relevance of
issues as they are raised during the discussion, and make rapid decisions on
whether to pursue a certain issue or redirect the discussion if it is not central
to the research objectives. Even though the discussion guide will be designed
to direct and focus the discussion, it is the moderator who must manage the
discussion around the key topics and bypass issues of only marginal relevance. In summary the moderator's imperative is to collect useable data,
therefore they must be aware of what information is desired and how it is best
obtained from participants.

The moderator also needs to pay attention to the *timing* and *pacing* of the
discussion. Pacing the discussion involves ensuring that all topics on the
discussion guide have been covered in sufficient detail by the conclusion of
the session. The group should not run over time and moderators have an
obligation to conclude the discussion at the time indicated at the beginning of
the session. It is easy for a discussion to remain focussed on a certain issue for
a lengthy amount of time, however moderators need to be aware of pacing the
group discussion through all intended topics. It is helpful for the moderator
to be aware of the relative importance of each question on the discussion
guide, the approximate discussion time to devote to each topic and which
questions can be skipped if time becomes short. A moderator also needs to be
sensitive to the timing of introducing new topics into the discussion. The
moderator needs to gauge whether a group has sufficiently 'warmed-up'
before introducing the central discussion issues. Sensing the timing within
a group is also necessary to identify when a group has naturally exhausted one

topic and is ready to move to the next issue. This sense of timing is particularly important when discussing more sensitive topics, as moving too quickly to the central issues when a group is not yet ready will affect the quality of the information gained. An example of this issue is shown below:

One of the research assistants mentioned that some people were put off by some questions, and he could actually see this because of their non-verbal communication . . . and after that they switched off and didn't want to contribute. He said it was when we talk about condoms . . . it was a question coming too suddenly, it's sensitive. That's what I would do differently next time, introduce it gently and try and justify why I am collecting this information. (Researcher, Zambia)

The moderator also needs to attend to ethical issues such as consent and confidentiality during the discussion. The moderator must seek informed consent from participants to take part in the research and seek their consent to tape-record the discussion (see Chapter 2 on Ethical considerations). Some participants may have been instructed to attend the group discussion by a community leader, and therefore have not been given the opportunity to decline participation. Participants who feel obliged to attend the discussion may be reluctant to fully contribute to the group discussion, which will impair the quality of the information gained.

Conducting focus group research in another country can be a difficult task, particularly when the research team are unfamiliar with the language of participants. Inexperienced researchers and those wanting to feel part of the data collection process may consider conducting the group discussion through an interpreter. This strategy should be clearly avoided. One needs to consider the practicalities of using an interpreter to conduct a group discussion and the effect this would have on the group dynamics. For example, the researcher would deliver a question to the group, which would be translated by the interpreter. Participants may then comment on the issues. The interpreter then needs to provide a summary of the issues back to the researcher, and then wait for the next question and so on. This is clearly an inappropriate strategy as the flow of responses through the interpreter will quickly stifle any group discussion and it will be reduced to a question and response session. While the translations are being relayed to the researcher the group remains inactive or will begin side-conversations, which is highly disruptive for group dynamics and any information in these side-conversations will be lost. It is always better to train a moderator in the study country to conduct the discussion in an appropriate language (see Chapter 4 on Training the focus group team).

In some situations the research investigators may wish to observe the group discussion in progress in order to identify whether the focus group methodology is being applied as intended, to become aware of the issues discussed and to observe the group dynamics. Even where the researchers are unable to understand the language, it is possible to gain a broad understanding of the issues raised and the context in which they are discussed. One strategy for doing this is to work together with the note-taker. If the researcher is seated by the note-taker, the note-taker can indicate which section of the discussion guide is currently being discussed, and quietly translate some of the key issues. In this manner the researcher can relatively easily gain a general indication of the issues being raised by participants, while also observing the group dynamics and conduct of the discussion. It is also possible that the presence of the researcher will encourage the moderator to explore the issues more fully; the presence of foreign researchers can also validate the research and give credibility to the need to tape-record and translate the discussion. At some points in the discussion the researcher may feel the need to encourage the moderator to explore certain issues raised in the discussion. These interruptions should be minimised due to the possible disruption to the flow of the discussion. However, there may be times when suggesting a probe is appropriate. It is important not to interject into the group and so spoil the group dynamics, but to alert the moderator of the issue to be explored further and allow them to probe the group at a suitable time in the flow of the discussion. Some experiences of this are shown below:

I used to ask the moderator to follow the question guide with his finger so I knew where he was up to. One research assistant would write key words on paper so I knew what the group was talking about. (Researcher, Pakistan)

I could observe the behaviour of the group even though I couldn't understand what was being said. Body language and behaviour on this particular topic was important as we were showing pictures and getting reactions to them. (Researcher, India)

I could understand about seventy-five percent of the Kikuyu language, so I could chip in if I felt that the moderator is not asking relevant things or missing things out. (Research student, Kenya)

Process of group moderation

A focus group discussion has a number of distinct stages, including the pre-discussion, introduction, central discussion, closing and post-discussion

Pre-discussion stage:
- Arrange venue (e.g. seating, equipment)
- Welcome participants
- Serve refreshments
- Identify participant characteristics (e.g. loud, quiet etc.)
- Manage seating (if possible)
- Administrative tasks (e.g. reimbursements, name tags etc.)

Introductory stage:
- Introduce research (e.g. purpose, organisation, use of information)
- Introduce moderator and note-taker
- Confirm consent for participation
- Seek consent for tape recording
- Assure confidentiality
- Outline group discussion process and 'guidelines' for group conduct
- Develop rapport with group
- Establish permissive environment
- Ensure first question is easy and all participants respond

Central discussion stage:
- Encourage discussion *between* participants
- Seek range of opinions and experiences
- Monitor participant contributions (e.g. quiet/dominant participants)
- Manage group dynamics
- Utilise non-verbal signals to promote discussion
- Use active and passive listening techniques
- Probe extensively around key questions
- Keep discussion focussed
- Determine whether responses answer the research questions
- Explore new issues
- Use appropriate level of moderator involvement (i.e. directive or non-directive)

Closing stage:
- Summarise key discussion issues
- Seek further issues not discussed
- Re-confirm confidentiality of data
- Respond to participant queries

Post-discussion stage:
- Provide incentives to participants (if appropriate)
- Distribute a post-session questionnaire (if appropriate)
- Conduct a debriefing meeting

Figure 9.2   Moderator's tasks at key stages of the discussion

stages. As the central figure in the group discussion, the moderator will need to be aware of the different roles and tasks to be conducted during each stage of the group discussion process. The key roles of the moderator in the various stages of the discussion are listed in Figure 9.2 and discussed below.

Pre-discussion

If a venue for the group discussion has been identified, the focus group team needs to arrive early to arrange the seating, equipment and to welcome participants. During the pre-discussion time participants may be served refreshments, and administrative tasks such as reimbursements may be conducted by the assistant. It is important for all members of the focus group team to be friendly and welcoming to participants by making small talk; however they should refrain from engaging in conversation about the research topic. If participants feel that they have informally shared their views on the issues with a member of the research team they may be reluctant to raise these again in the group discussion and the information may be lost.

The pre-discussion time can also be used for participants to complete a pre-session questionnaire, while they are awaiting the arrival of others. This questionnaire typically collects social and demographic information about each participant (see Chapter 10 on Recording the focus group discussion for an example). The pre-discussion period can also be a useful time for the research team to identify the characteristics of participants and whether there may be any particularly quiet or talkative participants. These individuals can then be seated in strategic locations in the discussion circle to assist the moderator in managing the group dynamics. The seating of these individuals may be achieved with the placement of name cards around the table. For example, a quiet participant should ideally be seated directly opposite the moderator so that full eye contact can be used to encourage discussion; a talkative participant seated at the moderator's side so that body language can be used to show reduced interest if they begin to monopolise the discussion. However, in some situations there will be little pre-discussion time as a group may have already been assembled before the research team arrives or the pre-discussion time is taken up with establishing participant's eligibility to the study (see Chapter 5 on Participant recruitment). In these circumstances the identification of participant characteristics and strategic seating cannot be controlled and the moderator will need to manage the group dynamics as the group progresses.

Introductory stage

The next stage occurs when participants are seated and the moderator provides an introduction to the group discussion. The atmosphere in a group discussion is often created in the first ten minutes; therefore the manner in which the moderator introduces the group is critical as it sets the tone of the discussion to follow. Too much formality by the moderator in the introduction can stifle the discussion, while overly informal behaviour by the moderator may mean that the discussion is not taken seriously. During the introduction the moderator needs to provide an overview of the research topic, indicate how the group discussion will proceed, and provide guidelines for the discussion, such as respecting the views of other participants, encouraging disagreement in opinions, and allowing only one member to talk at a time for clarity in the tape-recording. The moderator needs to provide enough information in the introduction to ensure that participants feel at ease and know what to expect of the group discussion (see Chapter 3 for an example introductory statement). This gives the participants *cognition* so that they know what is expected of them and feel comfortable with their role as a group member (Hennink and Diamond 1999). At the same time the moderator must try to generate motivation amongst participants, so that they feel their responses are valued and encouraged. Indicating the selection criteria for participants will reinforce the group homogeneity between participants and dispel any suggestion of a hierarchy in the group. It will also signal to participants that they were not targeted for any particular reason. The moderator also needs to introduce the note-taker and any observers in the room. Ethical issues also need to be reviewed and the moderator needs to seek consent to tape-record the discussion. If the group refuse permission to record the discussion the research team will be reliant on the note-taker to record the key issues discussed.

The first question to the group typically acts as an 'ice-breaker'. Often the moderator will ask each participant to introduce themselves in turn around the group and respond to a simple, often factual question, about themselves. This type of introduction ensures that all participants have contributed something from the beginning of the discussion, which helps participants to feel confident to contribute to the discussion. This type of introduction also helps the person who later transcribes the tape-recorded discussion to distinguish the different voices in the discussion. A more subtle reason for seeking contributions from each group member during the introductory stage of the discussion is that it helps to deter the development of *groupthink* (Janis 1982). Groupthink is 'the tendency for dissenters to suppress their disagreements in favor of maintaining consensus in the group' (Morgan 1997: 50). Seeking contributions from all group members early in the discussion allows everyone to provide their views before a group consensus or strong views emerge. The groupthink process can also be curtailed by continuing to seek a range of opinions from an early stage in the discussion. Finally, this type of introductory strategy is also useful if there are latecomers to the group, as they can still be integrated into the discussions at this stage.

Those who arrive after the introductions are best excluded from the discussion as it will be harder to integrate them once the discussion has commenced without disrupting the group dynamics.

Central discussion stage

The central discussion stage is where the moderator begins to direct the discussion towards the key research issues. Moving the discussion towards the key issues can be difficult to manage, as participants may contribute many views and issues at once and the moderator must try to remember these issues but explore each issue in turn to gain sufficient depth in the discussion. It is during the central stage of the discussion that the moderator will employ a wide range of moderation strategies in order to encourage discussion, manage the group dynamics, gain depth in the discussion, and encourage diversity in the contributions (see later section on Moderation techniques). Generally moderators will use extensive probing techniques during the central discussion stage as this is when the key research issues will be discussed and the greatest depth of information is required.

During the central discussion stage the moderator must continually assess whether the information from the discussion will be sufficient to answer the research questions. The moderator may need to continually re-direct or re-focus the discussion towards the key research topics. Inexperienced moderators may simply be relieved that there is some discussion occurring and pay little attention to whether the information is of adequate quality to meet the research objectives. A well-trained moderator is able to recognise when a group is not working well and re-direct the focus of the discussion so that the research objectives can be met. The moderator must take care not to be too directive of the discussion so as to stifle the revelation of new issues. Therefore, the moderator may begin to use non-directive moderation techniques during the central discussion stage to explore new areas and allow participants to define the issues raised. This style of moderation follows the general approach of grounded theory methodology, which allows respondents' issues to come to the fore without restraint from a facilitator (Glaser and Strauss 1967; Strauss and Corbin 1990). Throughout the central discussion stage the moderator must continue to provide positive encouragement for participants to share their views, through empathetic listening, eye contact with speakers, leaning forward and active listening.

Although the moderator will often use a carefully prepared discussion guide to direct the discussion, both the discussion guide and the moderator's skills work together to facilitate a successful discussion. A poorly developed guide will remain poor regardless of the skills of a moderator; similarly poor moderation cannot be salvaged by a good discussion guide. Thus, it is a combination of well-developed moderating skills and a carefully designed discussion guide that will lead to an effective group discussion. It is in the central stage of the discussion that this combination will be most crucial.

Closing stage

During the closing stages of the discussion the moderator may use a range of closing questions to finalise the discussion, such as the *all things considered* question, *advice to the Minister* question, and the *summary* question (see Chapter 3 for a discussion of closing questions). The moderator may summarise the main issues covered during the discussion and seek clarification on the summary or request participants to identify any issues missed. This approach provides a useful winding down of the discussion and ensures that nothing has been overlooked. In the last comments the moderator should thank participants for their contributions, reconfirm the value of the information received and respond to any final queries.

Post-discussion stage

At the completion of the group discussion the research team may ask participants to complete a brief (one to two page) questionnaire before leaving the venue. This post-session questionnaire can be used to collect demographic information from participants or more personal or sensitive information related to the research topic, but which are inappropriate to ask in the group setting. The post-session questionnaire may be preferable to a pre-session questionnaire as it avoids the potential of biasing the discussion by highlighting certain topics before the discussion commences.

The research team often holds a debriefing session after the group discussion to share impressions about the discussion and the information received. This meeting is useful to review the effectiveness of the group procedures, including the main themes discussed, difficulties encountered, moderator's technique, group dynamics, suitability of the location and so on. Reflecting upon these issues is particularly important after conducting the first group to identify any revisions to the moderator's technique or to the discussion guide.

Moderation techniques

Facilitating a group discussion is a complex and challenging role. The group moderator needs to ensure that the discussion remains focussed around the central research issues, yet allow sufficient divergence to identify new and unanticipated issues to emerge from the discussion. The moderator should encourage and manage a discussion, yet they should not dominate the discussion. The moderator needs to facilitate and channel the natural flow of the discussion, but not force it along a predetermined path. The moderator also requires skills to balance the contributions of participants by seeking responses from all participants and dissipating dominance by any one group member. These seemingly conflicting tasks are all required in moderating an effective focus group discussion. In some instances, achieving these objectives can occur through variable levels of moderator involvement. The following section describes various moderation techniques to encourage group discussion, seek diverse views, probe the discussion for detail and clarity, and utilise the non-verbal signals of participants to seek contributions to the discussion.

Level of moderator involvement

The level of moderator involvement in the discussion will vary according to the objectives of the research. A moderator may adopt a directive or non-directive style of moderation (Stewart and Shamdasani 1990). *Directive moderation* is where the moderator plays an active role in facilitating contributions and encouraging debate in the discussion, through probing and follow-up questions to the group. Directive moderation is used when the aim of the discussion is to elicit participants' opinions and experiences around quite specific, pre-determined issues. With this style of group moderation there is less spontaneity in the flow of the discussion as the moderator's task is to focus the discussion on specific issues and seek depth and detail in the responses on each issue. An alternative style of moderation is *non-directive moderation*, which allows the group discussion to flow more or less naturally with little involvement by the moderator. This type of moderation is useful when conducting exploratory research, as it allows greater opportunities for participants' views to emerge spontaneously and is heavily reliant on group interaction and independent discussion. It can also be used where the research objectives involve observation of the group dynamics and interaction between participants. In reality, the level of moderator involvement in the discussion may be somewhere in-between these styles and moderators can also switch from directive to non-directive approaches at different points in the discussion. A certain amount of direction and structure is useful in the early stages of the discussion and for managing the group dynamics, while in the central part of the discussion a less directive approach will enable spontaneous views to emerge more easily. Experienced moderators will be aware of the influence of different styles of moderation on the type and quality of the information obtained.

Encouraging and managing a discussion

The essential role of the moderator is to encourage a group discussion around the central issues of the research, but not to directly lead the discussion as in an interview. A group discussion is working well when the moderator has little input but is subtly managing the discussion through probing and re-direction of the contributions. A focus group discussion should never be reduced to a question and answer session resembling a series of in-depth interviews with a group of respondents. It should be a discussion *between* participants which is facilitated and guided by the moderator. Inexperienced moderators can easily fall into a pattern of asking participants for their contributions in turn and begin a pattern of serial questioning of participants. This will quickly create a sterile environment and stifle the generation of any group discussion. It also sets up the expectation in participants that they need to wait their turn to respond. Figure 9.3 shows a diagrammatic representation

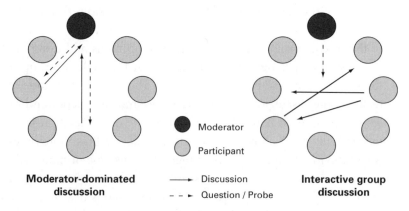

Moderator-dominated discussion

⬤ Moderator
◯ Participant

⟶ Discussion
--► Question / Probe

Interactive group discussion

Source: Adapted from Hennink and Diamond (1999: 130)

Figure 9.3   Styles of group discussion

of a moderator-dominated style of questioning participants compared with an interactive discussion between participants, with only little input from the moderator.

One of the benefits of collecting information from a group of people is the opportunity to use the energy of a group discussion and the interaction between participants to explore a topic in greater detail than in an in-depth interview format. For this to work effectively, the moderator needs to engage group participants in a discussion and encourage them to react to each other, rather than simply responding to the moderator (Greenbaum 2000). Using the group dynamics to encourage a discussion is one of the key skills used by the moderator. This involves using the issues raised by participants to foster a discussion between participants, so that each issue is discussed and debated in greater depth. This may begin when one participant states a certain opinion about an issue and a second participant highlights some concerns with that opinion. Rather than accepting that each participant directs their views to the moderator, the moderator seeks to connect the two participants, so that they engage in a discussion about their varying opinions. Once two participants are engaged in a debate, the moderator can begin to draw in other participants and foster a discussion within the group, perhaps by asking whether other participants share the same or different views, or highlighting that a participant touched upon the same issue earlier and may like to contribute. The net effect is that the moderator has taken the response from one participant and used it to form a *group* discussion, so that the entire group can be used to explore the range of views around a single issue (Greenbaum 2000; Fern 2001).

While a moderator's role is to encourage the discussion, they also need to manage the discussion to ensure that it does not deviate too far from the topics of interest. The dynamic nature of a group discussion means that participants can raise any issues during the discussion, some of which will be of marginal relevance to the research objectives. In managing the discussion the moderator needs to make quick decisions about whether to pursue a discussion of the issue raised, delay it until later in the discussion, or redirect the discussion away from issues of marginal relevance to the core research objectives. In order to make these decisions quickly the moderator needs to be clear on the primary objectives of the research and the purpose for which the information will be used. It is useful to remind participants at the beginning of the discussion that sometimes discussions diverge from the central issues, and there may be a need to refocus the group's attention towards the key issues. This ensures that participants understand why some issues are pursued in depth while others are discussed only superficially.

Careful listening

Often effective moderation involves not talking but careful listening and responding to the issues raised in the discussion. More experienced moderators spend a greater amount of time listening rather than talking, as the more opportunity participants are given to express their views the richer the output from the group discussion. Careful listening allows the moderator to identify the subtleties of the issues being highlighted and direct the flow of the discussion without the need for abrupt re-direction or introduction of a new topic. The moderator can listen to participant's comments and build on these to carefully guide the discussion onto further issues within the broad topic of the research, while maintaining the issues of importance to the participants (David and Sutton 2004). Although opportunities for subtle re-direction may not always arise, attentive listening increases the likelihood of identifying how to manage the discussion without disrupting its momentum. Fern (2001) distinguishes between passive and active listening. *Passive (or non-reflective) listening* is an empathetic style of moderation that encourages the natural flow of the discussion without influencing its direction. This may be done by making positive and encouraging gestures or comments and showing interest in each contribution. Some cultural groups may feel less threatened and participate more freely with such an approach. *Active (or reflective) listening* is where a moderator responds to participants comments more directly by seeking clarifications, amplification, explanations or examples. With active listening, the moderator is listening and digesting responses, mentally comparing these to comments received in other group discussions, and probing participant's contributions to the discussion. Fern (2001) identifies various types of reflective responses, such as clarifying, paraphrasing and summarising participant's comments in order to seek greater clarity and accuracy of understanding.

Utilising non-verbal signals

A moderator may also stimulate participants to contribute to the discussion through observing and reacting to the non-verbal messages of participants. Experienced moderators will become familiar with certain facial expressions and gestures which suggest an individual may want to contribute to the discussion, disagrees with a speaker, is puzzled by a comment or requires reassurance about an expressed opinion. Common indicators of disagreement or discomfort with the discussion include frowning, folded arms and certain facial expressions. Boredom is often suggested when participants lean back or look away from the group, while interest in the discussion is often signalled by sitting forward, alertness to the discussion and looking at speakers. Most moderators can feel a sense of interest or enthusiasm for a topic which is independent of the conversation that occurs (Fern 2001). These non-verbal signals can be utilised to great effect by the moderator to stimulate further discussion or elicit views from individual participants. For example, a moderator may say, 'You are nodding, did you have a similar experience you would like to tell us?' or 'I see that you are frowning, do you disagree with that opinion?' A moderator's recognition and utilisation of non-verbal signals can dramatically increase participation in the group discussion (Stewart and Shamdasani 1990). In international focus group research moderators need to be aware that the interpretation of non-verbal cues can differ by culture; however, many non-verbal signals are universal.

Probing

Probing is a technique used by the moderator to gain further clarity, depth and detail from participant's responses. A probe is used to stimulate further discussion or to focus the discussion to explore specific issues in depth. Effective probing can lead to increased richness in the information provided in the discussion and reflects the moderator's interest in the issues discussed. Greenbaum (2000) highlights the role of the moderator in probing a discussion to gain a deeper understanding of the issues:

An important implied role of the facilitator is the ability to use moderation techniques that will 'peel away the onion' and delve into the real reasons for the attitudes or behaviors that are indicated. An integral part of this is to leverage the energy of the entire group to explore the topic area in depth ... (Greenbaum 2000: 27).

It is useful for a moderator to use ample probing in the beginning of a group discussion to suggest to participants the level of detail that is sought in the discussion, but moderators also need to exercise caution not to over-probe as this may suggest to participants that the moderator is seeking a specific response that has not yet been voiced. Figure 9.4 describes various types of probes, each with a different purpose, which can be used by a moderator.

Ah ha probe	Used to acknowledge a participant's response and encourage further detail, e.g. *I see. Ah-ha. Yes. OK.*
Reflective probe	Involves paraphrasing a participant's comment to reflect these thoughts back to the participant for clarification, e.g. *So what you are saying is . . ..*
Expansive probe	Used to seek more information or an example of the issue, e.g. *Could you elaborate on that? Do you have an example? Can you describe that further?*
Silent probe	Involves the moderator pausing after a participant's contribution to enable the speaker to expand or another participant to contribute.
Group probe	Involves using one participant's point to probe the rest of the group for expansion of the issue, e.g. *Does anyone else have any experience of this?*
Group explanation probe	Asking the group to collectively explain an issue on which there appears to be a common consensus, e.g. *Everyone seems to understand this issue, can you explain it to me more fully?*
Ranking probe	Asking participants to determine the importance of an issue by ranking it against previous issues raised, e.g. *How important is this issue? Is it more of a problem than . . .?*
Participant gesture probe	Using the non-verbal signals of a participant to draw them into the discussion, e.g. *You look confused. Do you disagree with this issue?*

Figure 9.4   Types of probes

The simplest type of probe is the *Ah-ha probe* where the moderator makes positive noises, such as *Ah-ha, Yes, OK*, to acknowledge a participant's contribution and encourages them to continue describing an issue. The moderator needs to ensure that these brief one-word acknowledgements do not indicate a preference or value judgement about the comment, such as *Excellent, Great, I Agree*, as other group members may then try to make points that receive the moderator's praise (Krueger 1998b). The *Reflective probe* involves repeating a participant's remark or paraphrasing it, to reflect these thoughts back to the participant for clarification or expansion of the issue. The *Expansive probe* is commonly used to ask for more information or to request a tangible example of the issue. It may also be used to re-introduce issues raised earlier in the discussion that were not fully explored. For example, '*Earlier in the discussion several people mentioned the cost of services, can we talk a little more about this?*' One type of probe which is commonly overlooked is the *Silent probe*. Novice moderators are often uncomfortable when there is silence in a group discussion, however it can be used as a tool to actually promote further discussion. A well placed five-second pause after a participant's comment can enable the speaker to expand their point or allow another participant to contribute (Krueger and Casey 2000). The use of pauses is most effective when coupled with eye contact with the speaker. However, too long a pause can be uncomfortable for the speaker as they genuinely may have nothing more to add, and simply be waiting for moderator guidance.

The probes mentioned above involve the moderator probing the response of an individual participant, however probing strategies can also be used to probe the group as a whole. The *Group probe* and the *Group explanation probe* request further information or explanation of an issue from the entire group. This may involve the moderator highlighting an issue raised by one participant and seeking input from the rest of the group. For example, '*Mary has raised an interesting point, can anyone else think of an example of this?*' or '*Does anyone have a similar/different perspective on this point?*' or '*I see you are nodding, George, can you tell us your own experience with this issue?*' Some caution is needed in using the group probe as the participant who raised the initial issue may feel that their view is being challenged by the moderator asking for the reactions of others in the group. This can result in alienating the participant and disturbing the group dynamics if not done with care. It is often better to ask other members in the group whether they have had similar or dissimilar experiences rather than to ask if they agree or disagree with another participant (Stewart and Shamdasani 1990). The group explanation probe asks the group as a whole to explain an issue or phenomenon on which there appears to be a common view. This type of approach overcomes the situation where participants will simply say '*Yes, I agree*' to a certain point without providing their own experiences of the issue. It is sometimes useful for a moderator to indicate naivety about an issue to seek fuller explanations of the issue from the group. For example, in international focus group research the moderator may indicate that the information from the discussion will be used by foreign researchers who are unfamiliar with the local customs. This may provide sufficient justification for seeking detailed descriptions and explanations of issues which may be commonplace for participants (or a moderator). The *Ranking probe* asks the group to determine the importance of the issue under discussion in relation to other issues discussed. This is effective to stimulate a discussion about the merits or demerits of an issue. The *Participant gesture probe* works when the moderator utilises the non-verbal signals (e.g. body language or facial expressions) of participants to draw them into the discussion. For example, '*You look concerned, perhaps you'd like to share your thoughts on this issue?*' This strategy can equally be used to draw in those who appear to agree as well as those who seem to disagree with a speaker.

Encouraging diverse views

Often the purpose of focus group research is to seek a range of different perspectives on the research topic. Therefore, a moderator needs to draw out the diverse views of participants in the group. This involves the moderator specifically seeking alternative views from participants to those that have already been contributed. A moderator may use the following cues:

What do others think about this issue?

Does anyone else have a different opinion?

Does anyone recognise this situation?

Has anyone else experienced a different situation?

I see you are shaking your head – do you have a different opinion?

So far everybody seems to have the same opinion, do you know whether other people have a different view about this issue?

Probing for diverse views is also useful when participants in a group tend to agree with each other over an issue. Even though participants may share an opinion of the broad issues, their individual experiences of the issue may vary slightly, and learning of these subtle differences can improve the richness of the data collected. To seek diversity amongst participants who appear to agree with each other may be achieved by directly saying to the group, '*Even if you think your experience is just like everyone else's, don't just say "I agree." We want to hear your story because there's always something unique in each person's own experience*' (Morgan 1997: 53).

A further strategy to ensure that the discussion identifies a variety of responses is by avoiding the *deference effect*. This is where participants say what they think a moderator wants to hear rather than their own opinion about an issue (Bernard 1994). If participants all tend to agree with an issue or the discussion lacks diversity of opinions, it is possible that participants are agreeing with a perspective voiced inadvertently by the moderator. Clearly this situation is undesirable as the participant's true opinions of the issues discussed will not be identified. The deference effect can be avoided by clearly reinforcing to participants at the outset of the discussion that all views are valued and it is participants' own views which are being sought. A moderator should encourage both positive and negative comments and refrain from expressing their own viewpoint so that participants are not aware of the stance of the moderator on the issues.

Using stimulus materials

A group discussion may be refreshed by introducing a group activity or using stimulus material to provoke a discussion. In this way the participants are given an activity which is interesting and engaging, and the related discussion can provide researchers with valuable information. Figure 9.5 shows a

Figure 9.5   'Pile-sorting' activity during focus group discussion. Photo F. Kauser

'pile-sorting' activity during a group discussion, where women were asked to sort a list of pregnancy-related illnesses by various criteria. Group activities may be especially useful when group discussions are conducted amongst a group of conservative participants who may be uncomfortable in the group setting or feel that they have little to contribute to the discussion. Examples of stimulus activities include:

- A study on contraception in the United Kingdom introduced samples of contraceptive methods into a group discussion to identify participants' reactions to each method (Cooper *et al.* 1992).
- A study in Pakistan used a family planning clinic logo to identify community perceptions about the image of the clinic and the services provided (Hennink and Stephenson 2000).
- A study in India used cards with illnesses written on each, and asked participants to sort and rank the cards by various criteria (Kauser 2001).
- A study in the United Kingdom used posters of family planning services to identify young people's views on effective health promotion messages and the appeal of certain images (Pearson *et al.* 1996).

If group activities or stimulus materials are used in the group discussion, these activities need to be planned in advance and sufficient time allocated for the activity and related discussion.

Managing group dynamics

In every group discussion there will be a range of participants with varying characteristics, some will be quiet and others more dominant. It is the moderator's role to manage the group dynamics which result from the differing characteristics of participants, so that each member is given an equal opportunity to contribute to the discussion. Most group discussions will have some or all of the following types of participants; quiet, dominant, rambling and self-appointed experts (Walker 1985; Greenbaum 2000; Krueger and Casey 2000; Fern 2001; Litosseliti 2003). The moderator needs to be aware that the group may contain these types of participants and utilise a range of verbal and non-verbal strategies to manage certain personalities. Managing the group dynamics within a focus group discussion can be a challenging task, which becomes easier only with experience and knowledge of a range of techniques to manage certain types of participants. Some strategies for managing the group dynamics are described below.

A *quiet participant* will often remain silent during the discussion or provide only short responses when asked to contribute. It is easy for the moderator to ignore the quiet or shy participant, particularly if they are overshadowed by more outgoing and dominant participants. Quiet participants can have great insights as well as other participants, but it may take a little effort for the moderator to draw out their views. The moderator needs to reassure quiet participants that their contributions are equally valued, by using open body posture and eye contact to welcome their contributions. Gentle probing may also be effective in seeking their opinions; however, a moderator must be careful not to inhibit a quiet participant by making pointed remarks about their silence. Probing that reinforces the importance of their contribution is likely to be more effective, for example, '*Susan, we also value your views, do you have any experience of this issue?*' If a quiet participant contributes to the discussion spontaneously, it is important for a moderator to validate their response (Walker 1985). One method of doing this is to validate the comment and then ask for similar views from the rest of the group, for example, '*That was an interesting point Susan, what do others think?*' or '*Thank you, Susan. We have also heard this in other groups . . .*' There may be times when an entire group is quiet, perhaps they are young or culturally submissive. In these situations the moderator needs to take time to develop a permissive atmosphere within the group, reinforce the value of their contributions, and provide ample positive body language signals and verbal cues to invite contributions. A moderator must refrain from going around the circle and seeking responses from specific participants, as this may exacerbate a quiet group and become counterproductive. A group of quiet participants may also be a reflection of poor participant selection, whereby a hierarchy has developed within the group making participants reluctant to contribute.

There will often be a *dominant participant* in every group discussion. This person tries to monopolise or control the discussion either by being the first to respond to each issue or by giving lengthy responses to each issue. While these participants can make useful contributions to the discussion, the moderator needs to ensure that they do not monopolise the discussion to such an extent that the views of other participants are not heard. One of the most effective and subtle strategies to control a dominant participant is to utilise body language to signal reduced interest in their continued responses. A moderator may reduce eye contact with this participant, turn a shoulder towards them or look down at the discussion guide when they speak. If these strategies fail then a moderator may use verbal cues to redirect the discussion and seek the views of other participants; for example, *'Thank you for those views. Perhaps we can hear the views of others on this issue?'* or *'Would anyone else like to comment on this point?'* or *'Do others have any different or similar experiences?'* Some dominant participants will not respond to subtle body language cues or redirecting of the discussion, and a moderator may not be skilled enough in using these approaches effectively. In these situations a more direct approach may be required. Greenbaum (2000: 148) suggests a range of more direct approaches to handle dominant participants; for example, *'Bob, I can tell that you are very passionate about this issue, but we really need to hear how the others feel about it'* or *'Bob, we need to get inputs from everyone on this subject, and we will hear from you after some of the other people have expressed their views.'* If the participant continues to dominate the discussion, the moderator may intentionally ignore the dominant member when requesting response from participants by calling on other participants and refraining from making eye contact with the dominant member. After some time this approach is usually successful in equalising the contributions of group members. In some group discussion the other participants may begin to moderate a dominant participant by cutting them off or interrupting them to state their own views.

In unusual situations, the dominant person will continue to monopolise the group, in which case Greenbaum (2000: 149) suggests the most direct approach, such as stating: *'Bob, you must let other people in the group have their opinions – then we can hear from you'* or *'Bob, part of my responsibility is to hear from everyone in the room. You are making this very difficult, so it would be helpful if you would give the others time to share their thoughts before you give yours.'* Even in these situations a moderator needs to be as tactful as possible, so not to destroy the group dynamics. It must be remembered that a dominant person can be useful to call upon when the discussion falls quiet or at the beginning of a group to stimulate the discussion. If the dominant person is identified as such prior to the group discussion, the research team can seat this person at the moderator's side to make managing their contributions with body gestures more effective.

Some participants will be *self-appointed experts* who try to convince other participants that they are more knowledgeable than others in the group on the issues being discussed. They may do this by suggesting they have vast experience with the topic or due to their social position in the community. These participants are seldom true experts, but tend to offer their opinions as facts to intimidate other participants. This type of participant may cause other group members to feel that their contributions are less valued than that of the 'expert', they may feel reluctant to contribute their own views or defer their opinion to that of the 'expert' who they perceive to have more important opinions on the topic. The moderator needs to disempower the 'expert' participant by stressing that *everyone* in the group is an expert on the issue and this is why they have been invited to the discussion, and the research team is interested in the opinions of all group members. On some occasions there will be a *genuine expert* on the discussion topic amongst the group participants, perhaps a medical specialist where the discussion is about a specific illness. In this situation the moderator may recognise the expertise of the genuine expert, but emphasise that the researchers are interested in the experiences of all participants on the issue. The moderator may be tempted to call upon this person to clarify facts, but this is best avoided as it may create a hierarchy amongst participants.

A *rambling participant* is one who feels very comfortable in the group environment and tends to give long accounts of their experiences, which are often of marginal relevance to the discussion issues. Although it is important to identify the opinions of this type of participant, rambling participants are essentially time wasters, who impede the contribution of other members by monopolising the discussion with overly long contributions. The moderator has a limited amount of time in the group discussion to cover all the issues and seek a range of different views from all participants, so the rambling participant needs to be kept under control. The moderator may avoid eye contact with rambling participants, or redirect the discussion when they pause, or in extreme cases interrupt them to seek the views of others.

Common problems with moderation

Novice moderators may experience a range of problems with facilitating the group discussion. A range of common moderation problems and some of their causes are listed in Figure 9.6 and discussed below. First, a moderator may be unable to control the group discussion so that it diverges significantly from the key research issues. In addition, the moderator may experience difficulties with managing the group dynamics between participants so that certain participants dominate the group with issues of marginal relevance to the research. When the moderator is unable to control the discussion, this often reflects inexperience or lack of adequate training of the moderator. Many moderators will lose control of the discussion the first time they facilitate a focus group. In addition, moderators may not have received sufficient training in managing group dynamics or may not have adequate personal qualities to guide the discussion with authority. This problem may also be a reflection of a poorly designed discussion guide in which the issues are too broad and the moderator may be insufficiently skilled to define the issues during the discussion to provide a stronger direction for the discussion.

Loss of control of discussion

Possible causes:
Poorly trained moderator
Difficult group dynamics
Discussion guide too broad
Passive moderator
Moderator not focussing the discussion

Participants agree

Possible causes:
Group hierarchy developed
Moderator expressed own views
Deference effect created
Genuine agreement between participants
Participant selection issues

Frequent silences

Possible causes:
Moderator-dominated discussion
Question-answer pattern developed
Moderator not stimulating discussion
Inappropriate questioning
Sensitive issues raised
Mismatch in issues and participants
Poorly designed questions

Little discussion

Possible causes:
Moderator-dominated discussion
Poorly developed questions
Little probing
Moderator misguided on methodology
Issues lack relevance to participants

Superficial information

Possible causes:
Lack of probing
No permissive environment
Participants uncomfortable
Participants feel views not valued

Trying to reach consensus

Possible causes:
Poor introduction
Lack of moderator involvement

Figure 9.6   Common moderation problems

A second common problem in group moderation is that participants may simply agree with each other, resulting in a lack of discussion. This may be reflective of the composition of the group, whereby a hierarchy has developed between participants causing some members to agree with others whom they feel have more experience or a higher social status than themselves. A deference effect may have developed in the group discussion, whereby participants feel obliged to agree with the views of the moderator rather than express their own opinions. It may also be the case that participants genuinely agree on the issue discussed; however, if agreement persist on all issues, there is likely to be another underlying cause. This problem may also occur when participant selection has resulted in a group of individuals with extremely similar characteristics, such that there is little diversity in their experiences or opinions.

Third, a moderator may experience a group that frequently falls silent, rather than generating its own momentum in a discussion. This may be a symptom of a moderator-dominated discussion where the discussion is dependent on the stimulus of the moderator, rather than the dynamic interaction between the participants themselves. It is possible that a question and answer pattern has developed and when this stops the group is silent. The moderator may fail to stimulate participants' interest in debating the issues, or the moderator may be probing on inappropriate or sensitive issues that are unsuitable for a group discussion. A silent group may also be a symptom of a poorly developed discussion guide where the issues for discussion are at odds with the experiences of participants and thereby they genuinely have little to contribute to the discussion. The questions on the discussion guide may also be designed to elicit dichotomous responses rather than to stimulate discussion.

Fourth, a moderator may experience little discussion amongst participants, so that the group may begin to resemble a group interview rather than a discussion. This may be caused by a moderator-dominated discussion, where participants are given little opportunity to raise their own issues. A lack of discussion may also reflect poorly developed questions, which elicit only factual information or dichotomous responses rather than promote a discussion. Furthermore, the issues on the discussion guide may not be relevant to the participants, therefore they are unable to contribute to a discussion about these. There may simply be a lack of effective probing by the moderator, or the moderator may have insufficient skills to probe the discussion.

The fifth problem with moderation is a lack of depth in participant's responses, leading to superficial information. This is most often a result of a lack of probing of participants to fully explore each issue raised. Some moderators move too quickly through the discussion guide and will feel satisfied if only one participant has expressed a view rather than fully exploring the range of opinions of others within the group. The moderator may also be ignoring the probes on the discussion guide. In addition, the moderator may have failed to pay sufficient attention to creating a permissive environment, so that participants feel uncomfortable in the group discussion environment and fail to provide detailed responses to the issues. The style of moderation used may also suggest to participants that their views are not valued.

A further problem with moderation is that the participants feel compelled to reach consensus over the issues discussed. Valuable discussion time may be wasted in trying to come to an agreement over an issue, which is often not the purpose of the discussion. This problem may be a reflection of a poor introduction by the moderator who has failed to stress the desire for a range of different views on the issues discussed rather than reach a consensus. A moderator may also not be intervening to correct participants' assumptions that a consensus is required.

Key terms

The *moderator* is the key member of the focus group team, who facilitates the group discussion.

A *probe* is a reminder to the moderator to gain further clarity, depth and detail in specific issues raised by participants.

Cognition refers to the state of participants' understanding of what is expected of them as a group member.

The *deference effect* is when participants say what they think a moderator wants to hear rather than their true opinion.

Directive moderation is where the moderator has an active role in encouraging discussion and facilitating contributions, through probing and follow-up questions to the group.

Non-directive moderation occurs when the moderator allows the discussion to flow naturally with little moderator involvement. Often used when conducting exploratory research.

Active listening is where a moderator responds to participant's comments by seeking clarifications, amplification, explanations or examples.

Passive listening is an unstructured and empathetic style of moderation used to encourage discussion without influencing the natural flow of the contribution.

Groupthink is the tendency for participants who hold opposing views to those being discussed to withhold their views to maintain a consensus in the group.

Summary of key issues

- A focus group team typically comprises the moderator, a note-taker and occasionally an assistant. The common role for all team members during the group discussion is to create a friendly and welcoming environment for participants.
- The note-taker's role is to record the key issues raised in the discussion and participant's body language, which may be helpful in later interpretation of the data.
- The central figure in the group discussion is the moderator who is responsible for managing the group discussion using a pre-prepared discussion guide. The quality of the information gained in the discussion is a direct reflection of the moderator's skills in managing the discussion and the participants.
- The group moderator needs to ensure that the discussion remains focussed around the central research issues, yet allow sufficient divergence to identify new and unanticipated issues to emerge from the discussion.
- The level of moderator involvement in the discussion will vary according to the objectives of the research. A moderator may adopt a directive or non-directive style of moderation.
- A focus group discussion has a number of distinct stages, including the pre-discussion, introduction, central discussion, closing and post-discussion stages.
- Various moderation techniques can be used to encourage group discussion, seek diverse views, probe the discussion for detail and clarity, and utilise the non-verbal signals of participants to seek contributions to the discussion.
- A group discussion may be refreshed by introducing a group activity or using stimulus material to provoke a discussion.
- Every group discussion will comprise participants with varying characteristics (e.g. quiet, dominant). It is the moderator's role to manage the group dynamics amongst participants, so that each member is given an equal opportunity to contribute to the discussion.
- Common problems with group moderation include; a loss of control of the discussion, participants all agreeing on issues, frequent silences, little discussion created and participants trying to reach consensus.

10 Recording the focus group discussion

Chapter overview

Introduction

The systematic analysis of the information gained through focus group discussions is what distinguishes the academic use of focus group discussions from market research approaches (Bloor *et al.* 2001). Obtaining an accurate record of the group discussion is therefore critical. Focus group discussions are typically recorded in two ways, by using a tape recorder and by taking written notes during the session. Tape-recording the group discussion is most preferred, as it provides a verbatim record of the issues discussed and greatly increases the data quality. Tape-recording the discussion also overcomes the shortcomings of relying on written notes from the discussion, which may be incomplete, inaccurate or selectively recorded. Although tape-recording the group discussion remains the ideal, not all participants may give consent for tape-recording the discussion and therefore note-taking remains an important back-up. This chapter describes the methods of recording the information from focus group discussions, and highlights common issues with recording the discussion, particularly in international focus group research. The chapter also describes methods of collecting additional information about participants through pre- and post-session questionnaires.

Note-taking

Each group discussion should have a note-taker in attendance whose role is to make a written record of the key issues raised in the discussion. A note-taker should always be present even if the discussion is being tape-recorded, as the notes will be critical if the recording equipment fails, the recording is inaudible or the tapes are lost. The note-taker's role becomes essential if participants refuse permission to tape-record the session, whereby the note-taker's summary will be the only record of the information discussed. In this situation the note-taker's summary is used directly in the data analysis to identify the key themes discussed in the group. The note-taker's summary of the discussion is also a valuable *addition* to the tape-recording of the discussion. The written summary can include information that will not be available on the tape-recording, such as the body language and gestures of participants and whether parts of the discussion were lively or subdued, which can be invaluable in interpreting the information during data analysis. The written summary can also provide the transcriber with an overview of the issues discussed in the group before beginning the transcription process.

A note-taker should always be briefed on the requirements of their role (see Chapter 4 on Training the focus group team). The note-taker's role is to record the main issues raised in the discussion. Although it will not be possible to record everything said in a fast-paced group discussion, the notes should be sufficiently detailed to reconstruct the main flow of the discussion and paraphrase the range of issues covered, with some narrative extracts or brief verbatim comments, if possible. Note-takers need to be instructed to record the facts as they were discussed by participants without recording their own judgements or interpretation of the information. The notes taken should represent an objective record of the discussion. In addition, the note-taker may record any non-verbal signals of participants. A participant's body posture, facial expressions, gaze, shy laughter or silence may indicate a great deal of information about their interest in the topic, willingness to participate or reactions to issues discussed. As the note-taker will be seated outside the discussion circle they are in a good position to observe such body language. These non-verbal messages should be linked to the issue being discussed to help with later interpretation of the information during data analysis. It is important to remember that body language signals may have a different meaning in different cultural contexts. Ideally the note-taker will be from the same cultural background as the participants in order to correctly interpret the body language. However, some body language signals are universally understood.

Typically the notes will be taken in the same language as the discussion and later translated into the language of the research investigators. This strategy is recommended because a note-taker may experience difficulties if asked to simultaneously listen to the discussion, mentally translate the issues and record the summary in a second language. There would inevitably be a reduction in the quality of the information recorded as the note-taker may become distracted from the discussion by the task of translating particular words or phrases. In addition, note-takers should record any specific expressions, proverbs or words used by participants that describe specific concepts related to the topic of discussion. It is useful to preserve these phrases in the original language to enrich the information and provide a direct link to the participant's expressions (see Chapter 11 on Data analysis for a more detailed description of retaining such expressions).

The note-taker's summary needs to be clearly labelled to correspond to a specific discussion group and tape-recording. A note-taker's summary should be clearly structured, either by summarising the key issues under broad topic headings or by using the questions on the discussion guide. Some note-takers write skeleton notes during the discussion and expand these with fuller details directly after the discussion. Note-takers should be encouraged to write these notes in full within twenty-four hours after the group discussion or certainly before the next group discussion. The longer the time between the group discussion and revising the notes will result in a loss of recall in the detail of the discussion, or if subsequent groups are held the information from different groups may become confused. Figure 10.1 summarises the role of the note-taker in recording the discussion.

- Record the main issues raised in the discussion
- Paraphrase the issues discussed
- Develop an objective record of the discussion
- Avoid recording own interpretation or judgements about the issues
- Retain specific colloquial phrases or terms in local language
- Record body language and non-verbal signals of participants
- Write notes in the language of the discussion for later translation
- Clearly label notes to correspond with the discussion group and tape recording
- Structure notes by discussion topic or questions on the discussion guide
- Operate the tape-recorder
- Remind moderator of issues overlooked during the discussion

Figure 10.1   Guidelines for note-taking in focus group discussions

Video-recording

Video recording a focus group discussion is less common in health and social research than for market research purposes. A video recording can enable researchers to identify participants' actions, group interactions, body language and facial expressions in addition to the verbal dialogue. However, there remain continual concerns about the intrusiveness of video-recording a group discussion and the effect on participant spontaneity. Therefore, researchers need to carefully consider whether any additional information gained through video-recording will outweigh the potential intrusiveness of the approach and the impact on the discussion environment. In addition, there may be considerable effort required to transport and arrange the equipment in the field site, all of which make it a limited and little-used method to record focus group discussions in the health and social sciences (Krueger 1998b; Hennink and Diamond 1999; Litosseliti 2003). If video recording is considered, researchers need to be clear on the purpose of obtaining a visual record of the discussion and whether the data quality will be significantly improved by the use of video recording. If the quality of the discussion is the most important element of the research, then most researchers can rely on a tape-recording of the discussion.

Audio-recording

The most common method of recording the information from a focus group discussion is to tape-record the discussion. Tape-recording provides an accurate, verbatim record of the issues discussed which improves the data quality for analysis. A verbatim record of the discussion is necessary for data analysis involving the grounded theory methodology, which involves identifying common themes from the data and developing explanations (or theories) to provide a better understanding of the research problem (see Chapter 11 for further discussion of data analysis). In addition, tape-recording the discussion enables the researchers to highlight specific issues using quotations from the study population themselves. This is one of the traditions of qualitative research and provides a greater richness and detail to the data. Wherever possible, researchers should strive to tape-record the discussion to improve the quality of the research data, as is highlighted below:

When I worked in rural areas the field staff advised me not to use the tape recorder as people who had not seen one would be scared of it. So I didn't use it. I took notes, but it affected the quality, you just miss so much. (Research Student, India)

The moderator must observe ethical principles to seek consent from participants prior to tape-recording the discussion. This involves providing sufficient information to participants about the reasons for requesting the tape-recording, how the information will be used, and how participants' anonymity and confidentiality will be safeguarded. Participants may refuse permission to use the tape-recorder in which case the research team will be reliant on the written summary of the note-taker to recall the main issues discussed. In many situations, an initial refusal of the tape-recorder is a reaction to a lack of understanding about how the information will be used. Therefore, in seeking informed consent to the tape-recording, the moderator needs to take sufficient time to explain how the information will be used in the research project, and equally importantly what will not be done with the tape-recording, to dispel any fears about inappropriate use of the information. A common concern amongst participants unfamiliar with research is that the recording will be broadcast on the media and their voices will be recognised in the community. In politically sensitive areas there may be fears that the public release of the information will bring harm to participants, while other participants will simply fear unfamiliar technology. Clearly these concerns will not be evident in all sectors of the community, and may be more evident when working in remote or rural communities, or amongst less-educated populations. Experiences are different, however, and the recording of group discussions may be problematic in some contexts but not in others, as the experiences in Figure 10.2 demonstrate. Moderators need

---

It's quite a conservative area, some women thought that the recording was going to be played on the radio and their voices would be recognised. The young women were afraid that their husband or mother-in-law would hear the tape. We took a lot of time to explain why we needed the discussion taped, then they agreed. Researcher, Pakistan

There was some resistance in using the tape recorder. Some were worried that it will go to the TV or radio. Moderators told them it was purely for academic purposes and they showed them some letters ... The first impression about the tape recorder is negative, and really needs to be softened up so that they don't feel threatened. Adolescents were concerned that teachers or parents might find out what they said, but we stressed that there was no way that they would ever hear the tapes, this was very important. Researcher, Lesotho

Participants didn't mind the tape recorder, no one asked why it was being taped, although we explained this at the beginning. They just accepted it. Could be because they are used to being researched, this is not a new thing for them. Researcher, Kenya

---

Figure 10.2   Participant concerns in tape-recording the discussion

- Explain reasons for requesting a tape-recording of the discussion
- Stress the importance of capturing complete and correct information
- Reinforce the outcomes of the research
- Explain how the tape recording will be used (and not used)
- Describe how confidentiality will be safeguarded
- Inform participants that they are not obliged to accept the recording
- Invite questions to allay fears and misconceptions
- Seek consent for tape-recording the discussion

Figure 10.3   Guidelines for gaining consent for tape-recording

to become confident in explaining the use of the tape recorder and ensuring that informed consent for its use is obtained. This may be provided during the field training sessions. Figure 10.3 highlights some guidelines for gaining consent for tape recording the discussion.

In explaining to participants the need to tape-record the group discussion, moderators may highlight a range of issues. First, the moderator may explain that it is not possible for the note-taker to write down everything that participants say during the discussion, particularly with many people in the group, therefore the tape-recording will assist the researchers to accurately recall all the issues raised in the discussion. Second, the group discussions are being conducted to identify the views of participants, and the tape-recording will ensure that their issues are recorded exactly in the manner they were raised, and can therefore be accurately reported to the research investigators. Third, every point raised by participants is important to the research team and the tape-recording will ensure that all the information discussed is recorded and no issues are overlooked or misinterpreted, as they may be with using a note-taker. Finally, the moderator may highlight that the research investigators are unable to participate in the group discussions, or are unable to understand the language of the discussion, therefore the tape-recording will be used to develop a translation of the discussion for the research investigators to clearly understand the issues from the perspectives of the study participants.

After clearly explaining the reasons for seeking a tape-recording of the discussion and identifying how the information will be used, the moderator needs to seek consent for its use and respond to any remaining concerns raised by participants. The tape recorder should only be switched on after consent is given. If consent is refused the discussion should proceed with a note-taker recording the main issues of the discussion.

While much attention is often focussed on participants' negative concerns about the use of a tape recorder, it can also have a positive benefit on the

---

There was actually no problem with using the tape recorder. Women felt like 'the star of the show' and passed the microphone to each other. They all wanted a turn to hold the microphone. It seemed to empower the women to talk about their views. They felt important and privileged that someone came to sit with them. Research Student, India

They enjoyed it. Some of them wanted to hear their voices on tape. So at the end I played back the last one to two minutes, it made them laugh. Researcher, Malawi

They were all glad, they were too glad! And then they said oh we'll sing a song, we'll record a song! No, we had no problems at all with them accepting the tape recorder. Research Student, Zambia.

The men were very interested in the tape recorder, it helped start the discussion. They asked which brand it was, how much it cost and what it could do. Researcher, Pakistan

Figure 10.4   Benefits in using a tape-recorder

group dynamics and be beneficial to the group discussion. Some examples of this are shown in Figure 10.4.

Digital recorders are becoming increasingly popular for recording group discussions and interviews. This new technology offers several advantages over the traditional tape-recorder. Digital recorders store the audio information in a digital format, this means there is no longer a need for cassette tapes, which may become damaged or lost after the group discussion. The large memory space of digital recorders also means that many hours of recording can be stored on the device, so several group discussions may be recorded and stored. Unlike the audio-cassette recording, a digital recording can be copied instantly, enabling immediate back-ups of group discussions or sending the audio file to other members of the research team not at the field site. The quality of the audio recording on digital devices does not deteriorate over time, as would happen with a recording on a cassette tape. In addition, the use of a digital recorder can improve the ease of transcription by using transcription software, this overcomes the need to use a manual transcription machine with a pedal device to stop/start the cassette recorder during transcription. There also exists the potential for rapid analysis of digital data with an audio software package, however this remains an emerging area in qualitative data analysis. When selecting an appropriate digital recording device, it is important to ensure there is a USB connection to enable files to be transferred for analysis.

Practical issues

The recording device is generally placed in the centre of the discussion circle, or if an external microphone is used this will be placed in the centre and the recorder placed close to the moderator or note-taker. The audio equipment should be visible but not intrusive. A very useful strategy is to leave the recorder on for some time after the formal completion of the discussion, as participants almost always make important points after the conclusion of the discussion and these will be captured if the recorder is still running.

Selecting appropriate audio equipment to produce a good quality recording of the discussion is important. A tape-recorder suitable for one-to-one interviews may not necessarily produce a recording of sufficient quality in a group discussion, so attention to the microphone component of the unit is essential (Bloor et al. 2001). Built-in microphones may be adequate but often have limited sensitivity, therefore using an external, multi-directional microphone attachment is often more suitable for recording voices from several locations surrounding the microphone, as in a discussion circle. Some microphones have an auto volume control feature, which may be useful for individual interviews but is ineffective in a discussion group setting. This type of microphone will adjust for loud noises, such as a loud speaker, but if the next speaker is quieter their initial comments may be lost as the microphone adjusts the volume to capture the softer sound (Bloor et al. 2001). External microphones may also operate on a separate switch to the main tape recorder, and care needs to be taken to switch on both devices before recording the discussion. Although good quality recording equipment is important, highly sensitive microphones may not be suitable for research in some fieldwork contexts. When recording group discussions in community settings there is typically a lot of background noise (even with groups held indoors), as babies cry, doors slam, children shout, heavy traffic passes and car horns sound, in addition to several people talking in the actual group discussion. The tape-recording can often sound chaotic for the person trying to transcribe the discussion. Some high quality microphones will pick up the external sounds very clearly and this may make it difficult to isolate the voices of participants from other competing sounds. These issues need to be considered when selecting a suitable microphone. For example:

A good quality tape recorder is important, but very high quality microphones can actually distract from the quality of the recording, they are too good and also pick up the children outside and the man shouting that he is selling milk two lanes down! (Researcher, Pakistan)

If serving refreshments during the discussion, researchers should exercise caution in providing noisy food packets and remember that food and drink utensils can also create sounds which will affect the recording quality.

Often battery operated recording equipment is preferred due to the greater flexibility when at the research location, particularly in locations where there may not be a power supply or when the groups may be unexpectedly held outdoors. When using battery operated equipment it is worthwhile to select a device with a battery indicator and to carry sufficient spare batteries. When selecting cassette tapes, it is advisable to avoid the 120 minute tapes as they tend to be quite thin and may break with the continual rewinding during the transcription process (Bernard 1994). Finally, it is good practice to test the recording equipment before the commencement of each group discussion and to ensure that one member of the research team is responsible for the operation of the tape-recorder during the group discussion. It is easy for the moderator and note-taker to become absorbed in their respective roles during the group discussion, so that neither notices that the cassette tape needs changing or the battery level is low.

Pre- and post-session questionnaires

The tape-recording and the note-taker's written summary of the discussion will capture the main issues discussed within the focus group. However, researchers may also wish to obtain additional information about each participant. This may be demographic information or personal information related to the research topic but that is too sensitive to ask in the group setting. It can be useful to gain some information about the socio-demographic characteristics of participants to provide a context to the issues raised during the discussion. For example, a group discussion may focus on the use of family planning clinics; however, if information about participants reveals that most of the participants do not use contraception themselves this may provide an insight into their comments during the discussion. This back-ground information can be useful when describing the general characteristics of the study population, and during data analysis when comparing the information from various group discussions amongst participants with different contextual characteristics (Ulin *et al.* 2002).

Such information from individual participants can be collected through a post-session questionnaire, administered at the end of the discussion group, or occasionally at the beginning. Typically, a pre- or post-session question-naire is a brief (one or two page) short response questionnaire, which seeks information relevant to the topic of the group discussion as well as socio-demographic information. The questionnaire is confidential and anonymous

---

Young people's health study

Thank you for attending the group discussion today. We would also like to collect some personal information from each group member separately. This information will be strictly confidential and anonymous; so we do not need your name. The information you provide will be very useful in developing the report on Young People's Health in this city.

Please answer the following brief questions and place your form in the box by the door before you leave. We greatly appreciate your co-operation.

1. **Your age:** ....years
2. **Sex:** Male Female
3. **Are you still attending school?** Yes No
4. **If you've left school, what age did you leave?** ....years
5. **Have you ever smoked cigarettes?** Yes No
   If yes, at what age did you first start smoking? ....years
6. **Have you ever taken any illegal drugs?** Yes No
   If yes, which drugs have you tried?.....................................
7. **Have you ever had sex?** Yes No
   If no, your survey is complete. If yes please continue.
   At what age did you first have sex? ....years
   How many people have you had sex with? ....(number)
   Did you use contraception the first time you had sex? Yes No
      If yes, which method did you use? ....
   Have you ever used 'emergency contraception'? Yes No
      If yes, did you go to your regular doctor for this? Yes No

THANK YOU FOR COMPLETING THIS FORM

Figure 10.5 Example post-session questionnaire

as it may seek sensitive or personal information from participants. Figure 10.5 shows an example post-session questionnaire.

Key terms

A *verbatim record* is a word-for-word transcription of the group discussion taken from the tape-recording of the discussion.

Objective note-taking refers to the note-taker recording the issues in the way that they were raised by participants during the discussion, without making any judgement or interpretation of the issues.

Summary of key issues

- Focus group discussions are typically recorded in two ways, by using an audio-recorder and by taking written notes during the session.
- A note-taker should always be present even if the discussion is being audio-recorded, as the written summary will be critical if the recording equipment fails, the recording is inaudible or the cassette tapes are lost.

- If participants refuse permission to tape-record the session, the note-taker's summary will be the only record of the information discussed.
- The written notes should represent an objective record of the discussion.
- Researchers need to carefully consider whether information gained through video-recording will outweigh the potential intrusiveness of the approach and the impact on the discussion environment.
- Tape-recording the discussion provides a verbatim record of the discussion, improves data quality and is critical for systematic data analysis.
- Seeking informed consent to tape-record the discussion is essential.
- Careful selection of audio equipment is necessary, as equipment suitable for individual interviews may not be ideal for recording a group discussion.
- Researchers may administer a brief post-session questionnaire to collect socio-demographic information about each participant or information related to the research topic that is too sensitive to ask in the group setting.

Data preparation and analysis

Introduction

Data analysis involves synthesising the focus group data in a systematic manner to provide information that effectively responds to the research questions. Analysis of textual data can be a challenging task, as it involves identifying the meaning of information which is often in an unstructured and fragmented format because it originated from a group discussion. The large volume of textual data also poses a challenge to the analyst to identify how to segment the data into smaller, manageable parts for analysis. In essence, data analysis 'is the process of moving from raw interviews to evidence-based interpretations that are the foundation for published reports' (Rubin and Rubin 2005: 201). Textual data analysis needs to be conducted in a systematic, structured manner so that the conclusions reached are reliable and can be verified. This chapter describes the systematic process of textual data analysis from focus group discussions.

The data from focus group discussions are distinct from other types of qualitative data, because the information is collected from a discussion amongst a *group* of people. Therefore, the group context and the dynamic nature of a discussion need to be taken into consideration during analysis of the data. There are particular challenges in the analysis of data from a group discussion. First, the interaction between participants in a group discussion often leads to interrupted speech, contradictions of opinion, unfinished ideas, disagreements and misinterpretations between participants. These aspects of a group discussion can create difficulties when analysing the data if participants' comments are not considered in the context of a discussion. The analyst also needs to follow through each segment of the discussion to its natural conclusion, as opinions voiced early in the discussion may change once the issues have been debated amongst participants. It can also be difficult to determine whether frequently made comments reflect the views of the entire group or only of certain individual participants. All these issues require particular attention in the analysis of data from a group discussion.

This chapter provides an overview of the systematic process of analysing data from focus group discussions. The specific focus of the chapter is on the preparation of focus group data from international focus group research, with a discussion on issues of translation and transcription of group discussions conducted in another language. The chapter also identifies the particular challenges and strategies for the analysis of data from a *group* of participants. It is not the intention of this chapter to provide an extensive discussion on the analysis of qualitative data in general. This information is available in numerous other texts and readers are referred to the following: Dey 1993; Strauss and Corbin 1998; Denzin and Lincoln 1998a; 1998b; 2000; Krueger and Casey 2000; Silverman 2000; 2005; Punch 2005; and Richards 2005.

Principles of data analysis

There are a range of principles that underlie the analysis of qualitative data. These principles reflect the qualitative research paradigm in which the data were collected and guide the analysis of textual data. Each of these principles is described below.

Level of data analysis varies

The appropriate level of data analysis will vary for each research project, and is dependent upon the purpose of the research and the complexity of the study design. For example, focus group research may be conducted to identify broad issues or terminology to assist in the development of a survey questionnaire. In this situation, detailed analysis of the substantive issues in the data are not needed or appropriate to meet the research objectives. Similarly, focus group research may be conducted to broadly gauge community support or opposition to specific government programmes. If the group discussions highlight that the program is clearly favourable or unfavourable then only a brief report may be required to serve the purpose of the research, and detailed textual data analysis may not be required (Stewart and Shamdasani 1990). In other types of research, the purpose of the focus group discussions is to develop a greater understanding of a phenomenon or to explain certain behaviour. This type of research necessitates a much more detailed analytic approach that may require identifying important issues in the data or analysing the behaviour of sub-groups of the study population. This type of research will require detailed analysis of the focus group transcripts and a systematic approach to data analysis. This type of analysis is most often conducted when the researchers wish to assess the substantive issues raised in the discussion groups and when the analyst wishes to retain participants' descriptions of the issues and the context of the research problem. The findings of this type of research are often submitted to peer-reviewed academic journals for which systematic procedures and analytic rigor in the analysis are expected (Miles and Huberman 1994).

Analysis is an ongoing process

Qualitative data analysis is an ongoing process that begins during the data collection and continues until the final report is completed. Informal processing of the information begins during the data collection stage of the research, however the most formal part of the data analysis involves analysis of the transcripts of the focus group discussions. In addition, data collection and analysis are often conducted simultaneously, whereby analysis of the initial group discussions guides the subsequent data collection, so that the two

processes are conducted in tandem. As the data are being collected researchers examine the information, consider how it contributes to the research
problem and identify whether new issues need to be explored in subsequent
group discussions. Thus, the initial data analysis informs the data collection
in a circular manner. Conducting analysis of the data throughout the research
process improves the quality of data collection and the research results.

Remain close to the data during analysis

In qualitative data analysis the analyst remains 'close' to the data. The analyst
is continually reading the textual data, identifying patterns and issues in the
data, developing explanations and hypotheses with the data and then going
back to the data to verify the conclusions made. These conclusions may
stimulate further questions to be explored in the data, further analysis is
then conducted with the new queries, a more detailed hypothesis is developed
and again the analyst returns to the data to ensure that the new explanations
are supported by the information found in the data. Therefore, the analyst is
continually interacting with the data and returning to the data to check the
hypothesis and conclusions made at each stage of the analysis.

Analysis is circular, not linear

The analysis of textual data is not conducted in a linear sequence of stages,
whereby one stage is completed before the next is undertaken. Instead, data
analysis is a circular process whereby the stages of analysis may be repeated,
overlap or are conducted simultaneously. Qualitative data analysis often
follows an iterative spiral (Dey 1993; Rubin and Rubin 1995), whereby
researchers conduct some analysis, reflect on the findings, collect more
data, resume data analysis and gradually develop a greater understanding of
the research issues. Figure 11.1 outlines a series of stages in data analysis,
however, the analyst may return to any of the previous stages of analysis
before proceeding further, therefore qualitative data analysis is often
described as a circular and evolving process rather than a linear sequence of
stages.

Analysis is systematic and rigorous

Qualitative data analysis must be conducted in a systematic and rigorous
manner, following accepted procedures for the analysis. For example,

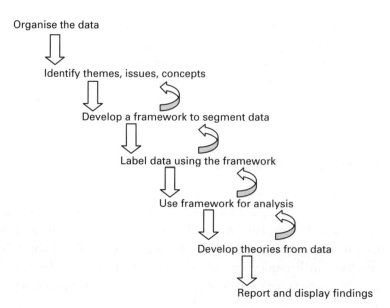

Organise the data

Identify themes, issues, concepts

Develop a framework to segment data

Label data using the framework

Use framework for analysis

Develop theories from data

Report and display findings

Figure 11.1   Process of inductive data analysis

discourse analysis, analytic induction, content analysis, or conversation analysis, are some of the approaches used in the analysis of textual data (Bloor *et al.* 2001). A systematic approach to data analysis is recommended to avoid bias and selectivity in the analysis process, and to ensure that analysis is conducted with the necessary scientific rigor in the procedure to produce quality research outputs (Krueger and Casey 2000). A part of rigorous analysis involves the use of verbatim transcriptions of the group discussions, so that the textual data represent an accurate record of the discussion issues and the context in which they were discussed. Systematic analysis also involves examining data from a variety of sources in the research project, such as the discussion transcripts, field notes, observer's notes, post-session questionnaire and debriefing notes, each of which will illuminate different aspects of the study findings.

Analysis can be verified

The process of analysis should be verifiable, so that another researcher using the same data will come to similar conclusions. Researchers should therefore document the process of analysis used, by noting how themes were developed from the text, clearly defining the labels used to segment the data, documenting the results of key text searches and how theory and explanations are supported by information in the text. Well documented analysis provides a trail of evidence to verify the validity and reliability of the findings and the conclusions generated from the data.

Process of data analysis

The essential process of qualitative data analysis is summarised in Figure 11.1 as a series of stages. However, the actual conduct of textual data analysis is not linear, as the various tasks are often conducted concurrently or repeated so that the process of analysis is circular rather than linear. The analysis of qualitative data involves first reading the textual data and becoming familiar with the information within the context of a group discussion. The data then need to be segmented into smaller, manageable parts for analysis. This segmentation is typically conducted by identifying themes within the data and analysing the data by each specific theme. Finally, the analyst needs to synthesise the analysis from the various themes to respond to the research questions and draw broader theoretical conclusions from the data. This process describes the typical academic approach to the analysis of textual data, and is detailed more fully throughout this chapter.

One of the central tasks of data analysis involves segmenting the textual data into smaller parts for analysis. The segmentation of the data serves both practical and theoretical purposes. From a practical perspective, focus group research produces a vast amount of textual data that can be unwieldy to analyse, therefore the data need to be broken up into smaller, more manageable, parts for analysis. For example, a single focus group discussion may produce between thirty and fifty pages of text. If there are ten focus group discussions in a study, the volume of data escalates to 300–500 pages of text. Analysing this volume of textual data as a whole is difficult, therefore the data are segmented. The textual data are also segmented for analytic reasons. Generally, the data needs to be segmented by meaningful characteristics or themes that emerge from the discussion. Analysis of the individual themes provides a more detailed understanding of each issue and enables a comparison of the issues between discussion groups or amongst sub-groups within the study population.

The analysis of textual data involves much reading and re-reading of the data and assessing the issues in the group discussion transcripts. While reading the textual data the analyst should consider both the content and the quality of the data. The first reading of the transcripts will focus on the content of the discussion, identifying the emerging issues and considering these within the context of a dynamic discussion. Second, the analyst should read for quality and credibility of the data to determine the plausibility of the issues discussed. Ulin *et al.* (2002: 158) suggest that information is more credible when: examples given are vivid and detailed, and when participants describe their own experiences rather than those of others; when participants highlight specific issues that provide contextual detail that adds understanding of the issues; when replies to open-ended questions are spontaneous rather than probed; and when the speaker does not later contradict themselves. Third, the data are read for patterns and relationships in the data, perhaps patterns of responses are evident amongst subgroups of participants or relationships between issues are apparent. Finally, the analyst should also remain aware of what is absent from the data, perhaps certain issues from the research literature are not discussed in the data transcripts. The researchers should then question the data to identify the reasons for this absence. This type of analytical reading often leads to early hypothesis development, which may be assessed during the detailed analysis. The stages of textual data analysis are described in detail below.

Stage 1: Data preparation

The first stage of data analysis involves preparing the textual data, by developing a written transcript of the group discussion from the tape-recording. Data preparation also involves cleaning, labelling and anonymising the data. These tasks need to be conducted carefully as the quality of the textual data will be reflected in the accuracy of the transcriptions.

Transcribing the discussion

The tape-recording of each group discussion needs to be transcribed into a written document, or *transcript*. The transcript is a complete record of the group discussion that enables a reader to 'see' everything that happened during the session. As such, the transcript can also be shared with the research commissioning agency to provide an indication of how the issues of interest were discussed in the group.

Transcribing the tape-recording of the group discussion is extremely time-consuming. A one-hour group discussion can take anywhere from five to eight hours to transcribe, and may generate over fifty pages of text (David and Sutton 2004). Most research projects will conduct numerous group discussions, so the time required for transcription and the volume of data created quickly escalates. The lengthy transcription time is partly due to the more complex nature of a group discussion compared with individual interviews. In a group discussion numerous people may talk at once, there are incomplete comments, interrupted or unclear speech, and a range of participant voices to identify, all of which make the task of transcription more difficult and time-consuming. One researcher's experience of transcribing focus group discussions is shown below:

It took so long. Oh, my goodness it took so long! We used to work day and night … and the batteries were running out, and you need to have electricity. It took such a long time because you listen to two sentences and you begin to write, then you've forgotten, you rewind, you go back, Oh! It took so long, it was probably the worst part of the whole process! (Research Student, Zambia)

Transcribing the group discussions can begin as soon as the first group is completed, it is not necessary to complete the fieldwork before beginning the process of transcription. There are numerous advantages to transcribing each group discussion after it is completed. The transcriptions enable the research investigators to identify the issues raised in each group discussion and the extent to which they contribute to a greater understanding of the research problem. This will enable the researchers to build on the information gained and identify new issues to explore in subsequent group discussions. If little new information is gained with each subsequent group this may indicate that sufficient groups have been conducted and the data collection should cease. However, for practical reasons it may be necessary to provide all the tape-recorded discussions to a transcriber at once, for example if the groups are held in remote areas of the study country.

Verbatim transcripts are essential for data analysis. A verbatim transcript is an exact word-for-word record of the discussion as it is spoken on the tape-recording, this includes the colloquial language used and the disjointed nature of people's speech. Speech is often in fragments rather than in complete sentences, there is repetition, hesitation, false starts, half-finished thoughts, pauses, rephrasing and short exclamations or utterances. These characteristics are all reflective of true speech and should be replicated in the transcript, even unfinished or interrupted speech or an utterance of agreement with a previous speaker should be included. If speech is inaudible or regional accents are difficult to understand, this should be indicated on the transcript. The words of all speakers should be transcribed, not only those of the dominant speaker, but also the contributions of quieter group members. The transcript should replicate speech as it occurs on the tape-recording, the words should not be 'tidied-up' but rather reflect the true character of the discussion, including all the grammatical inaccuracies and confused sentences. One of the uses of focus groups is to observe how people think and talk about certain issues, so too much editing is undesirable. Editing of transcripts to improve their readability should be avoided, if any editing is required to make the text readable it should be done in the reporting stage (Bloor *et al.* 2001).

A common problem with transcription is that a transcriber may develop a summary of the issues or paraphrase the discussion on the tape-recording rather than developing a verbatim transcript of the discussion. For example:

> But one person did not transcribe verbatim, they just did summaries. Questions were recorded with no response or a whole block of questions together and a paragraph of answers even though I gave them guidelines. They said that other agencies only ever want summaries. (Researcher, Kenya)

Summarising the discussion on the tape-recording involves the transcriber selectively identifying issues deemed important and omitting any other information. This may risk bias in the issues selected for inclusion in the summary. In addition, developing a summary of the issues on the tape-recording does not preserve the richness of the vocabulary and the expressions used by participants, so the original character and detail of the discussions are lost. The words of participants can often convey feelings about an issue much more strongly than a summarised account. There is also a great deal of information in the subtle utterances of participants which will be lost without a verbatim transcript. For example, if participants were asked, *'Would you use a women's health centre if one were available in the area?'* a summary of the responses may read, 'They all said yes' or 'they all agreed'. However, the actual discussion may have been the following:

M: *Would you use a women's health centre if one were available in the area?*
P1:   (pause) probably.
P2:   Yes, I think so.
P5:   I would definitely use it. I know many other women will too.
P3:   Yes, me too.
P4:   Of course, there is no place to go now, we need it.
M: *What about you, would you use such a service?*
P6:   Yes, but would it be a free clinic?

Although the extract above is brief, there is more information contained in the discussion than a general agreement about providing a women's health centre, such as hesitation in responses, the lack of other services, and concern over the cost. All this subtle information is lost with paraphrasing and summaries of the discussion, thus verbatim transcripts also improve the data quality. It is extremely important to transcribe *everything* that is spoken on the tape-recording, rather than transcribing only selected portions. Sections of the discussion which may seem unrelated to the core issues of the research may shed light on certain issues at a later stage in the analysis. At the transcription stage it is too soon to determine which information is more or less relevant to the research questions, therefore the transcription should include everything that is said on the tape-recording. Seemingly unrelated information is also important as it provides an indication of the amount of time spent on and off the research topic during the discussion. In addition, the questions, comments, probes and other dialogue of the moderator should also be transcribed. Some transcribers focus only on the words of the participants, but the moderator's comments and the resulting discussion should all be included on the transcript as they were spoken. Failure to do so will lead to confusion in trying to understand the flow of the discussion and the prompts which lead to participants' responses. Although it is a tedious task, the transcription should include everything that is spoken on the tape-recording, in the way that it was spoken.

The transcript of the dialogue of the discussion does not reflect the entire character of the discussion. In addition to speech, other oral communication can be indicated in the transcript, such as laughter or exclamations, as well as pauses and hesitancies in responding. This information can be included in brackets by the relevant comment in the transcript. For example, (pause), (hesitation), (laughter), (interruption by supervisor). This type of audible response can be heard on the tape recording, however, non-verbal communication, such as body posture, gestures or facial expressions can also convey information and it is equally important for such communication to be noted. Usually this will be included in the note-taker's observations of the discussion and kept as a memo to the discussion transcript.

Some transcripts will distinguish the comments of different participants with speaker identifiers. Although including speaker identifiers is not essential, it has the advantage of being able to identify whether a particular viewpoint is expressed by a range of different participants or simply the same individual repeating the issue throughout the discussion. Including speaker identifiers on the discussion transcript involves the transcriber distinguishing between the voices of different participants and assigning each a number. For example, comments by the first participant will be identified as P1 for each comment made, another participant as P2, the next as P3, P4, and so on.

Including speaker identifiers is a cumbersome task for a transcriber, and it can be difficult to identify individual voices from a tape-recording. A common strategy to assist the transcriber is for the moderator to begin the group discussion by going around the circle and asking each participant to introduce themselves. This provides a reference point for the transcriber to distinguish between individual voices and to identify the number of people in the discussion group. In addition, if the moderator addresses speakers by name during the discussion this can be beneficial for the transcriber. However, speaker identification is not always possible, particularly with short extracts of speech or where a participant simply acknowledges agreement with another speaker. If there is doubt about the speaker's identification this should be indicated on the transcript.

Finally, completed transcripts should always be reviewed for accuracy and completeness. This involves listening to the tape-recording while following the transcript to fill in any gaps, identify errors or omissions and clarify any ambiguous discussion. It is also important that the transcripts are correctly formatted if a data analysis package is to be used. It can be helpful for the analyst to conduct the task of reviewing the transcripts, as it is a useful way to become quickly familiar with the data.

Translating the transcripts

In international focus group research, the group discussions are typically conducted in the language of the study participants, which may differ from that of the research investigators. Therefore, the tape-recording of the discussions will need to be translated and transcribed into the language of the research team for data analysis. This process may involve first transcribing the tape-recording in the language of the discussion and later translating the written document. This process will produce two transcripts: one in the original language of the discussion and a second translated transcript. However, time and resource constraints lead many research projects to conduct the tasks of translation and transcription simultaneously, the outcome of which is a single transcript in the language of the investigators, with the tape-recording as the only record of the discussion in the original language. With this strategy the person conducting the simultaneous translation and transcription tasks should be carefully selected and adequately trained on the requirements of these tasks (see Chapter 4 on Training the focus group team).

Translation of the group discussion needs to be carefully conducted, as incorrect, incomplete or poor quality translations can seriously affect the quality of the data and limit the analysis. Consideration should be given to selecting an appropriate person to translate the group discussion. It may seem logical to seek a professional translator for this task; however, there are several reasons why this may not be appropriate. First, it may be difficult to find a professional translator familiar with the languages of the study population, particularly if working with remote or rural communities where specific dialects are spoken. The cost of professional translators may also be out of reach of most research budgets. Second, and more importantly, professional translators are often language specialists who may translate the discussion into more formal language than is desired. The outcome may be a transcription that is grammatically correct, but lacks the informal, conversational style of the discussion, excluding the colloquial expressions and all their nuances. It is imperative that the tape-recording is translated in the style of the discussion and retains, as closely as possible, the flavour of expression as spoken by the participants. Using professional translators may not achieve this objective. Finally, professional translators are often not familiar with the substantive issues, terminology or concepts of the research topic under discussion, and may therefore develop a rather sanitised transcript of the discussion. In selecting a translator it is often more appropriate to identify individuals who are native speakers of the required language(s) and who are broadly familiar with the research topic and the local culture. It is often possible to seek local professionals, such as teachers, health providers, tertiary students, or government officials, to conduct the translations. Similarly bi-lingual researchers in the study country may provide a translation while understanding the style of research enquiry required. The advantage of these individuals is their familiarity with the local language, cultural issues and expressions of the target population, which means that they are ideally placed to translate the discussion to reflect the style in which it was conducted. They may be best able to translate the concepts of the discussion into colloquial language and hence achieve more ordinary, familiar phrasing of the discussion which is appropriate for the conversational style of a focus group discussion. Seeking these local professionals for translating the discussion may be particularly useful when translation from regional dialects is required. These issues are also discussed in relation to the translation of the discussion guide in Chapter 3.

The individuals conducting the translation will require some training on the requirements of the translation and transcription. As many translators will be simultaneously translating and transcribing the discussion they will need to be trained on both processes. Training is critical to ensure accurate

- Indicate whether simultaneous translation and transcription is necessary
- Ensure adequate time and resources for translation
- Select and train an appropriate translator
- Develop a verbatim translation of the discussion
- Translate the *meaning*, rather than a literal translation of the words
- Retain vernacular style of language in translation
- Maintain selected key terms, phrases and local proverbs in original language
- Ask moderator to review translations
- Check translations for accuracy

Figure 11.2   Key issues for translating focus group discussions

translations and transcripts are developed. Figure 11.2 highlights the key issues for translating the discussion (see also Chapter 4 on Training the focus group team). Sufficient time and resources need to be allocated to the transcription/translation process in order to generate high quality textual data transcripts.

Perhaps the most important issue in translating the group discussions is to ensure that the translation conveys the *meaning* of the issues discussed rather than providing a literal translation of the words used. A literal translation of the words may make little sense. The translation needs to focus on conveying the meaning of the concepts, expressions, ideas and issues discussed, and this may require using entirely different words. So the task of translation involves more than simply translating the words, but also conveying the meaning of what is being said. This problem was encountered by a researcher in Lesotho:

One person translated the focus group literally and it sometimes made no sense, she did not translate the meaning she translated the words. In terms of translating what was said – the words – it was perfect. But the actual meaning of those words, the meaning of those expressions in Sesotho was completely different. She took verbatim to mean literal translation rather than capturing the meaning. So also knowing the culture is very important in this regard.

The need to translate the cultural meaning of the issues discussed underscores the importance of using a translator who is familiar with the language of the discussion, the cultural expressions of the target population and the way in which certain topics may be discussed in the community. There needs to be a careful balance between translating participants' words and conveying the meaning of the issues discussed.

The translation of the group discussion should retain, as much as possible, the vernacular style of speech of the participants. The words or expressions should not be formalised but reflect the true character of the discussion, including the grammatical inaccuracies of speech, confused sentences and interrupted comments. It is also important that the translation identifies any subtle differences in the style of language used to describe the issues being discussed. For example, in the Chichewa language of Malawi there are many terms for 'pregnant' which may imply a different meaning by the speaker, such as *Wa Mimba* (someone with a tummy), *Wodwala* (sick woman), *Wa Pakati* (an in-between state, between life and death). Translating all of these terms simply as 'pregnant' may lose the subtle differences in vocabulary used to describe pregnancy and what these may imply. The specific expressions for pregnancy may be retained in the original language with a brief translation in brackets as shown above. Remaining sensitive to these issues will ensure that the transcript retains the richness and detail of the qualitative data.

Translating a group discussion is a complex task and it is inevitable that some words or phrases will not translate easily. There may be specific phrases in the local language that represent recognisable concepts, and may be retained in the transcription in their original language. For example, in Pakistan the Urdu term *purdah* is a culturally specific term which refers to the separation of women from strangers and can be applied in many contexts; similarly *burqua* refers to a particular piece of clothing worn by women to preserve *purdah*; *izzat* refers to the concept of family honour and the resulting behaviour of family members; and *sathi* is a brand name that has become synonymous for condom use. Similarly in South Africa, the term *lobolo* refers to the practice of paying 'bridewealth' to the family of the woman; however, in India the term *dowry*, although a similar concept, involves the opposite exchange of wealth from the family of the bride to that of the groom. All these examples show that a single word in the local language can describe very specific concepts or practices in certain cultural contexts. Most studies will uncover a range of such terms and these words or phrases can be retained in the transcript in their original form, with a brief description in brackets. This provides the transcript with greater richness of detail and retains some of the cultural expressions used by participants.

In translating the tape-recorded group discussion it is also necessary to have some understanding of the cultural expressions and nuances in communication amongst the study population. The study participants may use a specific manner of communication, which may be misunderstood without some knowledge of their culture. Alternatively, there may be phrases or expressions that are used by a specific sub-group of the study population, such as adolescents or amongst certain professions. It is therefore important to ensure that the translator is not only familiar with the language but also the subtle manner of communication amongst the study population, to be able to correctly identify the meaning of certain parts of the discussion. For example:

Even if you know the language you can miss the point by not knowing the culture. In Sesotho they always start a sentence with 'No' and then give an explanation meaning 'Yes', this took some time to get used to. A simple thing like, 'Are you OK?' the answer might be 'No. I am fine', this is confusing if you don't understand the culture. These things pop up in the transcripts, so they might be interpreted to mean something different to what is said. So it is important to have someone with local knowledge or a local collaborator to help with the context or to explain the culture. This is very important. (Researcher, Lesotho)

Finally, the translated transcripts should always be checked for completeness and accuracy in the translations. The checks may involve listening to sections of the tape-recorded discussion and following the translated text to identify whether the translation has adequately captured the meaning of the discussion issues and there is no missing or misinterpreted information. Ideally these checks would be conducted by an independent person. It may be possible to ask an in-country research collaborator or a bi-lingual local professional, such as a teacher or clerk, to conduct quality checks on the translations.

Clean, label and anonymise data

Once the group discussions have been transcribed and translated, the data need to be cleaned, labelled and anonymised before formal analysis can begin. As with other types of research, data cleaning ensures that there are no errors or inconsistencies in the data. For textual data, this involves listening to segments of the tape-recording and following the transcripts to ensure completeness and accuracy in the written record of the discussion. If the data are translated, checking the translations is also advisable. During this process it is also worthwhile to check the quality of the data. For example, if the moderator asked a clearly leading question which may have influenced participant's responses, it is worthwhile to note this on the transcript or in accompanying notes so that this can be considered during the data analysis.

A critical task in data preparation is to anonymise the group discussion transcripts to ensure that ethical principles are maintained during data analysis. This involves removing from the transcripts any names of people, locations, places of employment or services, or any additional information which may reveal the identity of any particular participant in the group discussion. These identifiers may simply be left blank in the anonymised transcript or replaced with a code, number or fictitious name. An example

---

EXAMPLE 1: Original focus group transcript

R2:   I have been working in a private clinic as a technician for the last 12 years. I am 30 years old. I am married for 4 years. I have 2 children.

M: Yes sir?

R3:   I am Mohammed Shaikh. I am 31 years old and I have done MSc. I am working as a lecturer in chemistry in the Hyderabad Government College for the last 12 years. I am married and I have one daughter.

R4:   I am Jamil Ahmad.

M: Yes Mr Jamil?

R4:   For the last six years I have been married. I have two children. I have done a BSc. I am working as a site charge in the Iqbal Industries private consulting firm. I am 32 years old.

EXAMPLE 2: Anonymised focus group transcript

R2:   I have been working in a private clinic as a technician for the last 12 years. I am 30 years old. I am married for 4 years. I have 2 children.

M: Yes sir?

R3:   I am _____ . I am 31 years old and I have done MSc. I am working as a lecturer in _____ in the _____ Government College for the last 12 years. I am married and I have one daughter.

R4:   I am_____.

M: Yes (name)?

R4:   For the last six years I have been married. I have two children. I have done a BSc. I am working as a _____ in the _____ private consulting firm. I am 32 years old.

Note: The names used in example 1 are fictitious and do not represent actual individuals.

Figure 11.3   Anonymising focus group transcripts

extract of original discussion is shown in Figure 11.3 and the same extract once the identifiers have been removed from the transcript. It is the anonymised transcript that will be used in the data analysis.

Each discussion transcript should be clearly labelled with markers that make sense for the project. For example, research on Asian women (AW) may mark each discussion transcript AW1, AW2, AW3, etc. If the focus groups were segmented, it may be useful to indicate this in the labelling system. For example, if the study on Asian women was segmented by rural and urban location, the transcripts may be labelled as AWR3, AWU5 to denote Asian women, rural, focus group number 3, or Asian women, urban, focus group number 5 respectively. Labelling the discussion transcripts provides a clear reference point for the data and if these labels also serve as the filenames it allows certain group discussions to be quickly identified.

Data analysis will often involve comparing the issues discussed between group discussions with different types of participants (e.g. between male or female groups, urban or rural groups). Therefore, each discussion transcript needs to be labelled with any characteristics that may be useful in the data analysis. The labels may be included on a cover-page of the discussion transcript or if using a data analysis software the information may be entered on a template for each transcript, to enable only group discussions with certain characteristics to be included or excluded from the analysis. These types of labels typically include the overall demographic characteristics of the participants in the group, such as gender, age group, marital status, parity, socio-economic status, location of the group discussions or any other information that may be useful in distinguishing between the discussion groups. For example, a study on young people's health in Pakistan (Hennink *et al.* 2005) used gender, age group, city name and socio-economic status as labels for each discussion group, which were used extensively during the data analysis to identify patterns in the issues discussed between different discussion groups.

Focus group research will often have numerous documents that relate to each group discussion, such as the tape-recorded discussion, the original transcript, a translated transcript, the anonymised transcript, the note-taker's written notes, any debriefing notes, a post-session questionnaire (if administered), and any labels attached to each group discussion. It is worthwhile to consider a filing system that links all the relevant documents to each focus group discussion. Each of these documents will be used at some point during the analysis process, so it is important that they are easy to locate with clear labels.

Stage 2: Identifying themes in the data

The next stage of data analysis involves identifying how to segment the data into smaller, but meaningful parts for detailed analysis. Focus group research produces a large volume of textual data which can easily become overwhelming during data analysis. To effectively manage the volume of data for analysis, it is necessary to segment the data into smaller parts and analyse these smaller sections separately. However, the data should also be segmented into meaningful parts, such as segmentation by specific issues or questions. The task of the research team is to identify *how* to segment the data and by what criteria, and to develop a framework for segmentation.

Segmenting textual data provides 'analytical handles' on the data to enable detailed analysis of each segment or issue across the whole data set. It also enables the analyst to make comparisons or connections between the issues discussed by various sub-groups within the data. In order to make effective comparisons there needs to be clear markers in the data to highlight where specific issues are discussed. Without such markers the simple analytic task of comparing issues across discussion groups can easily become cumbersome. For example, group discussions on ageing may have discussed the physical effects of ageing amongst a range of other aspects of ageing. The analyst needs to identify the exact parts of each transcript that include a discussion on physical ageing, and focus analysis only on this issue. The analysts may then wish to compare how the issue of physical ageing is discussed amongst groups of men compared to groups of women. To make this comparison most effectively, the sections of each transcript where physical ageing is discussed need to be clearly marked. Identifying a framework for segmenting the data is a critical part of the analysis process. The level of detail in the segmentation will depend on the level of specificity required in the analysis.

What is a theme?

Textual data are typically segmented by themes, which are topical markers or focal issues of various parts of the discussion. Themes can be topics, issues, concepts, influences, explanations, events, ideas or other things which mark the central focus of a part of the discussion. For example, participants in a group discussion on 'access to health services' may raise issues such as location, cost, waiting time, prescriptions, parking, consultation times, emergency treatment and medical practitioners. All these issues may be considered themes or topics of the discussion. Some of these themes will be raised by participants themselves, while others may have been prompted by the moderator using topics on a discussion guide.

Identifying themes

Identifying themes in textual data involves reading and re-reading the group discussion transcripts to notice the issues or concepts under discussion. There are two broad approaches to identifying themes. The first involves identifying the issues raised by participants in the discussion. This approach uses the principles of Grounded Theory (Glaser and Strauss 1967) in theme identification, whereby the themes are identified *inductively*, that is, from the issues raised by participants themselves. The greatest advantage of identifying themes inductively is that it allows the analyst to identify the issues of importance to the participants and may also highlight issues that the researchers had not anticipated. Themes may be refined by noticing particular metaphors or anecdotes used by participants and identifying the meanings attached to these phrases in the discussion. Such expressions may reveal important cultural themes, particularly when similar accounts occur across different group discussions (Rubin and Rubin 2005). Once a number of themes have been identified in one group discussion, the analyst may identify whether the same ideas appear in other group discussions and whether the themes need to be further refined. Themes may be refined by comparing a range of issues within and across different group discussions to identify what the discussion collectively reveals (Rubin and Rubin 2005). For example, participants in several group discussions may highlight a range of issues related to seeking health care, such as: treatment fees, cost of transport, inability to pay for health care or weighing the cost of health versus the cost of food. These issues may *collectively* identify the underlying theme or influence of 'poverty' on seeking health care, thus poverty can be identified as a theme in this way.

The second approach to identifying themes involves using the explicit topic areas from the discussion guide to highlight the parts of the discussion devoted to each specific topic (Holliday 2002). For example, a discussion guide may have three main areas investigating 'symptoms', 'treatment' and 'effects' of malaria. The discussion will inevitably focus on these three areas which can be used initially as broad themes. Further themes can then be developed from the specific issues discussed under each topic. One of the shortcomings of identifying themes in this manner is that the analyst is imposing a range of themes onto the data and may lose sight of the unique issues raised by participants themselves. In reality many researchers use a combination of the two approaches to identify themes both from participants' issues and from the topic areas on the discussion guide.

Developing themes also involves sensitivity to what is happening in the data, by 'reading through or beyond the data' (Mason 2002: 149) to identify broader processes and concepts. It involves reading and thinking analytically about the data, rather than simply reading the content of the discussion transcripts. There are a number of ways to improve analytical reading of the data for theme development. First, knowledge of the research literature may help the analyst to recognise particular themes or cultural issues in the data. For example, knowledge of the research literature on marriage processes in Pakistan will mean that an analyst is aware of the prevalence of arranged marriages and the concept of dowry payments. This awareness will help the analyst to recognise whether these concepts are evident in the discussion transcripts or if there is some variation of these concepts that is specific to the study participants. Similarly, the analyst's personal or professional experience of the research issues can assist in recognising and understanding issues that are discussed in the data (Holliday 2002). However, such experience can also block an analyst from recognising new or unexpected variations in the issues, if only a certain pattern of behaviour is anticipated. Second, analytical or reflexive reading of the data can be developed by asking questions about the issues identified in the data, such as, *What is happening? To whom does it happen? How or why is it happening? Who is involved?* Searching the data for the responses to these questions may help to focus a theme or identify a concept in the data (Strauss and Corbin 1998). For example, if these questions were asked when reading the discussion transcript on the topic of contraceptive use in India, the analytical reading of the data may reveal the following information: the issue discussed is non-use of contraceptive methods, this is discussed only by newly married women, and the discussion frequently mentions the influence of a mother-in-law. Therefore, through an analytical reading of the data a theme of 'mother-in-law influence on contraceptive use' may be developed from this process. Finally, the validity of an emerging theme or concept may be tested by identifying whether the same issue is repeated in other parts of the transcript or in other group discussions. Such comparisons may also further refine the variations of the theme (Strauss and Corbin 1998). For a more detailed discussion of techniques for identifying what is happening in the data see Chapter 9 of Richards (2005).

While developing themes and identifying how to segment the data, it is important not to lose sight of the 'big picture', that is the broad issues that are raised in the discussion. Remaining aware of the broad issues is important as much of the analysis process involves segmenting the data and considering the smaller sections of the data, so the broader issues can easily be overlooked. Often these broader issues will provide the initial framework for the development of the main findings of the study (Vaughn *et al.* 1996) and developing theories or explanations of the issues discussed requires a broader perspective of the core themes and patterns in the data (Richards 2005). The broad issues in the study are often evident from the initial reading of the transcripts in their entirety and making notes on the prominent issues of each group discussion. These prominent issues can be determined through the consistency with which the issues are raised throughout the data, the intensity of the comments, the specificity of issues, and the words and body language of participants.

One of the difficulties in developing themes from group discussion data relates to the group context of the data. The analyst can easily become focussed on the small comments from individual participants and lose sight of how these fit into the context of a group discussion (Lofand and Lofand 1995; Bloor *et al*. 2001). The interactive nature of data from a group discussion may mean that an opinion or point of view mentioned in one part of the discussion may be later contradicted or further developed in another part of the discussion. Therefore, when developing themes from group discussion data the analyst needs to carefully study the context of each comment within the discussion and follow the arguments of individual participants as well as the group as a whole in order to uncover the key issues. For example, participants in a study on access to family planning services in Malawi (Hennink and Madise 2005) would often mention that the distance to the clinic was a problem, and that a clinic within walking distance was most desirable. If examining small segments of the data the issue of 'distance' may initially seem like an appropriate theme. However, as the discussion developed participants began to say that distance was not a problem, which contradicted their earlier statements. By following the line of the discussion through the transcripts it became apparent that distance *per se* was not the issue, but the greater the distance the higher the cost of transport, and poverty made payment for transportation difficult. Therefore, the issues of 'transport cost' and 'poverty' became the themes. It is therefore valuable to follow how each issue evolves during the course of the discussion to uncover the core issues or themes. The analyst also needs to be aware of individual contradiction of opinion, and whether this may be a result of the group process of moderating a participant's opinion or the adverse influence of the group situation on participants voicing their true opinions (Vaughn *et al*. 1996). In order for the analyst to follow the various arguments of individual participants through the transcript it is necessary to include speaker identifiers on the transcript that distinguish individual speakers. Some contradictions and ambiguity are inevitable in group data. However, during the discussion the moderator should work hard to clarify contradictions in the discussion and the analyst should be prepared to exclude from analysis segments of data where ambiguity cannot be resolved so as not to misrepresent the issues (Bloor *et al*. 2001).

As a range of themes are developed they should be clearly defined and listed in a codebook, as shown in Figure 11.4. The development of themes is an evolving process that continues through the analysis. Typically about one-third of the data will be read when initially developing the themes, then as data analysis progresses further themes may be added or modified, several themes may merge into one, or themes may be split into separate issues. The list of themes is never rigid and continues to develop over time. Themes can

Theme	Description of Theme
Private	Private fee-charging clinic, hospital, health facility
Government	Free of charge, government clinic, hospital, health facility
Service time	Time spent with doctor/nurse during consultation
Wait time	Waiting time for consultation while at health clinic
Number of people	Number of patients at health service
Staff attitude	Attitude of staff to patients (e.g. polite/impolite, etc.)
Know staff	Clients who know staff at health clinic receive better service
Staff training	Staff training issues
Attention	Attention received from clinic staff or health professionals (e.g. personal, friendly, welcoming)
Privacy	Privacy issues during consultation
Medicine	Drugs, effectiveness, stock of drugs, etc.
Diagnosis	Appropriate medical examination, thorough examination etc.
Cost	Cost of service, medicines, consultation etc.
Distance	Distance of health clinic
Hygiene	Hygiene of health clinic
Presentation	Presentation of health clinic (e.g. tidy, neat, messy, etc.)
Transport	Transport and travel issues to health clinic

Figure 11.4   Example list of themes

also be further segmented at a later stage if more detailed analysis is required or new research questions generated. The development of themes ceases at the point of *saturation* (Glaser and Strauss 1967), when no more new issues or concepts are identified in the data. The codebook of themes should include a clear definition of each theme so that the analyst can recognise when a particular theme is relevant to an extract of text. This is particularly critical when working in a research team, so that the themes are applied consistently by each member of the team.

Once a range of themes has been developed and defined, the research team can identify an appropriate mode of analysis, either to conduct the analysis manually or to select a textual data analysis program to manipulate the data. However, all tasks up to this point, such as data preparation and identification of themes, need to be done manually. It is important to remember that the data analysis can be conducted manually. Although computer software can not *do* the analysis, it can be very useful in manipulating the volume of data to make the analysis process quicker and more systematic. Therefore, the decision on the mode of analysis is often influenced by the volume of data and the purpose of the study. If there are only a small number of group discussions to analyse or the groups were conducted to inform a survey rather than for substantive content, then it may be advisable to conduct the analysis manually. However, with a large number of group discussions or a complex topic, a software package can greatly enhance data manipulation procedures, such as data retrieval, indexing, insertion of new codes, hyperlinks and data comparison. For an overview of selecting software see, for example, Miles and Huberman 1994: 311; Flick 1998: 250; Ulin *et al.* 2002: 148; Silverman 2000: 154; Silverman 2005 (Chapter 13).

Stage 3: Label data by themes

The next stage of analysis involves indexing the whole data set, using the themes as labels to mark specific segments of the discussion transcripts where the discussion relates to each theme. This is a systematic process of reading and re-reading the discussion transcript, examining the content of the discussion and marking each segment of text with appropriate theme labels. This process is often referred to as 'coding' the data and the theme labels referred to as 'codes'. Labelling the data is akin to indexing the data to identify specific sections of the text where a certain issue is discussed, which can make analysis of the large volume of textual data easier and more accurate. Labelling the data provides a structure to the discussion transcripts that enables the analyst to retrieve all segments of the data relating to a single theme, which can then be put into a separate file for analysis. Providing a structure to the data also facilitates closer comparison of themes between various subgroups within the data set, such as comparing the comments of men and women, older and younger, or urban and rural participants' comments about a specific theme.

The theme labels may be used to mark a single line of text, a paragraph or several pages. Several labels can be applied to the same piece of text if these themes are evident in that part of the discussion. The labelling process may be done by marking the margin of the transcript or in a computer analysis program by highlighting the text and selecting the pre-prepared labels from a menu. An example of labelled text is shown in Figure 11.5. The whole data set should be labelled. Labelling the text requires the analyst to carefully focus on the text to constantly judge what is being discussed, follow through arguments, identify underlying concepts and decide which labels are most appropriate. It is a difficult and time-consuming exercise, yet it is a critical step to conducting quality analysis.

The most common ways in which to apply labels to the data are to identify all mentions of a theme, whether each individual mentions a theme, or whether each group discusses a theme; these levels are in fact components of each other (Morgan 1997). Morgan (1997) highlights that one unique issue in labelling focus group data is to consider the unit of analysis that is being labelled; is it the group that is the unit of analysis or the individuals within the group? Nearly all analysts will assert that the unit of analysis is the group.

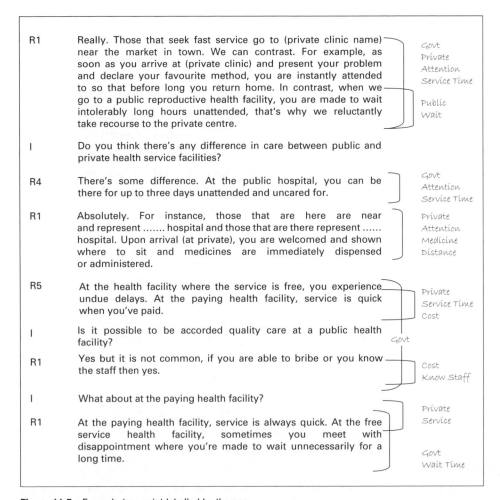

Figure 11.5   Example transcript labelled by themes

However, there is a need to recognise that focus group discussions are a product of the individuals within the group, yet the individuals are influenced by the group setting. Therefore, neither the individuals nor the group constitute a separate unit of analysis, but 'analytic efforts must seek a balance that acknowledges the interplay between the two "levels of analysis".' (Morgan 1997: 60.)

Stage 4: Using the framework for analysis

At this stage in data analysis the analyst will have read and re-read the transcriptions, identified key themes in the data, segmented and structured the data and applied theme labels to the entire data set. During these tasks the analyst will have become familiar with the content of the data, gained an impression of the issues discussed and the variation between discussion groups, begun to interpret the issues and formulate questions about these, and started to identify the emerging findings (Ulin *et al.* 2002). Therefore, by this stage in the analysis process the analyst has become quite familiar with the data and has already conducted a lot of informal examination of the data. The next stage of data analysis involves using the framework developed (i.e. the themes) to segment the data for detailed analysis of each data segment, then to link these analyses together to develop explanations or theories from the data that respond to the research questions.

Data analysis can be conducted at various levels from descriptive analysis of the issues discussed to more complex theory development. The appropriate level of data analysis will primarily be determined by the purpose of the study, but the quality and scope of the data may also define the level of analysis possible. For example, the purpose of a study may be to identify key issues around a topic, whereby descriptive analysis is sufficient. However, another study may intend to develop a theoretical explanation for certain behaviour but find that the anticipated depth or complexity of the issue is not apparent in the discussion groups, therefore the limited detail in the data mean that only descriptive analysis is possible. The following sections describe two levels of data analysis, descriptive analysis and more detailed analysis leading to theory development.

Descriptive Analysis

The first level of analysis is descriptive analysis. This involves examining each of the issues in the group discussion and describing the context of each issue. Descriptive analysis involves using the theme labels to identify all segments of text related to a specific theme and examining the discussion of each theme across the entire data set. This may be done by focussing on one theme at a time and examining each issue in detail. Descriptive analysis may involve:

a) identifying the issues discussed under a theme. For example, within a theme 'cost of health care' participants may agree that health care is expensive, but are most concerned about the registration or prescription cost rather than consultation fees. These are important distinctions;

b) describing all aspects of the theme discussed, both positive and negative. For example, under a theme 'quality of health care' participants may describe positive aspects of a health system and areas needing improvement. These details are particularly useful in evaluative research;

Features of a health clinic	FG1	FG2	FG3	Total participants	Total groups	
1. Staff attitude	1	1		2	2	
2. Confidentiality	1	11	111	6	3	
3. Length of consultation		1	1	2	2	
4. Gender of staff	111	11	11	7	3	← Important theme
5. Staff expertise		11		2	1	
6. Clinic location	1	11		3	2	
7. Image of clinic	1			1	1	← Marginal theme

Frequency of theme   Consistency of theme

Source: adapted from Hennink and Diamond 1999: 136.

Figure 11.6 Frequency and consistency of themes

c) noting the range of issues discussed under a theme and highlighting any common, recurrent issues;

d) noticing patterns in the discussion of themes, and whether certain themes are often discussed together. For example within the theme 'obesity' participants may often mention 'depression' and 'stigma';

e) comparing how the theme is discussed amongst various sub-groups in the study. For example, is the discussion of a theme more apparent amongst certain sub-groups? Is a theme discussed differently amongst certain subgroups in the study (e.g. between male or female groups)?

Descriptive analysis can also involve determining which themes are important and which are marginal within a study. Identifying the frequency with which an issue is mentioned in the group discussion may be a misleading indicator of its importance, as one participant may repeatedly mention an issue giving the impression that it is a group response rather than that of only one participant. Determining the importance of an issue in focus group research involves *descriptive counting*, which can be done by constructing a tally chart that lists the themes of interest in the first column and the number of focus groups in the remaining columns (see example in Figure 11.6). One tally mark is given each time a theme is mentioned by a different participant in each group discussion. The totals in the last two columns indicate the total number of participants who mentioned the issue (frequency) and the total number of groups in which the issue is mentioned (consistency) (Hennink and Diamond 1999). An important issue is one that is mentioned by many participants and across numerous groups, such as 'gender of staff' in the example. A marginal issue is mentioned infrequently by participants and in few group discussions, such as 'image of clinic', which is mentioned by one participant in only one group. It is important to note that descriptive counting is not conducted so as to report percentages or frequencies in a report, but as an analytic tool to identify whether there exist any patterns in responses across the whole data set. This strategy also enables 'group-to-group validation' (Morgan 1997: 63) of issues which reinforces the importance of issues by their recurrence in entirely different group discussions.

Although descriptive analysis often begins with identifying common and important issues in the data, it is equally important to understand how and why some types of participants differ with respect to the issues under investigation, which may lead to a better understanding of the research problem. Therefore, descriptive analysis should also focus on identifying patterns in the data and attaching some meaning to the patterns identified (Morgan 1997). This involves firstly comparing sub-groups of respondents to identify whether issues differ between certain types of participants. The issues discussed may differ by groups of male or female respondents, older or younger respondents and so on, or these sub-groups may raise different perspectives on the same issue. Once the analysis has established certain patterns in the responses the focus turns to searching the data for explanations for these patterns. It is when making comparisons between sub-groups of participants that the demographic labels of transcripts are crucial to easily identify the group discussions with certain types of participants.

Qualitative data analysis is often an iterative process, whereby the findings of data analysis inform subsequent data collection. This may occur when analysis of the first group of discussions is conducted and the findings reveal new questioning strategies to use in subsequent group discussions. This process is essential to grounded theory methodology, whereby qualitative research is an iterative and reflective process that links data analysis to further data collection. This process may occur if the descriptive analysis of the data identifies specific areas requiring further investigation. A limited number of additional focus group discussions may then be conducted to explore specific issues and provide information that gives a more detailed explanation of the research problem.

Theory development

The second level of data analysis involves the development of explanations, theories or conceptual frameworks from the data. Although theory can *guide* the research design and the analysis, particularly when a study is based around a hypothesis or theoretical framework, the process of data analysis can also *generate* new theories or explanations. Some studies are developed using a conceptual framework to determine the research hypotheses; in these situations the analysis will begin with analysing the themes that will directly inform the conceptual framework or hypothesis. In other studies researchers avoid imposing a theoretical framework on the data and allow a theory, conceptual framework or hypothesis to emerge from the data analysis; this is the inductive approach to textual data analysis. In reality, many studies may use a combination of both approaches in data analysis, whereby there may be a hypothesis about specific aspects of the research topic, while for other areas the analysis is largely inductive. The development of theory involves analysis at a greater depth than the descriptive analysis outlined above, however descriptive analysis is often conducted first to provide a baseline of findings from which theory development can begin. For further reference to developing theory from textual data, readers are referred to Miles and Huberman 1994; Denzin and Lincoln 1998b; Strauss and Corbin 1998; Wengraf 2001; Woolcott 2001; Silverman 2000 and 2005; and Rubin and Rubin 2005.

Developing a theory or conceptual framework from the research issues involves identifying patterns in the data and relationships between themes, then seeking explanations for these patterns and linking all these together into a hypothesis or conceptual framework that contributes to a greater understanding of the research problem. See Ritchie and Lewis (2003) for a more detailed description of using conceptual frameworks to build explanations from data. Conceptual frameworks are often displayed visually in flow charts or diagrams that aim to communicate the core issues in the data and their inter-linkages, while remaining faithful to the views of the participants (Woolcott 2001). Essentially the analyst is seeking to develop a story from the data that captures the essential meaning of the issues. For example, a study in Malawi (Hennink and Madise 2005) focussed on how to determine a client's eligibility for subsidised health treatment. One of the aims of this research was to conceptualise local perceptions of poverty so that local health workers could easily identify who would be eligible for subsidised health care. The focus group participants revealed a wide range of situations and factors that indicated poverty, and poverty was seen much more broadly than a lack of financial resources, although this was a primary indicator. During the analysis the numerous factors were conceptualised into three main indicators of poverty: physical indicators (appearance, health service use, contraceptive user), social indicators (parity, marital status, disability) and economic indicators (employment status, income, savings, assets) which could be used to determine poverty status. This conceptual framework of the research problem was developed through careful analysis of the issues, identification of the inter-linkages between issues and developing a broad framework to highlight the central themes, their inter-relationships and how they relate to the research problem.

In developing a theory or conceptual framework of the research issues, the analyst needs to ensure that the theory is 'grounded' in the data, in other words that it is well supported by the information in the group discussions, rather than the product of a researcher's subjective reading of the issues in the data (Strauss and Corbin 1998). Glaser and Strauss (1967) describe a range of tools and strategies that can be used to validate a theory against the data to show that it is grounded in the data. For example the *concept-indicator model* identifies how the data supports the development of a theory and which indicators, evidence or issues within the data contributed to the theory. Similarly, *negative case analysis* involves identifying cases that do not easily fit an emerging theory and analysing these to further refine a theory or suggest variations on a theory. For further descriptions of these tools see, for example, Glaser and Strauss (1967) or McKenzie *et al.* (1997).

Synthesis of findings

The final part of data analysis involves synthesising the research findings, both the descriptive analysis and any theory development, to respond to the research objectives. Although the research objectives will have guided the analysis process, the final synthesis of the data needs to explicitly respond to the research objectives, by providing a clearer understanding of the research problem, making an assessment of a research hypothesis or providing an overall evaluation of certain research issues. The final synthesis of research findings may entail describing the issues identified in the data and explaining the context of the issues and how these contribute to a greater understanding of the issues under investigation. In developing a synthesis of the findings the analyst may:

- describe the key issues raised in the discussion
- explain the context of the issues from the participants' perspective
- outline variations in the issues by sub-groups of participants
- provide a narrative to link the key issues to the research problem
- include extracts from the discussions to highlight issues
- identify strategies or solutions suggested in the data
- present the findings in a conceptual framework that shows how issues are related
- identify the areas requiring further investigation.

Some researchers develop a synthesis of the findings and verify the interpretation of the data in *feedback groups*. These are discussion groups held with a select group of participants towards the end of a study with the explicit purpose of validating the findings and recommendations of the study with the study population. Feedback groups enable a select group of the study population to comment on the accuracy of the research findings, the interpretations and the feasibility of the recommendation, and can sharpen the results and recommendations of the study. It is not always possible to conduct feedback groups in all research projects, particularly in international research where it may not be feasible to return to the study country. However, if the research is conducted collaboratively with researchers based in the study country, they may be able to conduct these feedback groups.

Key terms

A *transcript* is the written record of the group discussion as taken from the tape-recording.
Textual data refers to non-numerical data typical of qualitative research.
In-vivo refers to leaving in the transcript some words, phrases or proverbs in the language in which they were spoken, while the rest of the transcript is translated into the language of the research team.
Themes can be topics, issues, concepts, influences, explanations, events, ideas or other topical markers of the discussion.
Inductive theme development refers to the identification of themes from the group discussion data.
Coding, indexing, labelling refer to the process of marking various segments of the text according to a theme.
Grounded theory, developed by Glaser and Strauss (1967), refers to a process of analysing qualitative data whereby the issues are identified inductively from the data.
Theory in data analysis refers to linking a set of concepts or issues to develop an explanation for the occurrence of a specific phenomenon amongst a study population.
Descriptive counting is an analytical tool that involves identifying the pattern of issues or the balance of opinions within the discussion. It is not conducted to report frequencies or percentages in a report.
Context refers to the broader socio-cultural environment in which the research was conducted. It also refers to the environment in which the data were collected (e.g. group discussion).
Group to group validation involves identifying whether issues are evident in various group discussions. The importance of issues is reinforced by their frequent occurrence in entirely different group discussions.
Feedback groups involve taking the study results back to a selection of participants to validate the interpretation of issues and recommendations.

Summary of key issues

- The level and type of data analysis will be determined by the purpose of the study.
- Data analysis is not linear, but circular, whereby the stages of analysis may be conducted simultaneously, overlap, or be repeated in an iterative spiral.
- A verbatim, anonymised transcript of the discussion is necessary for detailed analysis.
- International focus group discussions are often conducted in local languages and need to be translated for data analysis. The translation should retain the colloquial, conversational style of the discussion.
- The overall process of qualitative data analysis involves reading the data, determining how to segment it into meaningful parts, analysing the various segments in detail, and identifying the meaning or explanations in the data to respond to research questions.
- Segmenting the data into meaningful parts for analysis involves identifying themes, issues or topics in the discussion and indexing the whole data set by these topical markers.
- Data analysis involves examining the collective segments of data on each theme, conducting detailed analysis and developing an explanation or theory from the data to respond to the research questions.
- Data preparation, identification of themes, and theme definitions need to be conducted manually. Computer software can assist in manipulating the data to make analysis quicker and more systematic, but can not *do* the analysis.
- Analysis should be verified by a 'trail of evidence' to demonstrate the validity of the conclusions.

12   Reporting focus group research

Introduction

Focus group research produces a large amount of information and it is often difficult to determine what should be reported, how to structure the information and how to utilise data extracts most effectively when reporting the research findings. As with all research reports, the structure and content of the report will be determined by the purpose of the study, the audience(s) and the key messages to be conveyed. Reporting the findings of focus group research involves identifying the core findings from the data and developing a narrative to communicate these findings to the target audience(s). The challenge is to develop a narrative that both integrates the central findings and provides sufficient depth and context to the issues reported. Qualitative researchers often focus on identifying the context surrounding the research issues, but then neglect to adequately report contextual issues in the study report. One of the traditions of reporting qualitative research is to use data extracts when reporting the study findings, by including quotations from participants. However, there is little guidance on the effective use of data extracts or on how to report study findings without the use of data extracts. This chapter discusses the fundamental issues in reporting focus group research, highlighting how to focus the research findings, effectively integrate data extracts and convey context in the report. In addition, the chapter discusses reporting the findings of focus group discussions in mixed-method research.

Reporting focus group research

Effective reporting of focus group research will be guided by the purpose of the study, the central findings of the research and the audience(s) to whom the results will be presented. These issues are identical to reporting the findings on any type of research project and are briefly highlighted below. Focus group research offers the benefit of integrating extracts of the group discussions into the research report to provide a direct and vivid link between the reader and the issues of the study population. The following sections describe how to effectively integrate data extracts into the research report, and provide suggestions for alternative ways of reporting the study findings without the use of data extracts. The following points summarise the issues to be considered in developing a report of qualitative findings:

- focus on the *central purpose* of the research
- determine the *audience(s)*
- identify the *key messages* to convey
- develop a *narrative*, an argument, a story to convey findings
- provide sufficient *depth* to the issues reported
- use the *textual data* effectively to support the findings
- convey the *context* of the research setting, methodology and findings
- *integrate* the findings with results of quantitative methods, if appropriate
- select an appropriate reporting *format*
- identify appropriate *dissemination* strategies.

Identify the purpose and audience

The central focus of any research report is to present the findings that respond to the purpose of the research. The purpose of focus group research will differ for each study and may be, for example, to improve service delivery, to evaluate a programme, to gauge public opinion, to understand certain behaviour, to influence policy development, and so on. The specific purpose of the research will guide the selection of issues to report, the reporting format, shaping of the conclusions and recommendations, and whether to use data extracts. Focus group research can produce a multitude of findings, complex inter-relationships between issues, various sub-issues and a lot of information that is related but peripheral to the core research topic. It is easy for researchers to become lost in the detail and volume of information and lose sight of the findings that respond to the basic purpose of the research. One of the challenges in developing an effective report is to remain focussed on the research objectives and continually assess whether the findings included in the report contribute to the research objectives or whether they are interesting but largely peripheral to the study purpose.

Researchers need to consider the type of audience for whom the report is being developed and how they may utilise the study findings. The manner in which the findings are reported needs to be compatible with how the findings will be used, so if results are intended to influence a change in policy or practice the readers need to be able to identify from the report: the rationale for change, the specific areas where change is needed, who may benefit from a change, the actions needed and the anticipated outcomes of a change. The audience may vary widely to include academic audiences, health practitioners, service delivery personnel, policy-makers, advocacy groups, non-government organisations or community members. It is also important to remember that there are likely to be numerous audiences who may use the study findings, requiring the presentation of the findings to be developed into a range of styles and formats. The type of audience will determine how the study findings are presented, in terms of the style, format and content of the report. For example, reporting the study findings to a policy audience may require a brief, concise style with only essential findings and recommendations included (e.g. bullet points, executive summary). While for academic audiences inclusion of the research methodology, theoretical framework and literature review would be required. Green and Thorogood (2004: 221) suggest that any or all of the following written outputs may be developed from a single study:

- one-page summaries of key findings for research participants
- short paper on key findings for practitioner journal
- progress reports and final report to study donor
- executive summary to policy-makers
- research article for peer-reviewed journal
- book chapter or monograph
- dissertation or thesis.

Identify the key messages

Reporting research findings involves identifying the core findings, set of issues or basic story which emerges from the research and developing a narrative to communicate these findings to the target audience. Identifying the key findings will help to structure the report and to determine which issues are essential for the report and which are peripheral. The challenge in focus group research is to develop a report that weaves together the important findings in a coherent narrative that is both relevant to the audience and considered accurate and complete by the study participants (Ulin *et al.* 2002). A study with multiple audiences may emphasise different findings for each type of audience or identify different messages for various target audiences. Once the central issues have been identified, the style and format for communicating these will be determined by the type of audience and purpose of the study.

Structure and format

The results of focus group research may be presented in a range of formats which vary in formality, length, writing style and readership. For example, the study findings may be condensed into a two-page policy brief, which highlights the essential issues in bulleted points. Alternatively, an article for a peer-reviewed academic journal would be longer and include methodological and theoretical justifications for the study, and conform to the conventions of academic writing. There are a wide variety of other formats in which qualitative research results can be presented, such as narrative commentaries, case studies, stories, visual presentations and so on. The most appropriate format(s) in which to present the research findings will be determined by the target audience and the messages that the researchers wish to convey with the findings.

Qualitative research results intended for academic audiences often adopt the structure of standard scientific reports (as shown in Figure 12.1), which may begin with a theoretical framework or hypothesis and present findings to support or counter these. Ulin *et al.* (2002) state that by using scientific writing conventions researchers may increase the likelihood of attracting the attention of scientists more familiar with quantitative research approaches and writing conventions, and indeed this approach may be entirely appropriate for structuring the results of some qualitative studies. However, Miles and Huberman (1994) point out that the reporting of qualitative findings

Introduction	Broad description of the research issue Purpose of the study
Background	Review previous related research Highlight gaps in previous research Identify the contribution of the study Present a theoretical framework or hypothesis Provide contextual and cultural information
Methods	Describe the research design Detail the data collection techniques Outline the process of data analysis Describe the research setting and participants Outline ethical considerations
Results	Present the research findings Highlight important linkages between issues
Discussion	Interpret the findings and link to previous research Identify how results fit conceptual/theoretical framework Discuss how results contribute to a better understanding of research problem Highlight the implications of the results Identify data limitations
Conclusion	Reinforce key points from research Outline recommendations for policy or practice Suggest further research required
Acknowledgements *References*	

Figure 12.1   Standard structure of scientific reports

may not start with a conceptual framework but rather aim to develop one from the research findings. These types of qualitative studies may therefore adopt a more circular approach to the analysis and structure of the research findings. The structure adopted should reflect the nature of the material to be presented, the needs of the target audience and the reporting conventions of the sources (i.e. journal, publisher and government report).

One frequently neglected area in reporting qualitative research is a lack of depth in describing the research methodology. Vaughn *et al.* (1996) reviewed 150 articles reporting focus group methodology and found that most studies neglected to describe the participant selection criteria and procedures, only reporting the number of participants. As with all types of research, adequately reporting the methodology is critical to aid interpretation of the findings, to enable the research quality to be assessed and to replicate the approach in future research. The methodology section therefore needs to adequately describe the research setting, study participants, participant selection, conduct of the group discussions, the discussion topics, treatment of the data (i.e. tape-recording, transcription, translation), data quality measures (i.e. validity and reliability), analysis procedures and data limitations.

A further limitation in the presentation of qualitative research is the frequent lack of narrative to link the various findings in a coherent way. The findings need to be presented in a logical manner that guides the reader through the various issues presented, identifies how issues are linked and how the collective results contribute to a greater understanding of the research issues. The research findings should support an argument through the document, with clear research questions (even if exploratory research) and use the research findings to support various aspects of the argument.

Using data extracts

One of the traditions in reporting qualitative research findings is to use extracts of data to highlight issues in the research report. This is typically done by including quotations from the group discussion or interview. The use of quotations in research reports provides the reader with an immediate link to the study population, and provides vividness, detail and context that are difficult to replicate by simply describing the issues. Glaser and Strauss (1967: 228) state that the use of data extracts can '... describe ... the social world studied so vividly that the reader, like the researchers, can almost literally see and hear its people ...' The use of data extracts is also a methodological tool to demonstrate that the results presented are the product of inductive analysis, whereby the issues highlighted emerged from the data rather than from an analyst's preconceptions. Presenting data extracts using participants' own words is also a philosophical commitment, that empowers the study population by giving voice to their issues, as well as conveying important contextual information to the readers, such as expression and emotion (Denzin and Lincoln 2000).

Quotations from the study participants are typically used in a descriptive way to illustrate the issues reported. However, the use of data extracts can also provide credibility to the issues highlighted in the analysis, by demonstrating that the issues raised are valid and originate from the data in the manner described by the researcher. Quotations can therefore help to convince a reader that the researchers' interpretation of the issues is correct and valid. However, the use of quotations to provide credibility to the research findings needs to be viewed with some caution, as a reader should not begin to expect a quotation in order to demonstrate the validity of an issue. It is entirely feasible that some issues may be well-grounded in the data, but evidence for this is spread throughout the data and there exists no explicit extract to be quoted, or an extract may not capture the issue clearly or succinctly enough (Corden and Sainsbury 1996).

Although the use of data extracts is common when reporting findings from qualitative research, there is little guidance on how to use or select quotations effectively. Researchers should consider the following issues when using quotations from qualitative data:

- What is the purpose of including the extract?
- Is the extract clear and relevant to the discussion?
- What does the extract demonstrate? (i.e. common or atypical perspective)
- How was the extract selected?
- How many extracts are needed for an issue?
- How is the extract referenced?
- What is the balance between data extracts and text?
- Does the extract need editing?
- Is the extract anonymous?

Researchers should first consider the reasons for including a data extract. It is important to remember that the data extract should contribute to the issues being discussed in the text. If it does not contribute anything that cannot be stated in the text then it should be omitted. There is little sense in including a quotation that is merely repetitive of the discussion in the text. However, data extracts used to illustrate an issue often convey more than the words spoken, the extract may also express a certain emotion or expression, or use language that conveys the controversy or sensitivity of an issue. The data extract may be included because it demonstrates not only the issue itself but highlights more subtle issues such as language, tone or feeling towards an issue. The data extract also needs to show relevance to the issue or argument being presented in the discussion and clarity in the point being demonstrated.

The purpose of including data extracts should guide the selection of extracts. The purpose may be to show the range of opinions expressed by participants; therefore each extract needs to demonstrate a different perspective on the issue. Similarly, extracts may be included to compare responses from different sub-groups of the target population (e.g. urban and rural residents), therefore extracts need to be selected from each sub-group. Alternatively, a single extract may be selected to illustrate particular norms or commonly shared views amongst participants. It must be clear from the text of the report what the selected extract represents. Researchers should also consider whether the extracts presented represent a balanced view of an issue. It may be necessary to include several extracts which present the issues from various standpoints to accurately demonstrate the issues in context. Finally, researchers should take care to avoid bias in the selection of quotations. A vivid or dramatic phrase may capture the attention of the researcher and the readers of the report, but the extract may be an atypical case. The inclusion of this type of extract gives certain issues undue importance in the report. Bogdan and Taylor (1975: 145) provide the following advice, '. . . *you should resist the temptation to overuse certain colourful materials at the expense of others. If you cannot find an alternative example, the point you are trying to make may not be as important as thought originally.*'

The use of quotations involves reporting speech, which often contains incomplete sentences, pauses, repetition and grammatical inaccuracies. These characteristics will often be retained in the original transcripts. However, at the reporting stage of the project some editing of the extracts may take place in order to render the quotations readable. Researchers vary in their willingness to edit data extracts; some will only include verbatim extracts from the transcripts, while others will edit to improve the readability. The only reason for editing an extract is to render it more readable in a report. Rubin and Rubin (2005: 262) state that 'as long as the meaning is preserved, the words that are quoted were actually said, and you mark the places where you made omissions, this practice is acceptable'. Where researchers decide to edit an extract, the changes should be clearly evident, so that a reader can distinguish the original statement from the modifications. Modifications to data extracts may include editing out sections of speech that are not related to the issue being reported, and replacing the missing words with ellipses (. . .), or inserting words into a fragmented comment to complete a sentence or make the comment more readable, the inserted words are included in brackets. Editing the textual data in this manner makes the text easier to understand, while clearly identifying the changes. However, hesitancies, grammatical mistakes and sentence fragments are left as spoken to retain the original character of speech.

The number of data extracts to include will be determined by the purpose of their inclusion in the report. If the purpose of including quotations is to highlight a typical or common issue amongst the study population, then a single quotation to illustrate that issue would be sufficient. If the purpose is to show a range of opinions, then one quotation for each point of view is necessary. Considering the purpose of a quotation will help to reduce the overuse of data extracts in a report. Researchers also need to consider the balance between the text or narrative of the report and the quotations from the data. The text of a report should provide a clear discussion of the findings, summarise the issues and guide the reader through certain arguments or explanations of the issues; relevant quotations from the data are then used as examples to illustrate specific issues in the text. The text is essentially the product of analysis, while the quotations represent the raw data. Too many quotations with little interpretive narrative not only bores the reader but equates to providing the reader with a range of raw data and asking them to draw their own conclusions. As with any scientific writing, reports of qualitative findings need to present an organised, coherent and logical synthesis of the information which reflects detailed analysis of the data, and only use extracts from the text to provide the contextual richness of the information.

The data extracts can be referenced to identify their exact location in the data set. The reference is placed in brackets after the quotation and may look like the following (OXF12: 515–520). This reference refers to focus group number twelve conducted in Oxford and is located at lines 515 to 520 of the transcription. This type of referencing follows the procedures for quoting from published literature and is generally only meaningful to the researchers. Attributing the characteristics of a participant or group to an extract is often more meaningful for a reader and can reinforce comparisons between subgroups, for example the attribution following a quotation may read 'young rural men', 'female health professionals' or 'health service managers'. In attributing the characteristics of the speaker or the group, care must be taken not to provide information that may reveal the identity of the participant. For example, if an extract is followed by (antenatal clinic manager, Kisumu) and there is only a single clinic in the town of Kisumu, then the anonymity of the participant will be compromised in the reporting of the data.

Reporting without extracts

Those inexperienced in reporting qualitative research may feel compelled to include data extracts in a report of the study findings. However, it is important to recognise that it is equally valid to report the findings of qualitative research without using any extracts from the data. There are numerous ways to present the findings of qualitative research, depending on the purpose of the study. Some suggestions arc outlined below.

Listing or ranking issues

A list of the issues raised in the group discussion may be included in the report. This list may be ranked in some way by participants during the

	Ideal qualities of a family planning clinic
Location	Walking distance or short rickshaw/tonga ride Little or no transport cost Close to home (within *Moholah*)
Opening hours	Regular and reliable opening hours (e.g. 8am–5pm, Monday–Friday) Emergency service arrangements (twenty-four hours) Open during school hours and evening service Closed Friday and Sunday
Premises	Neat and clean Well stocked with medicines Hygienic Functional Space for private discussion *Purdah* maintained Separate services for men
Services	Facilities for children and women's health Family planning services Range of effective methods (for both birth spacing and limiting) Infertility advice and treatment Treatment for sexual diseases Treatment of gynaecological conditions Operation facilities (caesarean and sterilisation)
Cost	Affordable fees (small fee or cost free) Subsidised assistance for poor Advice free of charge No disparity between prices advertised and charged

Source: Hennink and Stephenson (2000: 53)

Figure 12.2 A list of issues from focus group research

discussion or the issues may be grouped into categories by the analysts. Figure 12.2 shows the results of focus group research that identified a list of qualities of an ideal family planning clinic in Pakistan. These issues were grouped by the research team into various clinic characteristics and functions.

Presenting process information

The purpose of the focus group research may have been to identify a particular process (e.g. sequence of events, decision-making, lifecycle activities), therefore the findings may be presented in diagrammatic form. Presenting the results in diagrammatic form can effectively communicate the core research findings.

Conceptual frameworks

A qualitative study may have developed a conceptual framework to explain certain issues or behaviour. This conceptual framework may be presented in the report and the details discussed in the text.

Typologies

The research may have identified various typologies of behaviour, strategies or experiences, which can be described in the report (Ritchie and Lewis 2003). For example, various types of health-seeking behaviour (i.e. preventative, emergency, event-led, employment induced etc.) or types of contraceptive users (i.e. pregnancy prevention, safe sex, irregular, consistent). The presentation of typologies is useful for specifying the varying policy implications or interventions for each group.

Descriptive case studies

Presenting the results of the research in the form of a case study can be a useful way to convey a range of issues discussed by participants.

Conveying context in reports

Any social phenomenon needs to be understood within its own context, this may be the social, cultural, historical, economic or political backdrop in which the phenomenon is evident. These characteristics may influence the specific phenomenon being studied and will help to interpret the results of the study. The report of study findings needs to convey these contextual aspects to the reader throughout the research report. Qualitative research often sets out explicitly to explore the context in which social phenomena occur. Therefore, in reporting qualitative findings researchers need to reflect a range of contextual issues. The context of the research refers to both the socio-cultural milieu of the study setting and the context of the research methodology in which the information was collected. Conveying the context of the research helps the reader to develop a sense of the environment in which the research was conducted, the style of data collection and the broader background against which the results need to be assessed.

A range of contextual issues needs to be conveyed in reporting focus group research; this can be done in various ways throughout the research report, as summarised in Figure 12.3. Firstly, the background section of the report needs to highlight pertinent contextual issues relevant to the study topic, for example research on malaria treatment may provide a background on the prevalence of malaria, mortality rates, health structures providing treatment, drug availability and affordability, and preventative behaviour of the population studied. The background section also needs to describe the socio-cultural context of the research setting, by describing social and cultural norms

Background	■ Describe context of research topic (i.e. demographic patterns, policy and governance, financial, structural and historical issues) ■ Describe the socio-cultural context of the study setting
Methodology	■ Describe characteristics of the study population and sub-populations ■ Describe the context of data collection (i.e. group discussions)
Results	■ Identify issues within context of all study findings ■ Reflect context of the discussion ■ Provide perspectives of various stakeholders ■ Include quotations from the discussion ■ Include photographs of study setting, if appropriate
Interpretation	■ Reflect on contextual issues in interpreting study findings ■ Interpret study findings in context of data collection

Figure 12.3 Conveying context in reporting focus group research

of behaviour or beliefs related to the study issues. It is also important to provide a context to any sub-population studied, which may be defined regionally (e.g. urban poor, rural residents) or by certain demographic characteristics (e.g. adolescents, married men). The methodology section of the report should convey the context of the data collection. Providing an insight into the application of focus group methodology will enable the reader to correctly interpret the study findings, assess the data quality and understand any limitations in the type of data that can be collected using this approach. Reflecting on the influence of the methodology on the study findings is another way to bring forth the context of the methodology.

Context can be portrayed most directly in the results section of the report. The most direct way to convey context is to include quotations from participants in the study results. Verbatim extracts from the group discussion bring the reader directly into contact with the study population and convey a great deal of contextual information, not only in highlighting the issue itself but also in showing the expression and emotion with which it is conveyed. It may be appropriate to include longer quotations from focus group research to convey the context of a group discussion, and to include the question or prompts of the moderator. Including photographs in the report is another way to convey the physical context of the study setting, although care needs to be taken to preserve the confidentiality of participants if photos of the actual group discussion are considered. Another aspect of reporting context is to present the results from the perspectives of various stakeholders, such as community views, health service providers or policy-makers. Reporting the findings in this way will reflect the broader context of the issues.

Finally, context can also be reflected in the interpretation of the study findings by considering how each of the study findings is influenced by contextual influences. For example, research on family planning in culturally conservative settings may reveal limited contraceptive use amongst women, which needs to be interpreted within the context of the prevailing religious beliefs, socio-cultural pressures from family elders and prevailing social norms, such as pro-natalist attitudes within the study setting. The results of the study can then be interpreted within a wider framework of influences.

Reporting findings in mixed-method research

Many studies adopt a mixed-method research design, combining both quantitative and qualitative approaches. The main reasons for combining both approaches in a single study are to capitalise on the strengths of each approach as well as compensate for the weaknesses of each (Punch 2005), to mutually validate the findings of both approaches or to obtain a broader understanding of the study issue than can be gained using a single approach (Flick 2002). Often the qualitative and quantitative aspects of a study are conducted sequentially, for example focus group discussions may be conducted to identify issues or terminology to include on the quantitative survey, alternatively the group discussions may be held after the completion of the survey to seek explanations for the quantitative findings. Often both approaches will include similar components, albeit seeking different perspectives on these. For example the survey may collect data on the prevalence of an activity or attitude, while the group discussions seek to explain the activity, the influences or the context.

Reporting the findings of mixed-method research involves first analysing each type of data according to the procedures of the different research paradigms (i.e textual data analysis, statistical analysis). The way in which the results of each approach are presented will be determined by their purpose in the overall study design. Each approach may address a different study objective or the results of one approach may dovetail with the other and contribute to a more holistic understanding of the research problem. One of the issues in reporting the results of mixed-method research is the amount of data that are collected; researchers therefore need to be selective in determining the key issues to convey in the report. An effective approach to reporting the results of mixed-method research is to present the findings by key themes (Tashakkori and Teddlie 1998). The results of each approach will be reported under each theme, typically to provide a different perspective on the theme. For example, the survey results may show that only one-third of adolescent girls use condoms during first sexual intercourse, while the group discussions reveal a belief that a pregnancy cannot occur at first sex, thus the qualitative findings are used to provide context and explanation to the quantitative findings. The results thus guide the reader through the key findings of the research by identifying both the quantitative and qualitative findings for each issue, and then highlighting what the combined results mean. Once the results of key themes have been reported in this manner, the linkages between themes are discussed and referred to a theoretical framework (Ulin *et al.* 2002). By adopting this approach the results of each methodology are combined to jointly address the research objectives of the study as a whole. Occasionally the results of each approach will provide contradictory findings on the same issue. In this instance the researchers should try to identify why this may be the case; it may be a reflection of inadequate analysis or bias in the data collection or analysis. Where the researchers cannot explain the discrepancy, the contradictory data should simply be presented with sufficient information on the research process, so that the readers can assess the issues for themselves (Ulin *et al.* 2002).

Community dissemination of results

Focus group research involves interaction with the study population in gaining the required information and contact with community leaders to arrange the fieldwork. The research issues often have some policy relevance or recommendations regarding service delivery or changing certain practice that have implications for the study population. Often community members will enquire about how the study results will be disseminated and whether they will be informed about the results. The modes of research dissemination often overlook the communication of findings back to the study population, focussing instead on reporting to policy or academic audiences. However, community dissemination is also an ethical obligation of research and can be conducted in numerous ways. For example, a brief (i.e. two page) research summary may be developed to highlight key issues, main findings, and action points or recommendations. This summary can be disseminated back to the study community. Alternatively, meetings with selected community leaders can be undertaken to verbally discuss the findings and further activities, or a dissemination workshop can be conducted to more broadly disseminate the research findings in the study country, to which community members are invited. A dissemination workshop may invite a range of stakeholders including policy-makers, service providers, community advocates, community leaders, media representatives and so on. When the study community is unable to learn of the study findings or observe noticeable changes to the issues discussed there may be complacency in future participation in research activities.

Key terms

Dissemination refers to the communication of study findings to a wider audience.

Summary of key issues

- The purpose of the study and the target audience will guide decisions on the reporting of findings, selection of issues, inclusion of data extracts, format for presenting information, and shaping of the study conclusions.
- The use of quotations in reports is a tradition of qualitative research, but results can equally be presented without any data extracts.
- Conveying context in reports of international focus group research helps to provide a sense of the environment in which the research was conducted, the style of data collection and the broader background against which the results need to be assessed.
- An effective approach to reporting the results of mixed-method research is to present findings by key themes.
- Research dissemination needs to include in-country community dissemination, in addition to other forms of dissemination.

References

Akwara, P. 2002. 'Perception of Risk and Sexual Behaviour in Kenya', unpublished Ph.D. thesis, School of Social Sciences, University of Southampton, United Kingdom.

Allen, S. 2006. Informed consent document used in ongoing project 'Formative Focus Group and Interviews in Two African Capitals', Rwanda Zambia HIV Research Group (RZHRG), Emory University, Atlanta, USA.

Benaya, K. 2004. 'Factors Influencing Contraceptive Use and Method Choice Among Women and Men in Zambia', unpublished Ph.D. thesis, School of Social Sciences, University of Southampton, United Kingdom.

Bernard, H. 1994. *Research Methods in Anthropology: Qualitative and Quantitative Approaches*, second edition. Beverly Hills, CA: Sage.

Blanc, A. K. and Tsui, A. O. 2005. *The Dilemma of Past Success: Insiders' Views on the Future of the International Family Planning Movement*. A working paper. The Bill and Melinda Gates Institute for Population and Reproductive Health, Johns Hopkins Bloomberg School of Public Health, Chapter 5.

Bloor, M., Frankland, J., Thomas, M. and Robson, K. 2001. *Focus Groups in Social Research*. London: Sage Publications.

Bogdan, R. and Taylor, S. J. 1975. *Introduction to Qualitative Research Methods*. New York: John Wiley and Sons.

Borrayo, E. A., Buki, L. and Feigal, B. 2005. 'Breast Cancer Detection among Older Latinas: Is it Worth the Risk?', *Qualitative Health Research* 15(9): 1244–63.

Chimbwete, C. 2001. 'Socio-Demographic Aspects of Young People's Reproductive Behaviour in Malawi', unpublished Ph.D. thesis, University of Southampton.

Cooper, P., Diamond, I., Gould, C., High, S. and Partridge, J. 1992. *Choosing and Using Contraceptives: Consumers Experiences in Wessex*, Department of Social Statistics, University of Southampton. Report to the Wessex Regional Health Authority Measures in Family Planning Steering Group.

Corden, A. and Sainsbury, R. 1996. *Using Quotations in Qualitative Research*. Paper presented to the Fourth International Social Science Methodology Conference, University of Essex, United Kingdom, 1–5 July 1996.

David, M. and Sutton, C. 2004. *Social Research: The Basics*. London: Sage Publications.

Denzin, N. and Lincoln, Y. 1998a. *Strategies of Qualitative Enquiry*. London: Sage Publications.
  1998b. *The Landscape of Qualitative Research: Theories and Issues*. London: Sage Publications.
  2000. *Handbook of Qualitative Research*. Second Edition. Thousand Oaks, CA: Sage Publications.

Dey, I. 1993. *Qualitative Data Analysis: A User Friendly Guide for Social Scientists*. London: Routledge.

Diamond, I., Stephenson, R. and Sheppard, Z. *et al.* 2000. *Perceptions of Aircraft Noise, Sleep and Health*. United Kingdom: Civil Aviation Authority.

Farquar, C. and Das, R. 1999. 'Are Focus Groups Suitable for "Sensitive" Topics?' in Barbour, R. and Kitzinger, J. (eds.) *Developing Focus Group Research: Politics, Theory and Practice*. London: Sage.

Fern, E. 1982. 'The Use of Focus Groups for Idea Generation: the Effects of Group Size, Acquaintanceship, and Moderator on Response Quantity and Quality', *Journal of Marketing Research* 19: 1–13.

Fern, E. 2001. *Advanced Focus Group Research*. Thousand Oaks, CA: Sage Publications.

Flick, U. 1998. *An Introduction to Qualitative Research*. London: Sage Publications.

      2002. *An Introduction to Qualitative Research*. Second Edition. London: Sage Publications.

Gibbs, A. 1997. 'Focus Groups', *Social Research Update, Issue 19*. Department of Sociology, University of Surrey, United Kingdom.

Glaser, B. and Strauss, A. 1967. *The Discovery of Grounded Theory: Strategies for Qualitative Research*. New York: Aldine de Gruyter.

Green, J. and Thorogood, N. 2004. *Qualitative Methods for Health Research*. London: Sage Publications.

Greenbaum, T. 2000. *Moderating Focus Groups. A Practical Guide for Group Facilitation*. Thousand Oaks, CA: Sage Publications.

Griffiths, P. L. and Bentley, M. E. 2005. 'Understanding Indian Women's Perceptions of Overweight: A Study of Lifestyle and Obesity Risk Factors', *European Journal of Clinical Nutrition* 59: 1217–20.

Hennink, M. and Diamond, I. 1999. 'Using Focus Groups in Social Research', in Memnon, A. and Bull, R. (eds.) *Handbook of the Psychology of Interviewing*. John Wiley and Sons Ltd.

Hennink, M., Diamond, I. and Cooper, P. 1999. 'Contraceptive Use Dynamics of Asian Women in Britain', *Journal of Biosocial Science* 31(4): 537–54.

Hennink, M., Diamond, I., Clements, S. and Johnson, F. 2002. *Evaluation of Marie Stopes Family Planning Programme: Pakistan*. Report of Phase II: Evaluation. University of Southampton, UK.

Hennink, M. and Stephenson, R. 2000. *Evaluation of Marie Stopes Family Planning Programme in Pakistan*, Report of Phase I: Baseline. University of Southampton, UK.

Hennink, M. and Simkhada, P. 2004. 'Sex Trafficking in Nepal: Context and Process', *Asia Pacific Migration Journal* 13(3): 305–38.

Hennink, M. and Madise, N. 2005. 'Influence of User Fees for Reproductive Health in Malawi', *African Population Studies* 20(2): 125–41.

Hennink, M., Rana, I. and Iqbal R. 2005. 'Knowledge of Personal and Sexual Development Amongst Young People in Pakistan', *Culture, Health and Sexuality* 7(4): 319–32.

Holliday, A. 2002. *Doing and Writing Qualitative Research*. London: Sage Publications.

Janis, I. 1982. *Groupthink*. Second edition. Boston: Houghton Mifflin.

Jarrett, R. 1993. 'Focus Group Interviewing with Low Income Minority Populations: A Research Experience' in Morgan, D. (ed.) *Successful Focus Groups: Advancing the State of the Art* 184–281. Newbury Park, CA: Sage.

Jourard, S. 1964. *The Transparent Self*. Princeton, NJ: Van Nostrand.

Kauser, F. 2001. *Maternal Health Care Utilisation Among the Urban Poor of Maharashtra, India*, unpublished Ph.D. thesis, University of Southampton.

Kitzinger, J. 1994. 'The Methodology of Focus Groups: The Importance of Interaction Between Research Participants', *Sociology of Health and Illness* 16: 103–21.

Krueger, R. 1988. *Practical Guide for Applied Research*. Thousand Oaks, CA: Sage Publications.

1998a. *Developing Questions for Focus Groups*. Focus Group Kit 3. Thousand Oaks, CA: Sage Publications.

1998b. *Moderating Focus Groups*. Focus Group Kit 4. Thousand Oaks, CA: Sage Publications.

Krueger, R. and Casey, M. 2000. *Focus Groups: A Practical Guide for Applied Research*. Third Edition. Thousand Oaks, CA: Sage Publications.

Kumar, R. 2005. *Research Methodology: A Step-by-Step Guide for Beginners*. Second Edition. London: Sage Publications.

Lazarfeld, P. 1986. *The Art of Asking Why*. New York: The Advertising Research Foundation.

Lennon, A., Gallois, C., Owen, N. and McDermott, L. 2005. 'Young Women as Smokers and Nonsmokers: A Qualitative Social Identity Approach', *Qualitative Health Research* 15(10): 1345–59.

Litosseliti, L. 2003. *Using Focus Groups in Research*. London: Continuum.

Lofand, J. and Lofand, L. 1995. *Analysing Social Settings*. Third Edition. Belmont, CA: Wadsworth.

Madise, N., Hennink, M. Dambula, I. and Kainja, E. 2000. *Meeting Demographic Targets and User Fees for Family Planning Methods: Can Both Work in Poor Countries?* Paper presented at the Workshop on Reproductive Health Research in Developing Countries, 7 June 2000, London School of Hygiene and Tropical Medicine.

Marin, G. and Marin, B. 1991. *Research with Hispanic Populations*. Newbury Park, CA: Sage Publications.

Mason, J. 2002. *Qualitative Researching*. Second Edition. London: Sage Publications.

Mauthner, M., Birch, M., Jessop, J. and Miller, T. 2002. *Ethics in Qualitative Research*. London: Sage Publications.

Maynard-Tucker, G. 2000. 'Conducting Focus Groups in Developing Countries: Skill Training for Bi-Lingual Facilitators', *Qualitative Health Research* 10(3): 396–410.

McKenzie, G., Powell, J. and Usher, P. 1997. *Understanding Social Research: Perspectives on Methodology and Practice*. London: Falmer Press.

Meyers, G. 1998. 'Displaying opinions: Topics and Disagreement in Focus Groups', *Language in Society* 27(1): 85–111.

Miles, M. and Huberman, A. 1994. *Qualitative Data Analysis: An Expanded Sourcebook*. Second Edition. London: Sage Publications.

Morgan, D. and Krueger, R. 1993. 'When to Use Focus Groups and Why', in Morgan, D. (ed.) *Successful Focus Groups: Advancing the State of the Art* 3–19. Newbury Park, CA: Sage Publications.

Morgan, D. 1997. *Focus Groups as Qualitative Research*. Second Edition. Qualitative Research Methods Series 16. Thousand Oaks, CA: Sage Publications.

Morgan, D. and Scannell A. 1998. *Planning Focus Groups: Focus Group Kit 2*. Thousand Oaks, CA: Sage Publications.

Nuffield Council on Bioethics 2002. *The Ethics of Research Related to Healthcare in Developing Countries*. Bedford Square, London: Nuffield Council on Bioethics.

Patton, M. 1990. *Qualitative Evaluation and Research Methods*. Second Edition. Newbury Park, CA: Sage Publications.

Pearson, S., Cornah, D. and Diamond, I. *et al.* 1996. *Promoting Young People's Sexual Health*. United Kingdom: Health Education Authority.

Punch, K. 2005. *Introduction to Social Research: Quantitative and Qualitative Approaches*. Second Edition. London: Sage Publications.

Richards, L. 2005. *Handling Qualitative Data: A Practical Guide*. London: Sage Publications.

Ritchie, J. and Lewis, J. 2003. *Qualitative Research Practice: A Guide for Social Science Students and Researchers*. London: Sage Publications.

Rubin, H. and Rubin, I. 1995. *Qualitative Interviewing: The Art of Hearing Data*. Thousand Oaks, CA: Sage Publications.

2005. *Qualitative Interviewing: The Art of Hearing Data*. Second Edition. Thousand Oaks, CA: Sage Publications.

Scheyvens, R. and Storey, D. 2003. *Development Fieldwork. A Practical Guide*. London: Sage Publications.

Schinke, S. and Gilchrist, L. 1993 'Ethics in Research', in R. M. Grinnell (ed.) *Social Work Research and Evaluation*. Fourth Edition. Illinois: F. E. Peacock publishers.

Silverman, D. 2000. *Doing Qualitative Research: A Practical Handbook*. London: Sage Publications.

2005. *Doing Qualitative Research*. Second Edition. London: Sage Publications.

Stephenson, R. 2000. *The Impact of Rural-Urban Migration on Child Survival in India*. PhD thesis, University of Southampton.

Stephenson, R. and Hennink, M. 2004. 'Barriers to Family Planning Services Among the Urban Poor in Pakistan', *Asia-Pacific Population Journal* 19(2): 5–26.

Stewart, D. and Shamdasani, R. 1990. *Focus Groups: Theory and Practice. Applied Social Research Methods Series*, Volume 20, Newbury Park, CA: Sage Publications.

Strauss, A. and Corbin, J. 1990. *Basics of Qualitative Research*. Newbury Park, CA: Sage Publications.

1998. *Basics of Qualitative Research: Techniques and Procedures for Developing Grounded Theory*. Second Edition. Thousand Oaks, CA: Sage Publications.

Tashakkori, A. and Teddlie, C. 1998. *Mixed Methodology: Combining Qualitative and Quantitative Approaches*. Thousand Oaks, CA: Sage Publications.

Thorne, B. and Henley, N. 1975. (eds.) *Language and Sex: Difference and Dominance*. Rowley, MA: Newbury House.

Ulin, P., Robinson, E. and Tolley, E. *et al.* 2002. *Qualitative Methods: A Field Guide for Applied Research in Sexual and Reproductive Health*. North Carolina: Family Health International, Research Triangle Park.

Ulin, P., Robinson, E. and Tolley, E. 2005. *Qualitative Methods in Public Health. A Field Guide for Applied Research*. San Francisco, CA: Jossey Bass.

Varga, C. A. 2003. 'How Gender Roles Influence Sexual and Reproductive Health Among South African Adolescents', *Studies in Family Planning* 34(3): 160–72.

Vasquez, M. and Han, A. 1995. 'Group Interventions and Treatments with Ethnic Minorities', in Aponte, J., Rivers, R. and Wohl, J. (eds.) *Psychological Interventions and Cultural Diversity* (pp. 109–27). Boston: Allyn & Bacon.

Vaughn, S., Shay Schumm, J. and Sinagub, J. 1996. *Focus Group Interviews in Education and Psychology*. Thousand Oaks, CA: Sage Publications.

Walker, R. 1985. *Applied Qualitative Research*. Aldershot: Gower.

Wells, W. 1979. 'Group Interviewing', in Higgenbotham, J. B. and Cox, K. (eds.) *Focus Group Interview: A Reader* (pp. 2–12). Chicago: American Marketing Association.

Wengraf, T. 2001. *Qualitative Research Interviewing*. London: Sage Publications.

Woolcott, H. 2001. *Writing Up Qualitative Research*. Second Edition. Thousand Oaks, CA: Sage Publications.

World Medical Association (WMA) 2000. *Declaration of Helsinki. Ethical Principles for Medical Research Involving Human* Subjects, adopted by the 52nd WMA General Assembly, Edinburgh, Scotland.

Index